Routledge Revivals

National School Policy

Published in 1996, this book presents a broad overview of the development of educational policy for schools in England and Wales since Margaret Thatcher's Conservative administration took office in 1979. It reviews the separate strands of education policy as it relates to curriculum, equal educational opportunities, diversity and choice and management policies, and combines these with an overall appraisal of the direction of the schools system in the two decades before it was written. The book thereby provides a comprehensive text for undergraduate and postgraduate students which raises issues for debate and includes support material for discussion. It will also be of interest to school governors, educationalists and all those who care about the direction of educational change.

National School Policy

Major Issues in Education Policy for Schools in England and Wales, 1979 Onwards

Edited by Jim Docking

Routledge
Taylor & Francis Group
Routledge Revivals

First published in 1996
by David Fulton Publishers

This edition first published in 2018 by Routledge
2 Park Square, Milton Park, Abingdon, Oxon, OX14 4RN
and by Routledge
711 Third Avenue, New York, NY 10017

Routledge is an imprint of the Taylor & Francis Group, an informa business

A Library of Congress record exists under LCCN: 96223579

ISBN 13: 978-1-138-57811-1 (hbk)
ISBN 13: 978-1-351-26532-4 (ebk)
ISBN 13: 978-1-138-57814-2 (pbk)

David Fulton Publishers Ltd
2 Barbon Close, London WCIN 3JX

First published in Great Britain by David Fulton Publishers in 1996

British Library Cataloguing in Publication Data

A catalogue record for this book is available from the British Library

ISBN 1-85346-396-5

Contents

Preface vi

Contributors v

Chronology vii

Introduction x
Jim Docking

Part I CURRICULUM POLICY

1 The National Curriculum: Foundation Subjects 1
Augustine Basini

2 The National Curriculum: Themes and Issues 15
Roger Marples

3 The National Curriculum: Assessment 30
Derek Shaw

4 Pre-School Provision 44
Peter Jackson

5 14–19 56
Roger Marples

Part II EQUAL EDUCATIONAL OPPORTUNITIES

6 Special Educational Needs 71
Derek Shaw

7 Race 86
Augustine Basini

8 Gender 100
Elaine Sillitoe

Part III DIVERSITY AND CHOICE

9 Diversity 112
Peter Jackson

10 School Choice 126
Jim Docking

Part IV MANAGEMENT POLICY

11 School Management and Funding 139
Helen Johnson

12 School Governance 151
Michael Creese and Peter Earley

13 Staff Appraisal 163
Di Bentley

14 Inspection and Advice 175
David Rowles

15 Performance Measurement and Targets 187
Helen Johnson

Index 199

Preface

For some time now members of the education policy course team at the Roehampton Institute London have felt the need for a text which equips students with the main facts regarding changes in school policy since 1979 while also discussing some of the controversial issues. We wanted something that was informative, up-to-date and reasonably comprehensive, but also provocative.

The fact that we have produced nothing until now is less due to our inertia than our judgement that anything published today will be out of date tomorrow, so rapid has been the pace of educational change. The spring of 1996, however, seemed an appropriate time for a book of the kind we envisaged. For one thing, the main thrusts of Conservative education policy are now abundantly clear, whatever further measures there may be. True, a Bill affecting nursery provision and grant-maintained schools is going through Parliament even as this book is published, there are prospects of change at 16-plus following the report by Sir Ron Dearing and a White Paper has been announced to expand selective education; but at least we have been promised a period of no major change in the National Curriculum and assessment arrangements until the next century. Moreover, this book appears during the run-up to a General Election, in which education is set to be a major focus for debate. Now therefore seems the right time for a book which summarises where we are, reflects on why and how we got here, points to some of the main contentious issues and reflects on the ways forward.

We believe this book will appeal not only to students on relevant courses in higher education (our core audience) but also to a wider readership – local councillors, parents, governors, teachers and lecturers, officers in the education service, politicians of all parties and everyone who cares about the direction of so much educational change.

J.W.D.
April 1996

Contributors

Augustine Basini was formerly Deputy Principal of Digby Stuart College at the Roehampton Institute London, where he is now an education tutor and coordinates courses in education policy and urban education.

Di Bentley, an Assistant Dean at Roehampton Institute London, is about to take up the directorship of the School of Education at Sheffield Hallam University. She has written extensively on educational topics, particularly on science and health education.

Michael Creese is a former head teacher, County Coordinator for Governor Training in Suffolk, and a Training Officer with Action for Governor Information and Training. He was awarded a doctorate for research into governor–teacher relationships, and is author of *Effective Governors, Effective Schools: Developing the Partnership* (1995).

Jim Docking was formerly Head of Education at Whitelands College and Chairman of the School of Education, Roehampton Institute London, where he is now a research associate and visiting lecturer. His books include *Primary Schools and Parents: Relationships, Rights and Responsibilities* (1990) and *Managing Behaviour in the Primary School* (2nd edition, 1996). He is co-author of *Exclusion from School: Supporting Disaffection at Key Stage 4*, editor of *Education and Alienation in the Junior School* (1990) and co-editor of *Special Educational Needs and the Education Reform Act* (1992).

Peter Earley is a lecturer at the Oxford Centre for Educational Management, Oxford Brookes University. He has also worked at the National Foundation for Educational Research, where he directed a major national project on school governing bodies.

Peter Jackson lectures in education and the philosophy of education at the Roehampton Institute London and is a member of the education policy course team. He is co-author of *Educating Young Children: A Structural Approach* (1992).

Helen Johnson is a principal lecturer at the Centre for Educational Management, Roehampton Institute London. She was formerly Director of Postgraduate Programmes at the CIPFA Education and Training Centre.

Roger Marples lectures in education at the Roehampton Institute London and is a member of the education policy course team. He is currently editing a book on the aims of education and has published in British and American journals on topics relating to the philosophy of education.

David Rowles is a principal lecturer at the Centre for Educational Management, Roehampton Institute London. He was formerly Senior Inspector of Schools for the London Borough of Merton and is now an Ofsted inspector.

Derek Shaw is an engineer-turned-teacher who taught in both primary and secondary schools. He is an INSET and MA tutor in special educational needs at Roehampton Instititute London; his research interests include cognitive modifiability and mediation theory.

Elaine Sillitoe lectures at the Roehampton Instititute London. She is a parent (of a son and a daughter, in that order) and governor of an infant school and a junior school in North London.

Chronology

1975	**Sex Discrimination Act** Discrimination on grounds of sex unlawful
1976	**Race Relations Act** Discrimination on grounds of race unlawful **James Callaghan's Ruskin College Speech**
1977	**Taylor Report** *A New Partnership for Our Schools*
1978	**Warnock Report** *Special Educational Needs*
1979	**Education Act** LEAs no longer required to submit plans for comprehensive secondary education **Keohane Report** *Proposals for a Certificate of Extended Education*
1980	**Education Act** Assisted places scheme Registration of independent schools Parents' right to state a preference for the school they want their child to attend Independent local appeals committees for admissions LEAs and governors to provide information about schools Parents to be represented on governing bodies LEAs not obliged to make educational provision for under–5s except for children with special needs
1981	**Education Act** Concept of special educational needs replaces previous categories of handicap LEAs to identify and assess children with special educational needs Important rights for parents in the assessment and statementing processes Children with special needs to be educated normally in mainstream schools **Rampton Report** *West Indian Children in Our Schools*
1983	**White Paper** *Teaching Quality*
1985	**Swann Report** *Education for All* **White Papers** *Better Schools* and *Education and Training for Young People* **Certificate of Pre-Vocational Education (CPVE)** introduced

1986 **Education (No.2) Act**
New membership arrangements for school governing bodies
Annual governors' report and meeting
Sex education the responsibility of school governors
Political issues must be taught in a 'balanced' way
Governors to 'use their best endeavours' to ensure identification of children with special educational needs and suitable provision for their education
Corporal punishment prohibited in maintained schools and those on assisted places in independent schools
General Certificate of Secondary Education (GCSE) replaces GCE O level and the Certificate of Secondary Education (CSE)
National Council for Vocational Qualifications (NCVQ) established to approve National Vocational Qualifications (NVQs) and General National Vocational Qualifications (GNVQs)Ï

1987 **TGAT Report on assessment and testing**
AS Level introduced
Technical and Vocational Education Initiative (TVEI) introduced nationally
City Technology Colleges Trust founded to coordinate the CTC programme

1988 **Education Reform Act**
National Curriculum and assessment
National Curriculum Council and School Examinations and Assessment Council
Open enrolment
Local Management of Schools
Provision for schools to transfer from LEA to grant-maintained status
State funds for City Technology Colleges
Inner London Education Authority abolished
Local Government Act
Teaching the acceptability of homosexuality as a 'pretended' family relationship made unlawful
Higginson Report *Advancing A–Levels*

1990 **Diploma of Vocational Education** replaces CPVE

1991 **School Teachers' Pay and Conditions Act**
Teacher appraisal
White Paper *Education and Training for the 21st Century*
Parent's Charter
National Records of Achievement established

1992 **Education (Schools) Act**
Ofsted and Office of HM Chief Inspector of Schools in Wales established
Schools to be inspected every four years by teams of independent inspectors
School league tables introduced

1993 **Education Act**
Funding Agency for Schools and Funding Council for Wales
Simplified arrangements for becoming a grant-maintained school
Measures for dealing with 'failing schools'
Category of 'indefinite exclusion' abolished
National Curriculum Council (NCC) and School Examinations and Assessment Council (SEAC) replaced by the School Curriculum and Assessment Authority (SCAA)
Time limits for statements of special educational needs
Secretary of State to issue a Code of Practice for children with special needs
Sex education compulsory for secondary children but not primary
Parents allowed to remove their children from sex education lessons
Technology Colleges established

1994 **Dearing Report** *The National Curriculum and its Assessment*
DES Code of Practice *The Identification and Assessment of Special Educational Needs*
Common Funding Formula for GM schools pilot scheme

1995 **White Paper** *Competitiveness Forging Ahead*

1996 **Nursery Education and Grant-Maintained Schools Bill**
GM schools permitted to borrow against their assets
Voucher scheme for pre-school education
Dearing Report *Review of Qualifications for 16 to 19-year-olds*

Introduction

Jim Docking

Whatever view people take about education policy since the Conservatives won the general election in 1979, they are agreed that the changes have been radical, pervasive and controversial.

In this book, we do not attempt to cover exhaustively all the policies which have affected schools, and we certainly do not claim to offer a definitive statement of the law in this respect. Rather, the authors, many of whom are members of the education policy teaching team at the Roehampton Institute London, have each provided a personal perspective on a key aspect of national school policy, working to a common format:

- an **Introduction** to set the scene
- an explanation of **The Policy** (with a summary of **Key Points**)
- **Issues for Debate**, exploring areas of controversy
- **Questions for Discussion**
- **Further Reading**
- **References**

The chapters are grouped in four parts: curriculum policy, equal educational opportunities, diversity and choice, and management policy. In Part I, the first three chapters focus on the National Curriculum. Augustine Basini notes how this country now has its first statutory curriculum, even though attendance at school has been compulsory for over a century. But because the National Curriculum was introduced hurriedly and without a coherent philosophy, it has been subject to numerous revisions costing hundreds of millions of pounds. Duncan Graham, who managed the innovation under three Education Secretaries, has described it as 'wilful distortion for political ends'. For all its virtues in providing every child with an 'entitlement' and promoting 'differentiation' to ensure all pupils have access to the curriculum, from the start it has been beleaguered with charges of centralism and bureaucracy. In Basini's view, the slimmed-down prescriptions following the Dearing review, though welcome, do not address some of the fundamental issues at stake, such as what should constitute an appropriate experience for primary school children.

In Chapter 2. Roger Marples examines the haphazard way in which curriculum areas not easily subsumed under subject headings – such as sex education, moral development and economic understanding – have been introduced in a piecemeal fashion, with coherence lacking once again. In particular, he attacks the assumptions hidden in the official guidelines for the cross-curricular themes. Whilst the controversial nature of economic issues, the concept of citizenship, relations between the sexes and so on is given lip service, the prevailing message seems to be that children should be taught to understand but not critically evaluate.

Derek Shaw, in Chapter 3, then unravels the complexities of the highly contentious arrangements for assessing children's achievement in the National Curriculum. After tracing the development of assessment from the original Task Group to the post-Dearing changes, he explores the role of the national standard assessment tasks (SATs) and raises questions about their scope, reliability and validity. He then describes how the Task Group's central role for teacher assessment has been significantly marginalised, simply supplementing SATs for matter not covered in the national tests. Noting the comment of Richard Daugherty, a member of the former School Examinations and Assessment Council, that 'teacher assessment was not seen by the policy-makers ... as an important component of the system', he refers to evidence that short external standardised tests in America have proved emotionally valueless and are being abandoned. The Americans, says Paul Black, who chaired the Task Group, 'see us marching backwards into unprofitable ways from which they are now escaping'.

Moving on to pre-school provision, Peter Jackson in Chapter 4 notes the absence of any sustained initiative since the 1933 Hadow Report on nursery and infant education. John Major's announcement of a voucher scheme (for four-year-olds only) in the run-up to a general election may help redress this, but it masks the ideological conflicts embedded in all discussion about nursery provision. This Jackson illustrates by contrasting perspectives from four quarters: the academic researchers, with their emphasis on the effects of pre-school experience on 'positive behaviours'; HMI on the need to 'acclimatise four-year-olds to reception class work'; the independent sector which points to the less cost-incurring private nurseries that are 'unencumbered by the compensatory ideology which leads LEA institutions to see homes and families as somehow culturally deficient'; and the right-wing Centre for Policy Studies with its simple faith in the power of market forces. He asks whether it should be academic or developmental experiences which drive any policy to increase pre-school opportunities, and looks critically at the controversial voucher scheme, about to be introduced nationally.

Roger Marples in the last chapter in this section, surveys the minefield of provision for 14- to 19-year-olds. Tracing the tortuous path through various committees, reports, speeches and piecemeal development, he notes a growing consensus for provision that will increase post-16 participation rates in both education and training, address the vexed question of parity of esteem for academic and vocational qualifications, give opportunities for easy transfer between courses, make wider use of records of achievement and gain coherence where there is fragmentation and division. Writing before the Dearing report on 16-19 is published, Marples draws attention to two central conflicts in the debate: the insistence that A–levels must be retained as a 'gold standard' versus a more radical approach; and the acceptance of 'dual track' academic and vocational routes versus the belief that fluidity between different kinds of courses is the better way forward.

The first of the three chapters of Part II, which is concerned with equal opportunities, is about policy on special educational needs. In Chapter 6, Derek Shaw examines problems in the concept of 'special educational needs' and the circumstances that warrant special provision. After explaining the changes in policy since the Warnock Report of 1978, he asks whether a concept that encompasses a continuum of ability, with only those at the very end eligible for a statement, has outlived its usefulness. Even Mary Warnock has now claimed that 'as a basis for legislation ... it was disastrous'. Shaw discusses problems of statementing and resourcing special needs, integration versus segregation, and the predicaments produced by the National Curriculum, delegated funding, open enrolment and 'opting out'. He concludes by pointing out two fundamental difficulties: the amount of money the Government is willing to direct to children with special needs and whether delegating responsibilities to individual schools is in the best interests of the children.

Like 'special educational needs', the concept of 'race' is also beset with problems, as Augustine Basini observes in Chapter 7. After outlining current policies and explaining the difficulties in defining 'race relations', he notes the concerns that national policies will not promote racial equality. The reasons are various: the diminishing powers of LEAs to develop anti-racist policies; the Right's pressure to remove multicultural educational from the agenda and promote a monoculture; the conflict between the emphasis on maximising opportunities for parental choice and the desire to prevent racial segregation in schools; and the demands that testing make on bilingual youngsters. In Basini's view, however, the problem is also attributable to racist impulses in society and the failure to address the institutional processes that lead to the underachievement of black pupils.

In her discussion of equal opportunities for boys and girls, Elaine Sillitoe (Chapter 8) notes how gender differentiation has its roots in the domestic ideology and 'good woman' beliefs that have dominated provision for girls' education until fairly recent times. Echoing the sentiments expressed in the previous chapter, she suggests that the main counter-initiatives have come from local education authorities, whose sphere of influence in this respect is now irreversibly on the wane. In her view, the increased centralisation of education policy-making has meant less support for gender equality policies – though the compulsory core subjects at 14-plus mark an important step in equalising curricular opportunities. Elaine Sillitoe then discusses the impact of the 'hidden curriculum' on gender opportunities and whether it is boys or girls who are now the more disadvantaged.

Part III contains two chapters devoted to the theme of the 1992 White Paper – choice and diversity. On the question of diversity, Peter Jackson begins Chapter 9 by noting the difficulty in appealing to the evidence from other countries that a diversity of schools improves standards. Both France and Germany do better than Britain, but France, like us, is overwhelmingly comprehensive whereas Germany has developed separate technical schools. Jackson expresses concern at the paucity of opportunity to develop diversity of the curriculum, as distinct from diversity of school status. In his view, this is not just because British schools have to contend with the demands of the National Curriculum: it is a consequence of the odd-jobbing philosophy which has prevented policy-makers from indulging in more radical reforms. He also notes the tension between policies to promote parental choice and pressures to stop diversification of ability through selection. Lastly, he brings out the similarities and differences between the postmodernists and the neo-liberal marketeers. Both support diversity and choice, but whereas the marketeers believe that these will raise standards, the postmodernists see diversity as concomitant with society's increasing fragmentation and heterogeneity. In Jackson's view, 'a strong well-ordered state sector can withstand and benefit from a fringe of less mainstream institutions'.

In his complementary Chapter 10, Jim Docking recognises that, in the interest of consumerism, school choice is now firmly embedded in educational policies across the industrialised world, but that its role varies from country to country. In Britain 'parentocracy', as Philip Brown calls it, is a reaction to universal LEA-controlled comprehensive education and a wish to reinstate more traditional teaching methods in mainstream education; in Australia choice is mainly between the public and private sector, the latter receiving subsidies; in the Netherlands it involves creating new schools in response to the nature of local demand for diversity; while in some states in the USA it is easier for school diversity to flourish without the constraints of a national compulsory curriculum. Docking notes how both the promoters and critics of school choice appeal to the interests of freedom and democracy: the promoters regard it as necessary to hold back encroaching state power, while the critics are concerned that unfettered choice will lead to social divisiveness to the detriment of the development of citizenship. He examines evidence that the policy to empower parents is not in practice realised, and that although schools have changed in response to choice pressures, they have often done so more to promote themselves than to create a greater range of curricular opportunities.

The last five chapters which make up Part IV focus on management issues. In Chapter 11, Helen Johnson reviews the changes towards decentralised decision-making and delegated budgets. She then goes on to explore two sets of tensions which perpetuate the controversy surrounding these developments. The first resides in the impossibility of creating a funding system that is at once 'fair' and 'simple'. The second results from the wish to devolve responsibility for school budgets whilst ensuring their effective management. Among the other concerns which Helen Johnson examines is the lack of democratic accountability in the new centralised Funding Agency and other educational quangos.

In the next chapter, Michael Creese and Peter Earley explain the policy changes in school governance. They go on to question whether governing bodies really represent and are sufficiently accountable to the communities they serve, the extent to which governors are capable of fulfilling the role expected of them, and whether the partnership between lay governors and professionals is emerging as an effective working concern. The authors conclude with a plea to the professionals to draw governors further into the debate about school effectiveness and to provide them with training that will create more informed and influential discussions on strategies for school improvement.

In Chapter 13, Di Bentley explores the controversies surrounding teacher appraisal and whether we need a model of appraisal that rewards good teachers, promotes staff development, or weeds out bad teachers. Noting that teachers want appraisal predominantly to support their own professional development while the Government might be happier with one more directly linked to performance, she examines such contentious issues as performance-related pay and the link between appraisal and discipline. It is the latter, she thinks, which carries the greatest dangers: 'It would be a disaster for any school to undermine the trust which teachers currently have in appraisal as a system that at least does them no harm, provides a listening ear once in a while, and at best may well do them some good'.

In his examination of the growth of the new inspection system under Ofsted (Chapter 14), David Rowles (himself an Ofsted inspector) notes the evidence to suggest that, although the prospect of inspection motivates schools to improve their provision and practices, it is less certain that the actual experience of inspection results in further improvement. This leads him to discuss the wisdom of a policy which separates inspection from advice. He goes on to note the arguments of critics like Ted Wragg and Tim Brighouse, who lambaste inspectors for their mechanical and vague reports and criticise a system which imposes a 'tyranny of orthodoxy', failing to recognise the uniqueness of each school and the particular circumstances in which it operates. Rowles would like to see more discussion on whether the identification of individual teachers in inspection reports might highlight the achievements of thousands of outstanding members of the profession and help to re-create public confidence.

In the last chapter, Helen Johnson analyses the contentious issue of performance measurement and league tables. Noting that the public has a democratic right to demand value for public spending, she warns that performance indicators are not a neutral management tool. We have to ensure that all partners in the exercise have a sense of ownership of these indicators and share the values they represent. An important question is therefore: Who chooses the indicators and decides what is information? After discussing different kinds of qualitative and quantitative indicators, she explains the 'value-added' debate and the problems in interpreting value-added data. Whatever the controversies surrounding this issue, she concludes, the future of performance measurement is assured.

From this overview of recent developments, it is clear that no area of the education service has gone untouched. The changes have been achieved through an unparalleled spate of law-making and regulatory activity. Among the seven Education Acts since the beginning of the 1980s (with another promised) which have been directly concerned with schools in England and Wales, those of 1988 and 1993 were gargantuan pieces of legislation, with 238 and 308 sections respectively compared with 122 in the 1944 Act. As Bills, they were subject to endless revision, exposing the Government to charges that policy was being made on the hoof. Reviewing the 1993 Act, which was passed after 981 amendments, Rogers (1993) has noted that only the 1989 Broadcasting Bill had more amendments tabled, and only the Maastricht Bill took up more parliamentary time.

In its White Paper on school policy, the Government justified the changes in terms of 'five great themes' – quality, diversity, parental choice, greater school autonomy and greater accountability (DfE, 1992). Recent policy statements from the Labour Party (1995a, b) and the Liberal Democrats (1992) suggest that they do not part company with the Conservatives as far as these principles are concerned. Indeed, in some respects the opposition parties would pursue the White Paper's themes in more thoroughgoing 'right' ways – Labour by, for instance, setting a higher national target for delegating funds to schools, streamlining the processes by which incompetent teachers can be sacked, and endorsing setting by ability, the testing of five-year-olds and homework for primary as well as secondary pupils; the Liberal Democrats by giving more power to individual schools while replacing the highly prescriptive National Curriculum programmes with a 'Minimum Curriculum Entitlement'.

Of course, the opposition parties also entertain ideas that are far removed from Government thinking, especially over the role of local government in education. New Labour, for instance, besides promising to establish equitable funding between all types of schools, would set up 'a new partnership' to give greater emphasis to the power of local communities and local authorities – but the package would require LEAs to take greater responsibility for raising standards through the duty to produce three-yearly strategic development plans, with monitoring by Ofsted and the Audit Commission. The Liberal Democrats adopt the more anti-Government stance with their opposition to three sacred cows of the Conservatives – grant-maintained schools (but with a policy to introduce 'light touch' local control rather than abolish existing institutions), national testing (to be replaced by individual Records of Achievement from the early years), and A–levels (to be replaced by a modular 'English Baccalaureate' to meet the vocational as well as academic needs of post–14 students). Like Labour, the Liberal Democrats would shift the balance of power away from the centre and unelected quangos towards the local community, but LEAs would be transformed into 'fully democratically elected' Education Departments with increased accountability to parents and the electorate.

As recently as 1977, H.C. Dent could write that consultation and negotiation were the regular means employed in educational policy-making. What really made the English educational system 'tick', he said, was 'the fact that the various bodies who have to work in it – central and local administration, teachers and voluntary bodies – regard and treat each other as partners' (p. 47). He concluded his book by suggesting that if ever this 'all-pervading partnership' were to end, 'an entirely different – and I think much less happy – system would emerge' (p. 163). Reflecting on development since the 1970s, the reader might sadly comment: 'How time does fly!'

Significantly, the chairman-designate of the new Local Government Organisation, Sir Jeremy Bentham, has recently commented: 'We do not plead for partnership in the government of our country: we demand it' (*TES*, 5 January 1996). None the less, as the Labour Party (1995a) has recently acknowledged with approval, 'education is now at the top of the political agenda'. How policies will develop and change after the general election, we can only wait and see.

REFERENCES

Department for Education (1992) *Choice and Diversity: A New Framework for Schools.* London: DfE.

Dent, H.C. (1977) *Education in England and Wales.* London: Hodder & Stoughton.

Labour Party (1995a) *Diversity and Excellence: A New Partnership for Schools.* London: Labour Party.

Labour Party (1995b) *Excellence for Everyone.* London: Labour Party.

Liberal Democrats (1992) *Excellence for All: Investing in Education.* London: Liberal Democrats.

Rogers, R. (19930 *A Guide to the Education Act 1993.* London: Advisory Centre for Education.

Part I
CURRICULUM POLICY

CHAPTER 1

The National Curriculum: Foundation Subjects

Augustine Basini

INTRODUCTION

The National Curriculum, introduced in the 1988 Education Reform Act, is the most radical and important Government initiative since the 1944 Education Act, or, as Moon (1991) asserts, 'one of the most significant education reforms of this century' (p. ix). It is the first statutory curriculum in the history of British education. Attendance at school has been compulsory since 1880, but not until recently has an Act defined what pupils must be taught, with the exception of Religious Education (the 1944 Act). Now all 23,000 maintained schools and the 1000-plus grant-maintained schools in England and Wales must implement the National Curriculum of three core foundation subjects and seven other foundation subjects, as well as Religious Education (and a daily act of worship).

While Butler, the architect of the 1944 Education Act, had prescribed only Religious Education as a compulsory subject in schools, during the late 1960s a debate developed about the need for greater guidance and conformity concerning the content of the school curriculum. The so-called 'Great Debate', initiated by the Labour Prime Minister James Callaghan (in a speech at Ruskin College, Oxford, in October 1976) is frequently given as the pivotal date for the commencement of serious consideration of what was being taught in the schools. The argument concentrated on poor standards in comparison with other European countries and Japan, challenged the notion of the curriculum as a 'secret garden' and looked towards one that would meet national needs.

Also during this period 1974–79 (when the Conservative Party was in opposition) several radical Conservative Party 'think–tanks', such as the Institute of Economic Affairs, the Adam Smith Institute, the Centre for Policy Studies, the Hillgate group and the National Centre for Educational Standards (NCES), turned their attention to the reform of education and setting the political educational agenda for the time when the Conservative Party regained power. NCES was established in 1972 to campaign against 'progressive' teaching methods. The underlying ideology stressed the need for greater accountability from local education authorities (LEAs), schools and teachers, raising standards and returning to 'real' academic knowledge. There was a vigorous promotion of free market forces, competition, parental choice and satisfying the customer (a new notion in state education). The power of the local authorities was also to be severely curtailed by giving schools their own budgets – Local Management of Schools (LMS). It was not until the mid–1980s, however, (when the Conservatives had been in power for more than five years) that a White Paper, *Better Schools* (DES, 1985) set the context for the introduction of the National Curriculum by stating that 'the quality of school education concerns everyone', and that by the time pupils leave school they need to have acquired more than at present.

The historical and educational significance of the National Curriculum cannot be overstated. Yet its introduction in 1988 was very controversial. Even supporters of the Government were against the imposition of a 'centralised and bureaucratically set "Nationalised Curriculum"' (Whitty 1990, p. 25) which, it was argued, was against the Government's central policy of 'free market forces'. Chitty (1992) clearly enunciates this:

> Only members of the Hillgate Group actually wanted a National Curriculum, and they saw it largely as a tool of social control. Without their support, and the persistence of a significant section of the DES, the National Curriculum would never have found its way into the 1988 Act. (p.47)

Critics suggested that there had not been sufficient consultation, especially with teachers; that the curriculum structure was an obsolete grammar school type subject-based one that neglected important areas such as political awareness; and that there was excessive bureaucracy, overload of content and assessment procedures. Eventually, in 1993, the then Secretary of State for Education John Patten, after admitting that the Government had got its 'reforms' badly wrong, asked Sir Ron Dearing (Chairman of the Camelot Company and Chairman-designate of School Curriculum and Assessment Authority) to produce recommendations for slimming down the National Curriculum. The final Dearing Report was published on 5 January 1994. Its recommendations were accepted by the Government, and the Revised National Curriculum commenced in August 1995. The intention was that there would be no further amendments until the year 2000, though it will be 2003 before a cohort of pupils will have followed the new arrangements throughout their schooling.

THE POLICY

The National Curriculum as an entitlement for all pupils 15–16

Sections 1–25 of the 1988 Education Reform Act set out the general principles which must be reflected in the curriculum 'to be known as the National Curriculum'. Section 1(2) states that the curriculum of a school satisfies the requirements of the Act if it is 'a balanced and broadly based' curriculum which:

KEY POINTS
• An entitlement for all pupils aged 5–16 • Three core subjects and eight other foundation subjects • Cross–curricular themes and dimensions • A common structure for each subject • The concept of differentiation • The revised National Curriculum – August 1995

(a) promotes the spiritual, moral, cultural, mental and physical developments of pupils at the school and of society; and
(b) prepares such pupils for the opportunities, responsibilities and experiences of adult life.

The National Curriculum: From Policy to Practice (DES, 1989) was sent to all teachers in maintained schools. It stated the following key points:

1. That schools now, in law for the first time, have to provide a curriculum that is broad and balanced and meets the needs of each pupil;
2. That it is not sufficient for the school just to offer such a curriculum: it must be taken up by each pupil;
3. That the curriculum must promote development in all the main areas of learning and experience;
4. That the curriculum must develop the social and personal skills of the pupil.

Such a curriculum was seen as an entitlement for all pupils in maintained schools. The document went on to state the need for a curriculum that is clearly defined; that non-denominational religious education has a central role in promoting spiritual and moral development; and that while the National Curriculum foundation subjects provide a sound framework, attainment targets, programmes of study and assessment arrangements will help to improve standards in teaching and learning.

In the 1988 Act, the National Curriculum comprises a set of foundation subjects:

Core subjects

- English
- mathematics
- science
- Welsh, in Welsh–speaking schools.

Other foundation subjects

- art
- history
- geography
- a modern foreign language (for pupils 11–16)
- music
- physical education
- technology (including design); now design and technology and information technology
- Welsh, in schools in Wales which are not Welsh-speaking.

There is little legal distinction between core and other required subjects, though the core subjects were the first to be introduced. Religious Education was already a statutory requirement for all pupils in maintained schools. It is not one of the subjects that comprise the National Curriculum; instead, an 'agreed syllabus' is drawn up locally by the LEAs rather than at the national level. Following the acceptance by the Government of the recommendations of the Dearing Report (1994), art, music, history and geography are no longer compulsory during the last two years of compulsory education to allow more choice and flexibility.

From the start, it was emphasised that the foundation subjects were not a complete curriculum, and that the whole curriculum for all pupils would need to include cross–curricular themes and dimensions (DES, 1989). These will be explained in the next chapter.

A common structure for each subject

Each subject in the National Curriculum is structured using a common terminology:

- *Four Key Stages*, at the end of which every child is assessed:
  KS1 for pupils aged 5 to 7 (Years 1 and 2)
  KS2 for pupils aged 7 to 11 (Years 3 to 6)
  KS3 for pupils aged 11 to 14 (Years 7 to 9)
  KS4 for pupils aged 14 to 16 (Years 10 and 11)
- *Programmes of study for each subject*, defined in the 1988 Act as 'the matters, skills and processes which are required to be taught to pupils ... during each key stage'. Teachers' autonomy was recognised as space was to be made available to 'accommodate the enterprise of teachers' (DfE, 1995b, p.v).
- *Attainment targets* for the skills in each programme of study, defined in the Act as 'the knowledge skills and understanding which pupils of different abilities and maturities are expected to have by the end of each key stage'. They also act as criteria for assessment purposes.
- *Levels of attainment* for each attainment target which, following the Dearing Report, have since been modified to 'level descriptions of increasing difficulty [which] describe the types and range of performance that pupils working at a particular level should characteristically demonstrate. ... At the end of each key stage, teachers should judge which description best fits the pupil's

performance' (DFE, 1994, p.25). For art, music and physical education, end of key stage descriptions set out the standard of performance expected of the majority of pupils at the end of each key stage.

The concept of differentiation

Differentiation is a key concept in the National Curriculum. It is the process of matching teaching, learning and assessment to the needs of the individual pupil to ensure appropriate progress is being made. As Fitzgerald (1991) correctly points out, 'This is a difficult task for teachers with large classes, inadequate accommodation and insufficient resources' (p.11). But, however difficult, it is the teacher's task to monitor and record individual progress.

The revised National Curriculum

Following widespread criticism about excessive bureaucracy, content and assessment overload in the National Curriculum, the Secretary of State, John Patten, in April 1993 invited Sir Ron Dearing to review the National Curriculum and its assessment arrangements. He was asked to consider:

- the scope for slimming down the curriculum
- the future of the 10–level scale for assessment
- how to simplify the testing arrangements
- how to improve the administration of the National Curriculum and of the tests.

A wide-ranging consultation process was begun, particularly among teachers, headteachers and subject specialists. Staff from over 500 schools were consulted in nine regional conferences, and over 2,500 other schools, organisations and individuals sent in responses. An interim report was produced in July 1993 with the final report published on 5 January 1994.

The most important changes were:

- a slimming down of the mandatory curriculum for 5- to 14-year-olds, particularly outside the core of English, mathematics and science, releasing an average of one day a week for schools to use at their discretion
- from September 1996 onwards, more flexibility within the curriculum for 14- to 16-year-olds (KS4) for academic and vocational options
- a reduction in the number of attainment targets (to 25 at KS3)
- a simplification of the 10–level scale in the form of level descriptions to the end of Key Stage 3
- a review of all subjects, after which no further revision for five years
- a reduction in teachers' workload by simplifying the National Curriculum and reducing testing and recording demands
- limiting the national tests, until at least 1996, to the core subjects.

The Government accepted the recommendations. During 1994, subject advisory groups reduced the content and assessment procedures for introduction in 1995 for Key Stages 1 to 3, and 1996 for Key Stage 4. Information technology, originally incorporated into design and technology, is now a separate subject (DfE, 1995b). At Key Stage 4 (year groups 10 and 11), history, geography, art and music are no longer compulsory; the compulsory subjects have been reduced to English, mathematics, science and physical education and, from August 1996, design and technology, information technology, and a modern foreign language. Under the 1993 Education Act, sex education is also required at Key Stages 3 and 4. RE, although outside the National Curriculum, is still obligatory to 16 years. The present position is summarised in figure 1.1.

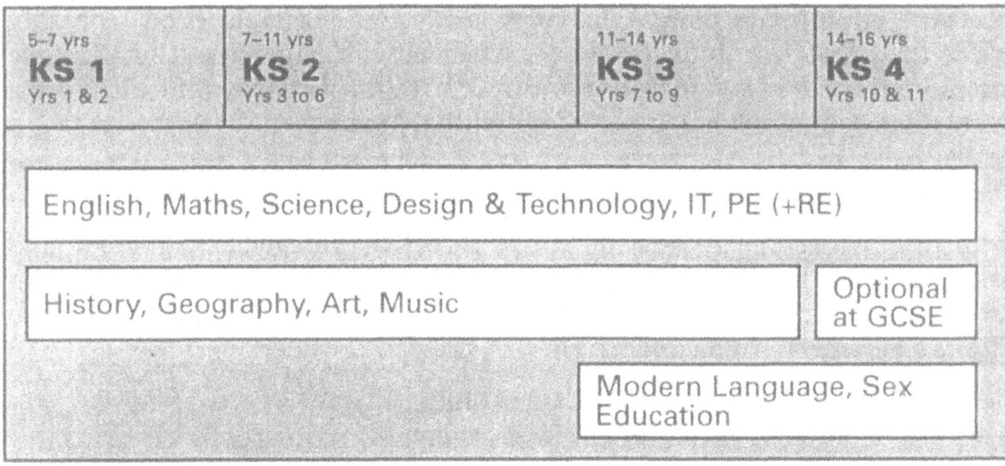

Figure 1.1 Revised National Curriculum

ISSUES FOR DEBATE

1. What is the ideology that underpins the National Curriculum?

The development of the National Curriculum needs to be placed in its political context. Since 1969 the Conservative Government has been in power for over 21 years and continuously since 1979. As we have seen, the 1970s saw the rise of the radical right and the era of the Black Papers (1969–75) vehemently criticising the educational system and schools in particular. Ball (1994) argues that during the 1970s and 1980s 'it became received wisdom within the Conservative Party that the school curriculum was out of control; that "real" knowledge was being replaced ... by an "ideological curriculum"' (p.33).

In spite of the priority which the Government says has been given to education policy, until recently there has been minimal consultation about its shape. Gilmore (1992) states that prior to 1987, education reforms were 'hammered out in ... no more than a month' and that consultation was inadequate, resulting in education legislation being rushed: 'During 1987 a new chapter for education was conceived and so speedily encapsulated in the Education Reform Bill of 1988 that it required hundreds of amendments. Yet again the Thatcher government legislated on the hoof' (p.205).

Egalitarianism began to lose its place in the educational debates (Feintuck, 1994, p.8). This came to full fruition in 1987 when the Secretary of State, Kenneth Baker, who was very keen to promote what would come to be known as the Education Reform Act 1988, stated that the age of egalitarianism was over, and there was a need 'to inject new vitality into the system [which] had become producer dominated' (cited in Maclure, 1992, p.xi).

The Government's proposed reforms, which emphasised the market forces philosophy, were seen by many educationists as potentially damaging and inappropriate for education (Wragg, 1988, p.5). The concepts frequently cited in education policy documents were free market forces, competition, privatisation, efficiency, cost effectiveness, value for money, choice, performance, standards, testing and accountability. Testing was considered to be crucial to improve quality control in schools. League tables were seen as a way to motivate schools to improve, with little regard given to different circumstances. Wragg (1988, p.11) regarded the Government's view of the curriculum and testing as 'survival of the fittest', while Ranson argued that the outcome was likely to be what it had always been in education: where those who can manipulate the system for their own purposes will be best served.

> Within the market place all are free and equal, only differentiated by their capacity to calculate their self–interest. Yet, of course, the market place masks its social bias. It elides, but reproduces, the inequalities which consumers bring to the market place. Under the guise of neutrality, the institution of the market actively confirms the pre-existing social order of wealth and privilege. (Ranson, 1988, quoted in Feintuck 1994, p.129)

Critics have argued that there is much confused thinking and contradiction in the 1988 Education Reform Act. In spite of the promotion of individual school autonomy in administrative matters, there has never been more central control of education, with the Secretary of State taking 418 new powers and adding over 200 more in the 1993 Act. Schools have to teach a prescribed curriculum and maintain a testing schedule; money and resources appear to dominate educational debate; and the National Curriculum promotes individualism at the expense of cooperation.

White (1993) argues that there is no well worked-out series of aims in the National Curriculum: 'The structural weakness of the 1988 Curriculum is plain. Its basis is the ten foundation subjects. What all these are supposed to be for has never been made clear' (p.9).

Kelly (1990) argues that there is 'no statement of philosophy or underlying ideals' (p.46) in the 1988 Act apart from raising standards. In his view, three major features characterise the ideology of the National Curriculum – instrumentalism, commercialism and élitism. As regards the first of these, Kelly suggests that the main concern of the constructors of the National Curriculum was with what education is for rather than what it is. Education was perceived as being preparation for adult life and employment, with very little consideration for the present. The emphasis was on economic considerations and preparation for the future rather than any development of intrinsic values.

The ideology of commercialism, says Kelly, is revealed in the imagery employed in the National Curriculum documentation – 'providers' of education, 'delivery' of the curriculum, 'machinery' to implement various aspects, 'users' and 'consumers' of the system, and the country's 'competitors'. Kelly, along with

Wragg (1988), Lawton (1992), White (1993), Ball (1994) and many others, argue that 'the picture is that of a factory–farming approach to schooling' (p.48). In contrast, the earlier Newsom Report (1963) had argued that 'An education that makes complete sense must provide opportunity for personal fulfilment – for the good life as well as for good living' (quoted in Kelly, 1990, p.50).

In the final analysis education is about promoting the kind of society we wish to establish. Tony Benn criticises both major political parties for failing to address this fundamental question:

> While we go on worshipping profit and neglecting need, prattling endlessly about productivity, competitiveness and economic efficiency, we are missing the central question, which is whether we want to be a community of interdependent people or driven back to the jungle where the strongest devour the weakest. (quoted in Kelly, 1990, p.50)

Lastly, Kelly (1990) argues that the National Curriculum – organised into subjects, with prescribed programmes of study and assessment and testing schedules – will promote élitism and 'selection by the back door'; and, by reinforcing the effects of competition on educational provision, is unlikely to meet the needs of the non–academic pupils.

There is general consensus among educationists that the National Curriculum was introduced without a coherent philosophy, was conceptually flawed and certainly lacked clarity. The consequence was the need to produce a new or revised National Curriculum six years after its introduction at a cost of £469 million (Hansard Vol. 235, no. 26, col. 287). As Lawton (1993) convincingly argues, 'The lesson which emerges from the 1988 National Curriculum is that educational planning – and in particular curriculum planning – should not be attempted with political timetables' (p.43).

Question for discussion

Should the National Curriculum have an overall aim? If so, what should it be?

---

2. What are the criticisms of the structure and content of the National Curriculum?

The original National Curriculum consultation document (DES, 1987) was issued during July and required responses by the end of September. The Government seemed to ignore the fact that schools were closed for at least five weeks during this period. As Golby (1987) states 'It is hard to escape the conclusion that "consultation" is an honorary term for a process more designed to secure unimpeded enactment of the wishes of central government than to provide a democratic forum' (p.3). According to Chitty (1992) there was a 'chorus of disapproval' by many teachers and educators (p.47). When Baker asserted that education should be led by its consumers not by its providers, the teachers received the message that their professionalism was undervalued and marginalised. As the Government was not prepared to disseminate the views of its critics, Haviland (1988) analysed the 20,000 replies received by the DES. Nearly 60 per cent of the responses concentrated on the National Curriculum.

Most approved the principle of *a* national curriculum, but also had serious reservations about the structure of *the* National Curriculum proposed by the Government.

Lawton and Chitty (1987) ponder what the consultation document might have looked like if HM Inspectorate's views of 'areas of experience' (similar to the National Curriculum in Scotland) had been the starting point for discussion[1] . They argue that 'Education is all about enriching a student's view of the world, not training him or her to give trite answers to complex questions, (p. 13).

Rather than broad areas of experience, we now have foundation subjects, a notion which has been criticised as being 'no more than lumps extracted from the curriculum *status quo* which the Government happens to approve of' as well as being both 'vague and mechanistic' (Chitty, 1992, p. 49). Merry (1991) suggests that

> the more fixed the curriculum becomes, the less it is able to respond to the real needs of individuals – any difficulties which arise are seen as the failure of the child to meet the demands of the curriculum rather than being seen as the failure of the curriculum to recognise and to meet the needs of the individual child. (p. 71)

It s true, of course, that since the 1970s some consensus had developed on the need for some form of common curriculum to ensure that children received a satisfactory experience throughout their schooling. However, as Coulby (in Bash and Coulby, 1989) argues:

> It is not the idea of a National Curriculum that has attracted protest, but the nature of the curriculum which is now being enforced, its mode of assessment and the high level of political control over it exerted centrally by the Secretary of State. (p. 55)

The concern has been that too much political control could lead to a more radical party political curriculum which could be extremist and doctrinaire. The time seems to be long past when the curriculum was seen as the responsibility of teachers and educators. Anthony Crosland, as Secretary of State for Education in the Labour Government of 1964–69, stated 'I didn't regard either myself or my officials as in the slightest degree competent to interfere with the curriculum. We're educational politicians and administrators, not professional educationists' (quoted in Francis, 1992, p. 11). How times have changed!

An insight into the mechanics of education policy-making in the late 1980s and early 1990s has been provided by Duncan Graham, the first Chairman and Chief Executive of the National Curriculum Council (NCC) between 1988 and 1991, and the person charged with introducing the new curriculum into all maintained schools in England and Wales under three Education Secretaries (Kenneth Baker, John McGregor and Kenneth Clarke). He tells how in 1990 the NCC had argued that the National Curriculum did not represent the 'whole curriculum', and that it had therefore decided to introduce a range of cross–curricula with published guidance on each one. The civil servants, however, had a strong desire to bring

---

[1] In 1977, HMI in a discussion document *Curriculum 11–16*, had suggested a curriculum based around eight 'areas of experience' (as distinct from subjects): the aesthetic and creative, the ethical, the linguistic, the mathematical, the physical, the scientific, the social and political, and the spiritual.

more central control to the curriculum as an effective means of increasing teacher accountability. Their response, according to Graham (1993), was dramatic:

> The roof fell in. A posse of civil servants descended on York (where the NCC was based) to tell the NCC that it could not continue work on nor publish the five booklets. They were a dangerous distraction, funds were not available. (p.20)
> There was a growing belief of [civil servants] in the Education Department that they knew best what should be in the curriculum even though they had never taught or been near a state school. (p. 22)

Graham accuses ministers of subverting the National Curriculum for political purposes ('a wilful distortion for political ends') and ignoring professional advice, and senior civil servants of obstructing the work of the NCC. Specifically, he accused Kenneth Clarke of subverting the history curriculum and interfering over teaching methods. Finally, Graham writes:

> I became acutely aware that in its implementation and substance this was a Civil Service driven curriculum and not the property of HMI [Her Majesty's Inspectors]. This was the first evidence of a huge *de facto* power shift in the way education was controlled in England and Wales. ... The National Curriculum was the [civil servants'] baby, their first major reform in Britain that had not been created by the educational professionals. (p. 30)

The civil servants and ministers were determined to amalgamate the NCC and the School Examination and Assessment Council (SEAC), established by the 1988 Act to supervise the curriculum and assessment procedures, so that a new single body could be under direct government control. In 1991 Graham, together with Philip Halsey, head of SEAC, suddenly 'retired'; they were replaced by a former member and former head of the Downing Street Policy Unit. In an editorial on 21 July 1991, the *Independent on Sunday* commented:

> When the history of twentieth-century British Education is written, the past ten days will be seen as a watershed. The Government has dropped any pretence that the National School Curriculum should be ideologically neutral. (Quoted in Chitty 1992, p. 82)

Question for discussion

Is it right that the content of the National Curriculum should be subject to the approval of the Secretary of State for Education, or should it be agreed by a body independent from the Government of the day?

---

3. Is the revised National Curriculum a fundamental improvement on the original version?

Following the publication of his interim and final reports on the revised National Curriculum, Dearing was generally seen to have 'dug the Minister out of a hole' and was for all practical purposes acting as the Education Secretary (*Education Guardian*, 14 December 1993, p.2). As we have seen, it had become generally accepted that the introduction of the National Curriculum was rushed, exceedingly bureaucratic and overloaded in content and assessment and testing procedures. The Government was desperate to get out of a mess exacerbated by teachers' antagonism and their boycotts of tests and assessment due to excessive work loads, a position which was upheld in the court. By comparing the documents pre- and post-Dearing, it is clear that something radical has taken place. For example, the proposals for the History National Curriculum (DES, 1991) was 237 pages (including 32 pages of introduction). The revised History National Curriculum (DFE, 1995a) is just 17 pages.

On becoming the new chief executive of SCAA in 1 October 1994, Nick Tate expressed confidence that the teachers would welcome the slimmed down curriculum which would allow them more flexibility: 'There has been a rolling back of the state in a sense because we are leaving more decisions to the schools'. He outlined the main tasks of SCAA in the *Education Guardian*, 20 July 1994, p.4:

1. convincing every teacher that the revised tests will give them useful information about their pupils' progress and how they compare against national norms. External markers will be employed;
2. monitoring the new curriculum 'from the day it is introduced' so that planning can be long term and strategic;
3. quality assurance work on public examinations. Support and guidance will be given to schools if and when they ask for it;
4. playing a creative role in the national debate about raising standards and challenging established practice and consensus which could lead to mediocrity.

While generally the Dearing revisions of the National Curriculum were welcomed, there were still misgivings exemplified by media headlines such as 'Unions split over the Dearing report' (*TES*, 7 January 1994), 'Unions divided over Dearing proposals' (*Independent*, 6 January 1994). The dilemma was mainly over whether teachers should continue to boycott even the reduced tests: 'It may seem politically expedient for teachers to do the tests this year but in the long run we will be left with results that are not valid' (*TES*, 7 January 1994). However, Robin Alexander and Jim Campbell, under the headline 'Curriculum imperialism' (*TES*, 28 January 1994) have gone full circle in the debate (comprehensively considered by Blenkin and Kelly, 1994) and challenged the basis of the Dearing curriculum. They ask what would be the most appropriate curriculum for primary education to meet the needs of children. Just by stating that a curriculum should be 'broad and balanced' does not make it so, they argue. Their complaint is that

> Any attempt to question the values underpinning these developments is met with populist hectoring about the need to forget the 'barmy theory' and get on with teaching children to 'read, write and add up' ... the model of high–priority basics and low-priority trimmings. (p. 8)

The writers maintain that the sharp divide between basics and the rest of the curriculum, and what the basics should comprise, need to be challenged. Dearing, they suggest, had missed the opportunity to establish a core curriculum comprising the essential skills and understandings drawn from all subjects:

> The larger questions about where the primary curriculum is going remain unaddressed, or at best are reduced to John Major's bizarre litany of Knowledge, Discipline, Tables, Sums, Dates, British History, Standard English, Grammar, Spelling, Marks, Tests, Good Manners and all the current guff of Back to Basics. (p.8)

They argue that primary schools have never neglected the basics and the importance of literacy is universally accepted.

On this view, it seems that the opportunity for a radical reform of the National Curriculum was missed. The debate is still urgently needed, but is unlikely to happen soon as no change is contemplated until the year 2000.

Question for discussion

What would you expect to be the main features of the debate for the next review of the National Curriculum?

THE FUTURE?

Graham (1993) reminds us that the National Curriculum is here to stay. No government is going to give up the power now held at the centre. The commitment is that there will be no substantial change to the curriculum for five years from August 1995. In the light of their experience from 1989 to 1995, teachers would welcome some stability to make the system work as well as possible for the benefit of all the pupils. However, given politicians' desire to be seen to try to raise standards and make schools more accountable, the publication of all test results might be imposed. In the meantime, only the core subjects will be nationally tested, and there is a danger that concentration will be given to these. As Graham points out, 'There is nothing broad and balanced about the three Rs' (p.117).

All the same, while there is still considerable disquiet about the National Curriculum, maybe in the final analysis guarded optimism is required in the hope that the revised arrangements will regenerate our schools and give teachers and pupils greater opportunity to raise standards through requirements that are more realistic and leave some space for school curricular development.

FURTHER READING

Ball, S. (1994) *Education Reform: A Critical and Post–structural Approach*. Buckingham: Open University Press. (Chapter 3 'Education, Majorism and the curriculum of the dead'.)

Blenkin, G.M. and Kelly A.V. (eds) (1994) *The National Curriculum and Early Learning:An Evaluation*. London: Chapman (Chapter 1 'Beyond the rhetoric and the discourse', Chapter 2 'Early learning and a developmentally appropriate curriculum: some lessons from research', and Chapter 10 'In conclusion: no improved quality without informed policy'.)

Chitty, C. (1992) *The Education System Transformed*. Manchester: Baseline Books. (Chapter 4 'The Education Reform Act 1988', Chapter 5 'Education reform reversals and amendments'.)

Chitty, C. and Simon, B. (eds) (1993) *Education Answers Back: Critical Responses to Government Policy*, London: Lawrence and Wishart. (Part II.)

Feintuck, M. (1994) *Accountability and Choice in Schooling*. Buckingham: Open University Press. (Chapters 1 and 2.)

O'Hear, P. and White, J. (eds) (1993) *Assessing the National Curriculum*. London: Chapman. (Chapters 1 to 6.)

Kelly,V. (1990) *The National Curriculum: A Critical Review*. London: Chapman. (Chapters 1–3, 6 and Conclusion.)

REFERENCES

Bash, L. and Coulby, D. (1989) *The Education Reform Act: Competition and Control*. London: Cassell.

Ball, S. J. (1994) *Education Reform: A Critical and Post–structural Approach*. Buckingham: Open University Press.

Blenkin, G. M. and Kelly, A.V. (eds) (1994) *The National Curriculum and Early Learning: An Evaluation*. London: Chapman.

Chitty, C. (1992) *The Education System Transformed*. Manchester: Baseline Books.

Department of Education and Science (1985) *Better Schools*. London: HMSO.

Department of Education and Science (1987) *The National Curriculum 5–16: A Consultation Document*. London: DES.

Department of Education and Science (1989) *National Curriculum: From Policy to Practice*. London: HMSO.

Department of Education and Science (1991) *Proposals for the History National Curriculum*. London: DES.

Department for Education (1994) *English in the National Curriculum*. London: HMSO.

Department for Education (1995a) *History in the National Curriculum*. London: HMSO.

Department for Education (1995b) *Information Technology in the National Curriculum*. London: HMSO.

Feintuck, M. (1994) *Law and Political Change: Accountability and Choice in Schooling*. Buckingham: Open University Press.

Fitzgerald, J. (1991) *Working with the National Curriculum in the Primary School*. London: Industrial Society Press.

Francis, P. (1992) *What's Wrong with the National Curriculum?*. Much Wenlock: Liberty Books.

Gilmore, I. (1992) *Dancing with Dogma: Britain under Thatcherism*. London: Simon and Schuster.

Golby, M. (ed) (1987) *Perspectives on the National Curriculum*. Exeter: School of Education, University of Exeter.

Graham, D. (1993) *A Lesson for Us All: The Making of the National Curriculum*. London: Routledge.

Haviland, J. (1988) *Take Care, Mr Baker!* London: Fourth Estate.

Kelly, A. V. (1990) *The National Curriculum: A Critical Review*. London: Chapman.

Lawton, D. (1989) *Education, Culture and the National Curriculum*. London: Hodder & Stoughton.

Lawton, D. (1992) *Education and Politics in the 1990s: Conflict or Consensus?* London: Falmer.

Lawton, D. (1993) 'Is there coherence and purpose in the National Curriculum?', in C. Chitty and B. Simon (eds) (1993) *Education Answers Back: Critical Responses to Government Policy*. London: Lawrence and Wishart.

Lawton, D. and Chitty, C. (1987) 'Two concepts of a national curriculum', in M. Golby (ed.), *Perspectives on the National Curriculum*. Exeter: School of Education, University of Exeter.

McGill, P. (1994) 'Tate à tête'. *Education Guardian*, 20 September 1994, p.4.

Maclure, S. (1992) *Education Re-formed*. London: Hodder & Stoughton.

Merry, R. (1991) 'Curriculum lessons from Europe'. *British Journal of Special Education*, 18 2, 71–74.

Moon, B. (1991) *A Guide to The National Curriculum*. Oxford: Oxford University Press.

Pring, R. (1989) *The New Curriculum*. London: Cassell.

SCAA (1994) *The National Curriculum and Its Assessment: Final Report*. (The Dearing Report) London: SCAA.

White, J. (1993) 'What place for values in the National Curriculum?' in P. O'Hear and J. White, (eds) *Assessing the National Curriculum*. London: Chapman.

Whitty, G. (1990) 'The New Right and the National Curriculum: state control or market forces' in M. Flude and M. Hammer (eds) (1990) *The Education Reform Act, 1988: Its Origins and Implications*. London: Falmer

Wragg, T. (1988) *Education in the Market Place: The Ideology Behind the 1988 Education Bill*. London: NUT.

CHAPTER 2

The National Curriculum: Themes and Issues

Roger Marples

INTRODUCTION

Schools have a statutory obligation under Section 1 of the Education Reform Act 1988 (ERA) to provide a 'broad and balanced' curriculum which:

- promotes the spiritual, moral, cultural, mental and physical development of pupils of the school and of society
- prepares pupils for the opportunities, responsibilities and experiences of adult life.

Whatever one's views on the National Curriculum, there were many schools, prior to its inception, whose curricula could be described as anything but 'broad and balanced' or directly concerned with life after school (Smith and Tomlinson, 1989). None the less, personal and social education was well established in secondary schools, and many primary schools were beginning to make formal provision for what, in the view of many teachers, was not being addressed in the mainstream curriculum – issues such as health and sex education, moral education, consumer education, social and life-skills. That all this was quite familiar to the authors of the National Curriculum is evident in the DES consultation document *The National Curriculum 5–16* (1987). But, having devised a subject-based curriculum, there was precious little room for other issues with a legitimate claim in any curriculum aspiring to breadth and balance.

THE POLICY

Within a year of the Education Reform Act, the National Curriculum Council (1990a) acknowledged that the National Curriculum was not the 'whole curriculum', and in the following year sought to redress this deficiency by producing a document entitled *The Whole Curriculum*.. The first page stated that 'the National Curriculum alone will not provide the necessary breadth'. The ten subjects combined with RE were regarded as a 'foundation' to which needed to be added not only additional subjects such as a second language or economics (particularly at Key Stage 4), but also cross-curricular elements and extra-curricular activities. The cross-curricular elements were identified as:

- *dimensions*, e.g. equal opportunities, with special reference to gender, ethnic minorities and special educational needs

KEY POINTS

- The National Curriculum is not the 'whole curriculum'
- Foundation subjects should be supplemented by additional subjects, cross-curricular elements and extra-curricular activities
- Political issues must be taught so as to give 'a balanced presentation of opposing views', and political activities by juniors are forbidden (Education (No. 2) Act 1986, ss.45-6)
- Sex education:
- This is compulsory in secondary schools and special schools with secondary-aged pupils but discretionary in primary schools
- It must be taught with 'due regard to moral considerations and the value of family life'
- Governing bodies must produce a policy statement
- Parents can withdraw children from sex education lessons which are outside National Curriculum subjects
- It is unlawful to teach the acceptability of homosexuality as a pretended family relationship

(Education (No. 2) Act 1986, s.s.45-6; Education Act 1993, s.241; Local Government Act 1988, s.88)

- *skills* in communication, numeracy, study, problem-solving, personal and social matters, and information technology
- *themes*, e.g. economic and industrial understanding (EIU), health education, careers education and guidance, environmental education, and education for citizenship

The five themes were acknowledged as being in no way conclusive but were considered as 'pre-eminent' and 'essential parts of the whole curriculum'. During 1990 the NCC produced five documents in the *Curriculum Guidance* series devoted to each theme, the principal recommendations of which are outlined below.

Education for Economic and Industrial Understanding

The aim of EIU, we are told in *Curriculum Guidance 4* (NCC, 1990b), is to help pupils make decisions about how they contribute to the economy through their work, how to organise their finances and how to spend their money. Industrial understanding is required in order to help them contribute to an industrialised, highly technological society.

From the start it is recognised as controversial that pupils should be encouraged to explain their own and other people's values and beliefs, although the curiously hybrid nature of EIU, with its uncomfortable mixture of economic concepts and skills appropriate to adult life and the world of work, seems to go unrecognised. The authors fight shy of a succinct definition of EIU, and rely instead on a broadly-based list of knowledge, understanding, skills and attitudes. Pupils are expected to acquire:

- knowledge and understanding of key economic concepts such as production, distribution and supply, how business creates wealth for individuals and the country, and the organisation of industry and industrial relations
- analytical, personal and social skills, ranging from the ability to collect, analyse and interpret economic data, to the ability to cooperate as part of a team in enterprise activities
- attitudes such as respect for evidence and rational argument and concern for human rights as these are affected by economic decisions.

EIU is supposed to be for all pupils of whatever background or ability and is expected to be delivered *within* most if not all subjects. The content is left much to individual teachers, but the result is something less helpful than it might have been to those teachers without a background in economics or industry.

Health Education

Health Education has a longer history in schools than EIU, and *Curriculum Guidance 5* (NCC, 1990c) is not the first advisory document on the subject. Apart from the Health Education Authority's *Schools' Health Education Project 5–13* (Cowley, 1983), a useful HMI paper was produced in 1986 as part of the series *Curriculum Matters*. *Curriculum Guidance 5* differs from these in selecting nine discrete components which it sees as constituting a coherent HE programme. These are:

1. substance use and misuse
2. sex education
3. family life education
4. safety
5. health related exercise
6. nutrition
7. personal hygiene
8. environmental aspects of HE
9. psychological aspects of HE.

Most of the document is devoted to what children should know and understand at each Key Stage in each component. There is an interesting section devoted to curriculum 'mapping' designed to show the contribution each component can make to the National Curriculum, Personal and Social Education, child development courses and other cross-curricular themes. It is for the most part a helpful document and considerably less daunting than EIU.

Policy on sex education is enshrined in law which has changed since the publication of *Curriculum Guidance 5* in 1990. At that time, governing bodies of maintained schools were required under the Education (No.2) Act 1986 to determine whether or not sex education should be part of their secular curriculum, and to provide a separate written statement of policy with regard to the content and organisation of sex education. The Act also required of LEAs, governing bodies and head teachers that any sex education provided should 'encourage ... pupils to have due regard to moral considerations and the value of family life'. The Local Government Act 1988 made it illegal to teach the acceptability of homosexuality in terms of family relationships. In addition, the Statutory Orders outlining the science curriculum provided for the coverage of sexual development and reproduction as well as provision in Key Stage 3 for the ways in which health may be affected by diet, lifestyle, bacteria and viruses (including HIV).

The 1993 Education Act changed some of the legal requirements significantly:

- Sex education is now a compulsory part of the National Curriculum for secondary age children, with governing bodies no longer having discretion whether or not it should be taught except in primary schools.
- Since August 1994 it has no longer been a requirement of the science curriculum to refer to HIV/AIDS, sexually transmitted diseases or any aspect of sexual behaviour other than biological aspects, though sex education outside the National Curriculum subjects is expected to include these topics.
- Parents now have the right to withdraw their children from sex education lessons outside the National Curriculum, with the result that some children may not receive information about sexually transmitted diseases.

Careers Education and Guidance

Like Health Education, Careers Education and Guidance has had a long history, albeit of widely varying quality. By the mid–1980s, all schools, including primary schools, were being exhorted to take the subject seriously. The White Paper *Better Schools* (DES, 1985) argued that helping pupils acquire knowledge and skills relevant to adult life was a major objective of education; and in a joint DES/Employment Department Paper *Working Together for a Better Future* (1987) the same message was reiterated, together with the requirement that LEAs and individual schools produce policy statements. The following year HMI produced *Curriculum Matters 10: Careers Education and Guidance 5–16*, which provided a rationale for the subject as well as guidance on implementation. It was again insisted that Careers Education should begin in primary schools and that a taught element should exist in all secondary schools. By 1990, when *Curriculum Guidance 6* was produced, the NCC had much on which to rely, and the suggested aims clearly reflect those outlined in *Curriculum Matters 10*. Pupils are expected to:

- know themselves better
- be aware of education, training and career opportunities
- make choices about their own continuing education and training and about career paths
- manage transitions to new roles and situations.

Such aims are designed to promote personal and social development and to challenge stereotyped attitudes to education, training and career opportunities, as well as promote five strands in pupils' development each of which should permeate the curriculum at every Key Stage. These are:

- *Knowledge of self*: qualities, attitudes, values, abilities, strengths, limitations, potential and needs
- *Roles:* position and expectations in relation to family, community and employment
- *Work:* application of productive effort including paid employment and unpaid work in the community and home
- *Career:* sequence of roles undertaken through working life and the personal success, rewards and enjoyment they bring
- *Transition:* development of qualities and skills which enable pupils to adjust to and cope with change, e.g. self-reliance, adaptability, flexibility, decision-making, problem-solving.

Environmental Education

Everything we do has environmental consequences. This has always been the case, but in recent years we have become more aware of global warming, the greenhouse effect and acid rain. The result has been that governments the world over have been forced, in ways scarcely imaginable even a decade ago, to concern themselves with ecological and environmental problems. Part of this concern has been manifested in an increased governmental awareness of the importance of environmental education. In 1987, the World Commission on Environmental Development published the Brundtland Report, *Our Common Future,* which called for a 'vast campaign of education, debate and public participation'. In the same year, the European Year of the Environment was marked by the production of education packs for each school by the Council for Environmental Education, and the following year the EC Council of Ministers agreed to take concrete steps to promote environmental education throughout the Community.

Curriculum Guidance 7 (NCC, 1990e) was thus a response to the importance of education in increasing awareness and concern about the environment. It sees the aims of environmental education as threefold:

- to promote opportunities to acquire the knowledge, values, attitudes, commitment and skills needed to protect and improve the environment
- to encourage pupils to examine and interpret the environment from a variety of perspectives
- to arouse pupils' awareness and curiosity about the environment and encourage active participation in resolving environmental problems.

Education for Citizenship

In the 1960s, it was not unusual to find 'civics' courses in schools for which one could obtain a certificate from the Royal Society of Arts. In addition there were A-levels in something called 'British Constitution'. More recently, the Politics Association has been instrumental in establishing politics in schools, for which there is an A-level and a journal, *Teaching Politics*. 'Political literacy' is considered to be one of the principal aims of political education, and there have been numerous publications in which this notion has been explicated. 'Education for Citizenship' is a relative newcomer to educational discourse, in spite of the efforts of the Council for Education in World Citizenship, which for years has been attempting to raise the profile of this aspect of education. There now exists a Citizenship Foundation, a Centre for Citizenship Studies in Education and an Institute for Citizenship Studies which provide support for teachers.

In 1988, the Speaker of the House of Commons set up a Commission on Citizenship to consider how to promote 'active citizenship' not merely in schools but in the wider community. The first recommendation of its report (Speaker's Commission, 1990) states that

> the study and experience of citizenship should be part of every young person's education ... from the earliest years of schooling ... into the post-school years within further and higher education and the youth service. (p.xix)

The Report's influence is immediately obvious in the definition of education for citizenship employed by *Curriculum Guidance 8* (NCC, 1990f). Education for Citizenship 'develops the knowledge, skills and attitudes necessary for exploring, making informed decisions about and exercising responsibilities and rights in a democratic society' (p.2).

Eight knowledge components, all of which are duly recognised as being interrelated, are suggested:

- the nature of community
- roles and relationships in a pluralist society
- the duties, responsibilities and rights of being a citizen
- the family
- democracy in action
- the citizen and the law
- work, employment and leisure
- public services.

Guidance is also given on education in the values implicit in citizenship, such as independence of thought, a constructive interest in community affairs, a willingness to examine evidence and opinions, and to discuss differences in attempts to resolve conflicts (p.4).

ISSUES FOR DEBATE

1. Problems of coherence

As was suggested earlier, it was not long after the creation of the National Curriculum before the NCC acknowledged that the core and foundation subjects were not the whole curriculum. This itself is a problematic concept in that it is not at all obvious what sort of thing a 'whole' curriculum would amount to. The problem with any such notion is that it suggests that there is nothing more to include, which is very odd indeed.

In the days before the National Curriculum many teachers, especially in primary education, began their curriculum planning with the pupil at centre stage. Admittedly a lot of this was ill-conceived and surrounded by confusion, such as the not infrequent failure to distinguish between children's best interests and that in which they are interested, but at least there was something at the centre trying to hold the curriculum together. The subject-based National Curriculum is, for the most part, a series of discrete and disconnected entities with each element, as David Hargreaves (1991) puts it, 'like a brick out of which children are expected to construct something meaningful'. However, in reality, says Hargreaves, the National Curriculum is more akin to a bomb site of disconnected bricks and fragments.

If the themes identified by the NCC are essential to personal and social well-being and thus have a justifiable place in the curriculum, there are ways of bringing a measure of what Hargreaves calls 'experiential coherence' to the curriculum whereby children (and their teachers) see the bricks (if that is what the individual tasks required of them are like) as having the potential to construct a meaningful and enduring edifice. One such way has recently been suggested by Chris Watkins (1995), who argues that the construction of a Personal and Social Education (PSE) curriculum should begin with the needs of the individual child, focusing on what he calls a person's 'seven selves' – bodily self, sexual self, social self, vocational self, moral and political self, self as learner, and self in the organisation. Here the 'whole person' rather than the 'whole curriculum' occupies centre stage.

This, of course, is only one suggestion among many others that cannot be pursued here, but it does raise a whole series of questions relating to the nature and status of both PSE and the various themes identified by the NCC, as well as the relationship between them. As recently as 1989, the NCC saw PSE as 'arguably the most important of the cross-curricular dimensions to which schools need to give attention'; and a recent Ofsted report (1994) acknowledges its importance, even if its interpretation of PSE bears little relation to the personal and social issues in the NCC *Guidance* documents. The result is one of confusion concerning both the status of PSE in official thinking and the role of PSE staff in incorporating the cross-curricular themes. The confusion arises from not addressing the needs of the whole child from the outset and in addressing each separately. The lack of coherence was exacerbated by arranging for each *Curriculum Guidance* paper to be written by different people and at different times. It is not surprising, therefore, that teachers remain confused and not a little daunted by what is expected of them.

When it comes to implementing the themes, there is evidence to show that most schools are less than enthusiastic (e.g. Whitty *et al.*, 1993). Teachers, pupils and parents have been led by Government rhetoric to accept that what really matters are 'proper' subjects. While both Environmental Education, and Economic and Industrial Understanding appear to bear some relationship to traditional and recognisable disciplines, it is not clear that the same can be said for Citizenship, Health Education and Careers Education. If they *are* proper subjects, why are they not part of the core and foundation lists, and why are they not examined? Nowhere in the *Curriculum Guidance* booklets are the themes referred to as a child's 'entitlement'. Little wonder that so many schools are not giving them the priority they undeniably deserve, and that they appear to enjoy less credibility than mainstream subjects. One of the principal difficulties associated with implementing the various themes is how progress is supposed to be monitored and evaluated. The virtue of attainment targets is that they at least force teachers to address questions relating to progression. All this requires proper coordination if all that is achieved is not to be either lost entirely or become so hit-and-miss, with overlap and repetition, that the end result is a hotchpotch deservedly lacking in status or credibility.

Question for discussion

In the year 2000, the National Curriculum may be reviewed again. Should 'cross-curricular themes' be given a higher profile? If so, what principles should inform the new policy framework to achieve this?

---

2. Problems with particular themes

Official documents such as *Curriculum Guidance 4–8* leave one with mixed feelings. On the one hand, it is encouraging to see that the forces of reaction, which were so prominent a feature of the Thatcher era, appear to be losing the debate. It is now being recognised, albeit somewhat belatedly, that there is such a thing as society and that schools have an important function in preparing young people for life within it. On the other hand, one is saddened, if not entirely unsurprised, by the quiescence in so many of these documents. Apart from paying lip service to the controversial nature of the material, there is little recognition of the richness of debate and ideological conflicts surrounding such things as the economy, the nature of work, the role of the family, the causes of poverty and ill-health, and environmental degradation. One has only to read the aims and objectives listed to appreciate how much importance is attached to understanding and apparently so little to criticism. There is, as we shall see when looking further at some problems within particular cross-curricular themes, if not a celebration of individualism with its association of rationality as enlightened self-interest, then a very strong emphasis on individual choice where the marketplace is seen as both given and good.

Economic and Industrial Understanding

As a discipline, economics is riddled with disagreement and competing views, and a failure to acknowledge this renders the whole enterprise inherently problematic. It is fair to say that most teachers do no have a background in the subject and may well experience difficulties in trying to grapple with complex economic concepts. Economics is not unique in this respect; much the same could be said of many concepts with which other themes are concerned. It is certainly insufficient a reason for denying children an understanding of economic concepts for, if Bruner (1960) is to be believed, any subject can be taught in an intellectually honest way to any child of any age or ability. Nevertheless, even if Jamieson (1991) is correct in claiming that it is unhelpful to begin with concepts and better to ask students questions about problems that puzzle them (e.g. 'Why is this price at this level?'), such an exercise will inevitably be more profitable where both teachers and taught have some familiarity with concepts and the disputes surrounding them. Again, EIU does not permeate the core and foundation subjects in a straightforward way. And if the coherence of economic understanding, and the other subjects in which such concepts are supposed to figure, is not to be seriously undermined, teachers will of necessity require much in terms of knowledge and skills. Until such time as additional resources are found for requisite training, it behoves us to remain sceptical about the quality and extent of the children's understanding at the various key stages.

A second problem concerns the approach adopted by *Curriculum Guidance 4*, which is seriously open to question. It minimises the controversy in what it readily admits to be a controversial subject, and substantially ignores the importance of issues such as exploitation, ownership and property rights, equitable distribution of profits, opportunities for decision-making within organisations, alienation and the division of labour. As Morrison (1994, p.8) says:

> Even though the document calls for a 'balanced presentation of opposing views' and for pupils to be 'encouraged to explore values and beliefs' ... its silence on what those might be is a most eloquent denial of their importance. It sees the rewards of wealth accruing to those individuals and communities possessed of 'business enterprise' [and] it assumes that industry and industrial relations are fixed – '*the* organisation of industry and industrial relations' [his emphasis]. It leaves the consideration of alternative economic systems until pupils have reached Key Stage 4, by which time many of them will have become saturated with the values of the existing economic system.

As far as 'enterprise' and its encouragement of mini-enterprises are concerned, one might well ask why children should be involved with any such thing, given its questionable intrinsic value. Why should we accept *Curriculum Guidance 4* when it says that 'pupils need to understand enterprise and wealth creation and develop entrepreneurial skills' (p 4) without further supportive argument? Surely it is possible to appreciate how an industry or business works without developing such skills in children? As Alistair Ross (1995, p.83) reminds us:

> Neither these understandings nor this skill are required by most children in order for them to become producers or consumers. Perhaps the intention was not so much that

> people 'understand' enterprise and wealth creation, but a desire that the population appreciate the need for the entrepreneur ... to be allowed free rein ..., Most people do not need [entrepreneurial] skills *per se*, [but perhaps it is] convenient if they develop the attitude that the outcomes of the application of these skills are so important that those exercising them should be held in proper esteem and privilege.

Health Education

It would be difficult to dispute the necessity of including any of the recommended nine components (see p.17) in a decent health education programme. Each one merits a chapter in its own right, but this section will focus on one of the most contentious – sex education. What is problematic is that this should be taught within the context of 'the value of family life', as required under the 1986 Act. Some, of course, would see nothing wrong in this – indeed as a component of health education, family life education (while not uncontroversial) is worthy of inclusion. But it needs to be handled with greater sensitivity than current officialese would suggest. The DfE Circular on sex education (1994), while recognising that many children do not have two parents, exhorts pupils 'whatever their circumstances to raise their sites' (p.6), thereby implying that certain family structures are better, or more valuable, than others. It is important to recognise value judgements for what they are, but pupils have a right to an education which will enable them to decide for themselves whether the rearing of children by single or homosexual or lesbian parents is acceptable, or indeed whether sexual relationships should be bracketed so firmly with family life issues.

A number of commentators have pointed to the individualistic bias implicit in *Curriculum Guidance 5*, with its emphasis on the importance of individual responsibility, choice and decision-making (see Morrison, 1994, pp.10–11, and Ross, 1995, Ch.4). Personal choice is emphasised in discussions of substance use and mis-use, sex education, health-related exercise, food and nutrition, and environmental aspects. All this is to ignore the fact that opportunities for choice are frequently determined by levels of income and education; and in a society which is reluctant to control the manipulation of information by vested interests within the food, drink and tobacco industries, it is absurdly late to delay the politics of health care to Key Stage 4.

Of course, individuals have a major responsibility for their own health, but subjects of such importance cannot be addressed in a social and political vacuum when there is reason to believe that inequality is the single most important factor affecting the nation's health. Even the DHSS (1976) has acknowledged the epidemiological evidence that direct government intervention in public health, housing and welfare has been more beneficial than medical treatment itself. In spite of the general recognition that 'the provision and acquisition of information alone is unlikely to promote healthy, or discourage unhealthy, behaviour' (*Curriculum Guidance 5*, p.7), the guidance for each component at every Key Stage emphasises knowledge and understanding of what individuals can do for themselves, with little if anything on the importance of values and attitudes or developing the capacity for social criticism.

Environmental Education

Curriculum Guidance 7 is understandably less 'individualistic' than the others, given the nature of the problem. While it would be absurd to minimise the effects of greater sensitivity on the part of individuals to such things as pollution, planning, design and conservation, the official advice creates the impression that increased knowledge and awareness will suffice. There is a complete avoidance of environmental ethics, and the tone adopted throughout does nothing to suggest that there might be anything questionable in the adoption of an anthropocentric or technocentric standpoint – a little more awareness here, or care there, and we shall all be all right. In all the proposals for work at the different Key Stages, there is not a hint of a suggestion that *sustainable* development might require a drastic change in life-styles requiring draconian legislation. Further, the whole thing is written as if *Curriculum Guidance 4* did not exist, with the consequent failure to recognise the tension involved between preparing children to become entrepreneurs, with its uncritical acceptance of the economic system and associated way of life, and the need for economic growth which is both ecologically sound and sustainable.

In a hard-hitting critique of *Curriculum Guidance 4* and *7*, John Ahier (1995, p.152) has this to say,

> Although they [aim] to provide guidance to professional adults ... they prematurely simplify and resolve the content of those concerns [which results in] a politically vacuous, benign context in which rational individuals combine their attitudes, skills and knowledge in the pursuit of their own ends ... These are ideological simplifications, in which more of the oppositional and critical positions on the environment and the economy are missing, notably those which are critical of our society's political and economic institutions, and those which see the need for more or less fundamental changes in culture and personal life.

Education for Citizenship

If we are supposed to be educating children for their future role as citizens, it is incumbent upon us to be clear about what the notion entails. 'Citizenship' is a deeply contested concept, the interpretation of which is inevitably coloured by one's ideological convictions. Some would interpret it in quasi-legal terms by reference to certain rights, such as the right of abode or the way voting rights are allocated. 'Good citizens' in one interpretation might be expected to accept their station with equanimity, combined with a willingness to work hard to ensure the maintenance of the social, political, economic and institutional *status quo*. It is their role to ensure that the boat is not rocked and existing social arrangements run smoothly. Stability and continuity are all important.

Another, and altogether more vibrant and dynamic model of citizenship demands more from citizens than a passive compliance with a particular state of affairs. On this model citizens are expected to participate actively in the body politic – not merely in terms of casting their votes in periodic elections, but shaping the social and economic conditions which govern our lives. Apathy, on such a view, is thus incompatible with being a good citizen. There are yet others, usually republicans, who refuse to accept that citizenship is compatible with the role of 'subject' of a monarch on the grounds that the opportunity to run for the position of Head of State is denied to them.

Assuming that agreement on the concept of citizenship is possible, we have still to determine what it is that we are citizens *of*. Are we citizens of England, the UK, the EC, or the world? Where do our duties and responsibilities as citizens begin and end? To what communities do we have legal ties and obligations, and upon what institutions – local, national or international – are we entitled to rely for protection, security and the dispensation of justice?

Curriculum Guidance 8 begins with a foreword by Duncan Graham, who 'defines' education for citizenship as something which 'helps [pupils] understand the duties, responsibilities and rights of every citizen and promotes concern for the values by which a civilised society is identified – justice, democracy, respect for the role of the law'. Yet again, understanding would seem to be more important than critical evaluation. Of course, it would be absurd to deny the importance of knowledge and understanding in empowering people, but the official guidance is replete with examples of understanding all sorts of things which facilitate the smooth functioning of existing society. As such it is highly complacent in refusing to acknowledge the necessity of making explicit the problematic status of the social, political and economic values underpinning the whole enterprise. Although it recognises that Education for Citizenship 'involves discussing controversial issues' (p.14), its silence on what these might be must leave many teachers at a loss as to how they might best proceed. It is all very well to invoke Sections 44 and 45 of the Education (No.2) Act 1986 in the demand for a recognition of 'all the views' presented in a 'balanced way'; but, when we look more closely at the areas of study, it is questionable whether *Curriculum Guidance 8* is itself consistent in this respect, given the implied assumptions on which so much of the context seems to rely.

There is, for instance, no mention of the role of the state nor a consideration of what is a burning issue in contemporary political philosophy, namely whether a liberal state should have no more than a minimal impact on people's lives (such as the provision of appropriate security whereby individuals are allowed to pursue their own good as they see it), or whether the state has a responsibility for ensuring the conditions for well-being (such as relief from poverty or the provision of health care and education). The relationship between the individual and society is assumed to be unproblematic, with nothing to indicate how the well-being of both is interdependent, and there is a very strong concern with the maintenance of 'order' and 'social stability'. What model of 'good citizen' is assumed here? Again, while there is a willingness to explore issues relating to justice, co-operation and discrimination, there is no mention of the problems facing ethnic minorities or with the ways in which they might feel excluded as 'citizens' in any way other than a juridical sense. Advice on teaching about the family is full of mixed messages. On the one hand, there is a willingness to 'distinguish myths and stereotypes from reality', while, on the other, an emphasis on the importance of family life for physical and spiritual well-being, as if family life were altogether less problematic than in reality it is. Single parent families are mentioned in the context of 'challenges' such as divorce and domestic problems, as though marriage was not itself a challenge.

The section 'Democracy in Action' raises important and perplexing questions. While there is the task of preparing pupils 'to participate fully as citizens ... in a democratic society', there is little to indicate what this involves or what a democratic society might be. According to advocates for representative democracy, there is little more to democracy than institutional provision for a competitive struggle for votes, with little or no opportunities for participation other than the selection of candidates. Participatory models, on the other hand, emphasise the importance of providing people with opportunities to participate in as many as possible of the major decision-making procedures affecting their lives. Even at Key Stage 4, *Curriculum Guidance 8* offers nothing more challenging than observing an election. Britain's political system is to be described and understood rather than challenged. If the authors are serious about the merits of participatory democracy, they must be prepared to acknowledge the implications of their own rhetoric for pedagogy, and for the importance of inculcating within pupils the wherewithal and disposition required if they are to be prepared for anything other than an attenuated form of democratic citizenship.

Question for discussion

Should school students be invited to challenge our political and economic institutions as well as to understand them?

THE FUTURE?

Like so much so-called educational reform, the attempt to broaden the National Curriculum may be described as too little too late. If the themes identified had been included in the National Curriculum from the outset, with each considered in relation to one another and in the context of the personal and social well-being of children, they might have been more enthusiastically welcomed by teachers. But this is water under the bridge. Meanwhile we should be grateful for any official approval of attempts to decompartmentalise the curriculum, but it remains to be seen whether or not schools have the will and the means required.

FURTHER READING

Buck, M. and Inman, S. (1992) *Whole School Provision for Personal and Social Development: The Role of Cross-Curricular Elements*. London: Goldsmiths College.

Dufour, B. (ed.) (1990) *The New Social Curriculum: A Guide to Cross-Curricular Themes*. Cambridge: Cambridge University Press.

Hall, G. (ed.) (1992) *Themes and Dimensions of the National Curriculum: Implications for Policy and Practice*. London: Kogan Page.

Siraj-Blatchford, J. and Siraj-Blatchford, A. (eds) (1995) *Educating the Whole Child: Cross-Curricular Skills, Themes and Dimensions*. Buckingham: Open University Press.

Verma, G.K. and Pumfrey, P.D. (eds) (1993) *Cross-Curricular Contexts, Themes and Dimensions in Secondary Schools*. London: Falmer Press.

Verma, G.K. and Pumfrey, P.D. (eds) (1993) *Cross-Curricular Contexts, Themes and Dimensions in Primary Schools*. London: Falmer.

REFERENCES

Ahier, J.(1995) 'Hidden controversies in two cross-curricular themes', in J. Ahier and A. Ross (eds) (1995) *The Social Subjects within the Curriculum: Children's Learning and the National Curriculum*. London: Falmer Press.

Bruner, J. (1960) *The Process of Education*. Harvard: Harvard University Press.

Cowley, J. (1983) *Schools' Health Education Project 5–13*. London: Health Education Council.

Department for Education (1994) *Education Act 1993: Sex Education in Schools* (Circular 5/94). London: DfE.

Department of Education and Science (1985) *Better Schools*. London: HMSO.

Department of Education and Science (1987) *The National Curriculum 5–16: A Consultation Document*. London: DES.

Department of Education and Science/Department of Employment (1987) *Working Together for a Better Future*. London: HMSO.

Department of Education and Science/HMI (1988) *Careers Education and Guidance from 5–6*. London: HMSO.

Department of Health and Social Security (1976) *Prevention of Health: Everybody's Business*. London: DHSS.

Hargreaves, D. (1991) 'Coherence and manageability: reflections on the National Curriculum and cross-curricular provision', *Curriculum Journal*, 2, 32–41.

Her Majesty's Inspectorate for Schools (1986) *Health Education from 5 to 16*. London: HMSO.

Jamieson, I. (1991) 'School work and real work: economic and industrial understanding in the curriculum', *Curriculum Journal*, 2, 55-67.

Morrision, K. (1994) *Implementing Cross-Curricular Themes*. London: David Fulton.

National Curriculum Council (1990a) *The Whole Curriculum*. York: NCC.

National Curriculum Council (1990b) *Curriculum Guidance 4: Education for Economic and Industrial Understanding*. York: NCC.

National Curriculum Council (1990c) *Curriculum Guidance 5: Health Education*. York: NCC.

National Curriculum Council (1990d) *Curriculum guidance 6: Careers Education and Guidance*. York: NCC.

National Curriculum Council (1990e) *Curriculum Guidance 7: Environmental Education*. York: NCC.

National Curriculum Council (1990f) *Curriculum Guidance 8: Education for Citizenship*. York: NCC.

Office for Standards in Education (1994) *Spiritual, Moral, Social and Cultural Development*. London: Ofsted.

Ross, A. (1995) 'The whole curriculum, the National Curriculum and social studies', in J. Ahier and A. Ross (eds) *The Social Subjects within the Curriculum: Children's Learning and the National Curriculum*. London: Falmer.

Smith, D.J. and Tomlinson, (1989) *The School Effect: A Study of Multiracial Comprehensive Schools*. London: Policy Studies Institute.

Speaker's Commission (1990) *Encouraging Citizenship*. London: HMSO.

Watkins, C. (1995) 'Personal-social education and the whole curriculum', in R. Best, P. Lang, C. Lodge and C. Watkins (eds) *Pastoral Care and Personal-Social Education: Entitlement and Provision*. London: Cassell.

Whitty, G., Rowe, G. and Aggleton, P. (1993) 'Subjects and themes in the secondary school curriculum', *Research Papers in Education*, 9, 159–180.

World Commission on Environment and Development (1987) *Our Common Future* (Brundtland Report). Oxford: Oxford University Press.

CHAPTER 3

The National Curriculum: Assessment

Derek Shaw

INTRODUCTION

The early discussions surrounding the move towards a National Curriculum took place against the background of the then prevailing view that what was taught, how it was taught and how pupils' learning would be assessed were matters for local education authorities and teachers, rather than central government. Though the Assessment of Performance Unit (APU) had been established in 1974, its purpose had been to *monitor* pupil performance and to *inform* the Education Secretary of educational standards and any discernible trends in those standards. The Government of the day did not seem to be intent on having a direct stake in assessment as it applied to individual pupils and schools. Indeed, it acknowledged concerns that critics of later legislation were to emphasise:

> 'League tables' of school performance based on examination or standardised test results in isolation can be seriously misleading because they fail to take account of other important factors such as the wide differences between school catchment areas.
>
> It has been suggested that individual pupils should at certain ages take external 'tests of basic literacy and numeracy', the implication being that those tests should be of a national character and universally applied. *The Government rejects this view.* (DES, 1977, p. 16, 18, emphasis added)

Richard Daugherty was a member of the School Examinations and Assessment Council (SEAC) policy committee on National Curriculum assessment. In his very informative book, he reviews the perspectives on the role of assessment as expressed in a succession of documents from the DES and HMI between 1977 and 1985. He concludes: 'There is no hint ... of schools and teachers being required, as distinct from encouraged, to assess their pupils' attainment at more regular intervals and on a more systematic basis' (Daugherty, 1995, p. 6). The shift that took place from this exhortational position towards one of direct intervention is, at least in part, attributable to the presence of Sir Keith Joseph as Secretary of State from 1981–86. At the North of England Education Conference in Sheffield in 1984, he emphasised:

- a commitment to higher standards
- examinations that focused on pupils' achievements (rather than on simply selecting or ranking them)
- the inclusion of parents and employers in the selection of educational objectives.

In the same year the DES published *Records of Achievement: A Statement of Policy* in which these principles were made clearly visible. Later in the 1980s, the General Certificate of Secondary Education (GCSE) examination introduced a system of *grade criteria,* and incorporated *coursework* into the assessment procedures. Though coursework had figured in the former Certificate of Secondary Education (CSE), it had not been part of the Ordinary level (O–level) examining process.

We see here an emerging set of considerations which subsequently become the basis of Government policy. Further wrangling would take place within the Conservative Party and within the Government in the transformation of these latent principles to legislative realities. Readers wishing to pursue this further are referred to Ball (1990), Knight (1990) and Lawton, (1992).

THE POLICY

KEY POINTS

- 'Assessment lies at the heart of promoting children's learning'
- Subject criteria for both primary and secondary age phases
- Attainment targets against which achievement is tested
- Initial acceptance of most of the proposals by the Government's Task Group on Assessment and Testing, but later radical amendments
- Assessment through
  - standard assessment tasks (SATs) at the end of each key stage
  - teacher assessments (TAs) throughout each key stage
- Level descriptors for assessing children's attainment
- Reporting and publishing aggregated results
- National administration of assessment

In January 1987, again at the North of England Education Conference, the Secretary of State, now Kenneth Baker, indicated that the focus on subject criteria already in place in the GCSE should be extended to the primary phase. Later Baker was also to make clear that he envisaged targets for the key stages which would act as criteria for testing, but would not emphasise simply the testable at the expense of other desirable educational outcomes and experiences. Further, he made it clear that teachers would be the principal assessors, with suitable moderation arrangements.

In July 1987, and prior to introducing to Parliament the Bill that would give force to these proposals, Baker established the Task Group on Assessment and Testing (TGAT) under the chairmanship of Professor Paul Black. Its brief was 'to advise on the practical considerations governing assessment within the National Curriculum' (DES, 1987, para. 1). The TGAT Report (DES, 1987) and its supplements (1988) set out a number of proposals to meet the Government's ambitions. Believing that 'assessment lies at the heart of promoting children's learning', the report ambitiously set out the four criteria for an assessment system that would guide its deliberations. They were:

- The assessment results should give direct information about pupils' achievement in relation to objectives: they should be criterion-referenced.
- The results should provide a basis for decisions about pupils' further learning needs: they should be formative.
- The scales or grades should be capable of comparison across classes and schools, if teachers, pupils and parents are to share a common language and common standards: so the assessments should be calibrated or moderated.
- The ways in which criteria and scales are set up and used should relate to expected routes of educational development, giving some continuity to a pupil's assessment at different ages: the assessment should relate to progression. (DES, 1987, para. 5)

The Report continued 'Unless the criteria are met, the potential of national assessment in assisting learning and supporting the professional development of teachers is unlikely to be realised' (para. 6).

These paragraphs related to several distinct purposes and interests. The concern with criterion-referencing reflects Joseph's earlier priority that assessment should focus on pupils' achievements in relation to previously set targets rather than to the achievements of other children (norm-referencing). The assertion that assessment is intrinsic to teaching and learning, i.e. is formative, was designed to appeal to teachers, confirming the centrality of the teacher in the learning process. The third criterion, moderation, underpinned ideas of reporting and, implicitly, accountability, both of which were high on the agenda of the Conservative Right at this time (and subsequently found endorsement across the political spectrum). The fourth criterion, progression, encompassed both teachers' and parents' concern for the progress of individual pupils, and also laid down a basis for judging the performance of schools. Indeed this is the essence of the 'value added' concept that was later to become so influential.

Related to these criteria, TGAT was also guided by four purposes of assessment:

- *formative,* so that the positive achievements of a pupil may be recognised and discussed and the appropriate next steps may be planned
- *diagnostic,* through which learning difficulties may be scrutinised and classified so that appropriate remedial help and guidance provided
- *summative,* for the recording of the overall achievement of a pupil in a systematic way

- *evaluative*, by means of which some aspects of the work of a school, an LEA or other discrete part of the educational service can be assessed and/or reported upon. (para. 23)

The Committee contrasted a broadly based process of assessment, commonly employed by teachers in their classrooms, with more focused tests undertaken to examine and measure specific elements of understanding, knowledge and skill. They pointed out the limitations of assessment in generating results which would enable comparisons to be made between schools and pupils, whilst recognising that such procedures have the capacity to offer 'richness of detail and a validity in context'. Turning to tests, the Committee highlighted the need for some aspects of assessment to be formally prescribed and undertaken in a closely monitored set of circumstances. It also argued that the style of 'test' need not be narrowly conceived as an 'externally-prescribed paper and pencil test, formal and unimaginative in scope, to be attempted in a set time on a formal occasion and marked according to set rules' (para. 45). Accordingly, it introduced the term 'standard assessment task' (SAT) to refer to a testing procedure that is both standardised and drawn from a diverse pool of activities, appropriate to the wide scope of achievement to be examined. The Report contained several significant comments which demonstrate that the Task Group was at least as aware as any of its critics of the balancing act that it was trying to accomplish 'We are required to propose a national assessment system which enhances teaching and learning without any increase in the calls on teachers' and pupils' time for activities which do not directly promote learning' (para. 24).

Judging from teachers' reactions since the system was introduced, readers may be tempted to conclude that this particular goal has proved elusive; but TGAT emphasised this consideration when justifying its attempt to avoid 'batteries of assessments and tests' in meeting its four purposes:

> Some purposes may, however, be served by combining in various ways the findings of assessments designed primarily for a different purpose. It is possible to build up a comprehensive picture of the overall achievements of a pupil by aggregating, in a structured way, the separate results of a set of assessments designed to serve formative purposes. (para. 25)

When the subject working parties began to produce their reports, it quickly became apparent that any attempt to conduct assessments across the whole of the National Curriculum would be a task of enormous proportions. Anticipating this, TGAT had proposed that 'an individual subject should report a small number (preferably no more than four and never more than six) of profile components reflecting the variety of knowledge, skills and understanding to which the subject gives rise. (para. 35).

In the way that National Curriculum has since developed, these 'profile components' came to be identified with attainment targets (ATs), each supported by a battery of 'statements of attainment'. The scope for assessable elements quickly became very great indeed, and generated over 1,000 statements of attainment. At the end of each key stage, these were used to judge at what point, on a 10–level scale, each pupil should be placed.

Sensitive both to teachers' professional concerns, pupils' learning and a broader public interest, TGAT attempted to locate its approach to the mechanics of assessment firmly within an 'educational' framework. Its 44 recommendations included the following:

- The 'standard assessment tasks' on which the national system would be based would employ a wide range of modes of presentation, operation and response (para. 50).
- Teachers' ratings should be moderated in such a way as to convey and to inform national standards (para. 62).
- The ages of the national assessment should be 7, 11, 14 and 16 (para. 92).
- National assessment results for any individual pupil should be confidential (para. 131).
- National assessment results for pupils ... aggregated at school level, should be published as part of each school's report (paras 137/138).
- Like all children, those with special educational needs require attainable targets to encourage their development and promote their self-esteem (para. 169).

Even a cursory glance at these proposals will reveal that a system incorporating all these principles would be both expensive and time-consuming. The point was not missed by other observers. As a result of a leaked memo, it became public knowledge that there was a difference of opinion between Downing Street and the Department over some of these proposals. In particular, concern was expressed over 'an enormously elaborate and complex system', and the high potential cost. In the event, though, the Department broadly accepted the TGAT proposals.

The passage of the Education Reform Act was followed by the establishment of two quangos to be responsible for administering the proposals relating to the National Curriculum. These were the National Curriculum Council (NCC) and the School Examinations and Assessment Council (SEAC). They have since been replaced by one body, the School Curriculum and Assessment Authority (SCAA).

The accumulating issues that have been discussed so far acted to compound other difficulties that were broached in Chapter 1. The upshot was an invitation to Sir Ron Dearing in 1993 to undertake a review of the existing arrangements for the National Curriculum and its assessment. Apart from being asked to review the scope for slimming down the curriculum, Dearing's remit was to consider:

- how the central administration of the National Curriculum and testing arrangements could be improved;
- how the testing arrangements might be simplified; and
- the future of the 10–level scale for recognising children's attainment.

On the first matter, readers will be unsurprised to read that Dearing concluded:

> The purpose of national tests is primarily to provide a summative contribution to the assessment of performance, and any diagnostic or formative elements should be subsidiary to that purpose and should only be included exceptionally where shown

> to be a cost-effective way of contributing formative information about a pupil. (Dearing, 1994: Appendix 1)

As regards ways of simplifying testing, Dearing echoed the view expressed by Gipps (1993) that one programme of assessment cannot fulfil four purposes, and he placed the emphasis squarely on summative assessment. In doing so, he also reflected the interest of Government in collecting information to serve as a basis for the evaluation and comparison of schools. In addressing the problem of teacher overload in assessing pupils according to numerous attainment targets, Dearing noted:

> There is no requirement to report National Curriculum levels for the non-core subject attainment targets at the end of the key stage. (Appendix 6, para. 21)

> There are *no requirements to keep records in any particular manner* nor to keep records against individual statements of attainment. Also, there is <u>no</u> requirement to keep evidence of the attainments of every pupil in every attainment target. (Appendix 6, para. 6, original emphasis)

Dearing also recommended that national tests at Key Stages 1–3 be limited to the core subjects, at least for the forthcoming three years.

The thorny subject of the original 10–level scale for assessment raised technical problems that go beyond the scope of this chapter. Dearing (1994) was clear, however, that the scale was 'unnecessarily complex and excessively prescriptive' (para. 2.28), and, after discussing possible solutions, he elected a 'keep and modify' option. What was needed, he said, was 'a definition of what is expected at each level, which is sufficiently clear to be of use to teachers but which avoids the excessive detail of the present approach' (para. 2.33). And so were born nine level descriptors (levels 1 to 8 plus exceptional performance). At the end of each key stage, teachers decide which level descriptor best matches pupils' achievement.

If Dearing was ready to see the importance of recognising the effects on teachers, he was none the less conscious of the important diagnostic and formative roles for teacher assessment that TGAT had underlined. Echoing the complaint from teachers about the lack of guidance in these matters, Dearing considered that the SCAA could provide guidance for the moderation of teacher assessment through continuing to produce examples of pupils' work at different levels and commentary explaining why the work met certain criteria. This particular recommendation has been followed by the publication of a series of booklets under the generic title *Consistency in Teacher Assessment: Exemplification of Standards*, (SCAA, 1995). A further recommendation was plainly at odds with the previously reported suspicions of teachers held by Ministers. 'Teacher assessment should have equal standing with national tests in reporting to parents and others by whatever means' (Appendix 1).

Two other matters emerging from the Dearing Review deserve a mention. The first was concerned with the effects of National Curriculum assessment on children with special educational needs, about which a further review was recommended. The second, which similarly is now subject of further work, is concerned with 'value-added', as described in the last chapter of this book.

ISSUES FOR DEBATE

1. What purposes do SATs serve?

The introduction of SATs has probably been the most contentious aspect of the National Curriculum. The difficulties are of two kinds: the preparation of the SATs themselves and the reliability of the test results.

Discussing the potential for the development of SATs, the TGAT Committee had exemplified the range of possibilities by describing three aspects (or modes) of the task, as follows:

- *presentation:* the method of delivery of the questions – oral, written, pictorial, video, computer, practical demonstration;
- *operation:* the expected method of working – mental only, written, practical, oral;
- *response:* pupils may answer in various ways – choosing one option in a multiple-choice question, writing a short prescribed response, open-ended writing, oral, practical procedure observed, practical outcome or product, computer input. (para. 47)

In this way the group hoped to avoid the pitfalls of narrow testing and, in consequence, achieve more dependable evidence of a pupils' achievements. The group's position was to develop the case for a multi-faceted assessment task, capable of performing the multi-purpose assessment which it had claimed possible. In some respects this area became the proving ground for what would follow.

The Government's first step was to invite bids from interested groups to undertake the development work for the SAT materials. In the event three contracts were issued, and each of the successful consortia prepared materials which were then piloted with a 2 per cent sample of seven-year-olds in 1990. This first attempt aimed to cover all the attainment targets; almost all the materials were cross-curricular and thematically based. The outcome was a workload that was condemned by teachers and ultimately recognised by the Government as excessively demanding.

Subsequent rounds of SATs, then, were to limit the range of subjects tested. Restricting the range, whilst practically and, in this case, politically, attractive, was one thing; selecting the attainments that would be assessed was another. Potential criteria were ease of testing, relevance to inter-school comparisons and the most important aspects of the education of seven-year-olds. Unsurprisingly, the primacy of reading, writing, handwriting, spelling and number was affirmed:

> In the name of 'manageability' the first steps had been taken, through the stipulation of what would be tested, to identifying a 'core within a core' – those elements of the statutory curriculum in the core subjects in which all pupils would be tested every year. (Daugherty, 1995, p. 42)

The whole episode can be represented in a variety of ways. For some it was a lost vision, failing to recognise breadth of achievement; for others it was a triumph for common sense and would bring the education service to account for what really mattered.

Question for discussion

Are SATs useful (and, if so, to whom?) if they are restricted to 'core' elements?

2. Are SATs reliable and valid?

There is an appealing simplicity about criterion-referencing: either an individual has achieved a competence or he has not. But what counts as demonstrating a competence? As Shorrocks and Nelson (1994) explain, there are two aspects of this – the domain definition and mastery definition.

The first of these concerns the areas of understanding, knowledge or skill to be addressed by the assessment. The problem is this: Can a child's performance in a subject be expressed in terms of an overall 'level'? Unfortunately, from the point of view of those constructing SAT materials, the collection of elements within a subject's statements of attainment are rarely neatly homogeneous. Where homogeneity is lacking there is an obvious difficulty in selecting the items for assessment. Problems arise also with the concept of mastery. Where the area under investigation (the domain) is poorly specified, then what should count as mastery of the domain is problematic.

Generally, these problems can be approached by sampling a wider range of elements from the areas in question. The difficulty here is that although increasing the size of the assessment materials makes the overall package more reliable, it also makes it more unwieldy. This raises the concern of 'manageability'. Greater reliability (or what Shorrocks and Nelson prefer to call 'dependability') has to be sought in an unhelpful climate. This is not to say that the task may not be achieved, but, as the writers state:

> The over-riding conclusion reached in the evaluation of the 1991 Key Stage 1 assessments was that the reliability, or more appropriately, the dependability of the scoring outcomes left a great deal to be desired. ... A valid, reliable and dependable assessment system, particularly in the earlier key stages, still seems a very long way off. (p. 45)

The attempt to solve this particular conundrum lies at the heart of the assessment debate. If the quality of the education service, and the progress of individuals within it, is to continue under public scrutiny (and few doubt that it should), then it is a matter of equal concern that the evidence informing that scrutiny should, itself, be shown to stand up to examination. In resolving this dilemma, it is interesting to note the opinion of Duncan Graham (in Graham and Tytler, 1993), the former Chairman and Chief Executive of the NCC.

> As far as testing at the ages of 7 and 11 is concerned, the moves towards a progressively simplified system will continue, if only because it is not possible either to validate by research the results of a system as complicated as that envisaged by the Task Group on Assessment and Testing (TGAT) in 1989, nor possible to resource it in terms of financial or staff costs. (p.127)

Question for discussion

How would you try to resolve the conflict between ensuring that tests are valid and reliable and ensuring that they are manageable and affordable?

3. What is the place of teachers' assessments?

TGAT had been in no doubt about the importance of assessments made by teachers in forming judgements of children's performance: 'We recommend that teachers' ratings of pupil performance should be used as a fundamental element of a national assessment system.' (DES, 1987, para. 60). This assertion was intimately connected to a view taken earlier in the report that the basis of national assessment be essentially formative. At the same time the Committee was also clear about the inherent dangers of relying on many thousands of teachers in many different contexts achieving comparability. The function of inducting teachers into a shared understanding of national standards was as much part of the system as the collection of data itself. Indeed, it was a pre-condition: 'Teachers' ratings should be moderated in such a way as to *convey* and to inform national standards.' (DES, 1987, para. 62, my emphasis).

In TGAT's view, two things were clear: that teachers would not have confidence in a system, or be committed to it, without active teacher involvement; and that achieving a trained teaching force would take time. The Group therefore set out a list of conditions which would have to be met to secure this professional commitment. The list included emphasis on recognising teachers' professionalism and the need for in-service training. However, as Daugherty's account of the early development of SATs at SEAC (he was a Council member) records, 'teacher assessment was not seen by the policy-makers in the Government and the DES as an important component of the system' (p.68). Daugherty also suggests that 'the purposes for which teacher assessment were best suited – the formative and diagnostic – were not a high priority for those policy-makers' (p.68). Despite the attention being given to SATs by the Department, it did not seem to be similarly acknowledged that, with the introduction of the National Curriculum in 1989, teachers were required to make assessments and keep records of their children's achievements on a day-to-day basis. No advice was forthcoming from central Government to assist them in this task. Indeed, it was not until December 1990 that there was any official guidance (SEAC, 1990), but this was significantly lacking in practical advice. When this situation is compared with the original TGAT prescription placing teacher assessment centrally in the assessment process, it seems that there had been a substantial shift in outlook since the Department's own publication, *National Curriculum: From Policy to Practice* (1989) which had restated the TGAT emphasis on teachers' assessments as Government policy.

The Chairman of TGAT, Paul Black, was subsequently to reflect on these changes in the following terms:

> The point to be underlined is not that TGAT lost the argument. We won the argument. The chilling feature is that in the world of political pressure to which education is now subject, that was of no consequence. (Black, 1993, p. 61)

In the same article, Black defends and reaffirms the TGAT view by reporting on developments in the USA, where the use of short external standardised tests was being abandoned 'because it is evident that they have done nothing to improve education ... They see us marching backwards into the unprofitable ways from which they are now escaping' (p. 64).

In trying to summarise thus far, we see the TGAT role for teacher assessment being significantly marginalised, reduced to providing evidence simply to supplement SATs where an attainment target is not represented in the SAT materials. Where SAT results conflict with teacher assessment, then the SAT result will be 'preferred'. Teacher assessment seems to be largely consigned to the purposes of formative and diagnostic assessment. The implicit assumption is that this activity will simultaneously produce the evidence that will enable teachers to report reliably on those aspects of the National Curriculum which are outside the scope of SATs. To this extent there appears to be a continuing role for teacher assessment.

The uncertainty which has surrounded the expectations placed upon teachers in discharging their responsibilities for assessment has been widely regarded as de-motivating. Many teachers and teacher groups had made considerable investments in time and energy in devising systems aimed at producing information that was both formative (influencing day-by-day teaching decisions) and, at the same time, able to generate a developing record of pupil achievement in the National Curriculum. What little support this has received from the centre has been seen as too little and too late:

> It was not only the volume of work which brought growing discontent as more and more teachers found themselves increasingly immersed in teacher assessment. It was the pointlessness of it all. (Daugherty, 1995, p.77)

Question for discussion

What should be the role of teacher assessment in the National Curriculum?

---

4. Report, publish and be damned?

The matters at issue here are whether the purposes of statutory assessment tasks have been reduced to reporting on schools, and whether the data that results from the standard assessments and forms the basis of 'league tables' is capable of representing a school's endeavours with its pupils.

As regards the first of these, the feature that stands out is the differing purposes that the assessments serve. TGAT had drawn attention to the various interest groups concerned with educational achievement – parents, individual pupils, other teachers, the school, school governors, employers, providing authorities, further education, education decision-makers, the general public. Each group would have interest in a different purpose served by assessments. In recognising the four purposes of assessment (see pp.32–3), TGAT had aspired to produce an assessment system that could satisfy all of these simultaneously. As we have seen however, developments in SATs and teacher assessment have compromised the TGAT vision.

As regards the second matter, reporting about schools has become a major concern. TGAT had underlined two factors that cause difficulty and concern when publishing the results of assessments. The first of these is concerned with National Curriculum assessment results as indicative of a school's overall performance. TGAT was clear that the results, though important, represented only one element of the multi-faceted nature of schooling:

> We recommend that the *only* [emphasis in original] form in which results of national assessment for, and identifying, a given school should be published is *as part of a broader report by that school of its work as a whole.* (para. 132, emphasis added)

The other problem is with the well-documented effects of socio-economic factors on educational performance. Put simply, the area in which a school is located is likely to be reflected in the academic success of its pupils – and this despite the school effectiveness studies that claim that schools are differentially successful. It is possible that a good school in a deprived area may achieve exceptional results but still fare poorly in inter-school comparisons. Similarly, a school may achieve results that stand comparison with other schools but its pupils may be under-achieving. In either case the reporting of 'raw' results alone tells an incomplete and potentially misleading story. Readers will be reminded of the quotation earlier in the chapter from the 1977 Green Paper, when the Government of the day rejected 'league tables' on precisely these grounds.

TGAT discussed the possibility of 'scaling' a school's results to make allowances for these background factors. Although it rejected this, the Report repeated the dangers of publishing raw scores alone, and came to the following conclusion:

> We recommend that any report by a school which includes national assessment results should include a general report for the area, prepared by the local authority, to indicate the nature of socio-economic and other influences which are known to affect the schools. This report should give a general indication of the known effects of such influences on performance. (para. 134)

The principle of holding schools accountable for their pupils' performance on both academic and other criteria has not been thought contentious. However, when schools are to be judged, it is clear that the indicators used must be beyond reproach. The dilemma here is that the movement towards simplifying assessment may act against the interests of making fair comparisons between schools, since too little assessment may not allow valid results to be drawn about the overall performance of a school. In addition results that claim to report pupil achievement may unfairly represent a school's efforts if it is not made clear, when the results are reported, that the school works in particular circumstances. A related problem concerns the distinction between children's actual level of attainment and the progress they have made (see Chapter 15)

In view of the difficulties associated with the undertaking, one might be forgiven for wondering why the Government was intent on pressing on with this approach. Three of the senior players in events, Black, Daugherty and Graham, who have figured in this chapter, leave us in no doubt about the influence of the

Conservative Party's right wing, as does Simon (1993, p.36) in a quotation from the *Independent*:

> The ideological thrust of the New Right in education was neatly summarised by Michael Fallon. ... What has been missing from British education, Fallon is reported as saying, 'is the discipline of the market-place', 'the power of the customer', and 'the engine of competition'.

The outcome was an interest in publishable results to provide information that would empower the customer (children's parents), and fuel the 'engine of competition'. In such an analysis schools will improve, as it were, automatically.

Question for discussion

Suppose league tables could give a reliable report of a school's overall performance and also do justice to the progress children had made in the school. Would there still be controversy about them?

THE FUTURE?

At the point when the Dearing Review has apparently caused peace to break out, at least on the National Curriculum assessment front, we are still left with the question of whether the new politically correct 'slimmed down' procedures can serve their purposes any better than their predecessors. It is true that teachers' complaints about workload have been calmed, but it is far from clear why reduced testing should produce data that is adequately reliable to make the inter-school comparisons that lie closest to Government claims to monitor the effectiveness of individual schools. Why, or how, reduced testing should enable a view to be taken about a school's performance in the broader sense, is no clearer.

Teachers' assessments have now been installed as the source of information in non-core subjects. Whilst some consideration is given to 'guiding' teachers, it is far from certain that the many teachers involved in their many judgements provide a reliable basis for comparative data. But given that Government support of training for moderation is ending, teacher assessment, despite Dearing, may return to the margins. The issue of 'league tables' is alive and well, and, more controversially, the Government intends to draft proposals for the national testing of five-year-olds to provide baseline data. Is the agenda for National Curriculum assessment any more settled now than it was when the Dearing Review was commissioned?

FURTHER READING

Broadfoot, P., Dockrell, B., Gipps, C., Harlen, W. and Nuttall, D. (eds) (1993) *Policy Issues in National Assessment*. Clevedon, Avon: Multilingual Matters.

Daugherty, R. (1995) *National Curriculum Assessment: A Review of Policy 1987–1994*. London: Falmer.

Dearing, R. (1994) *The National Curriculum and its Assessment: Final Report*. London: SCAA.

Department of Education and Science/Welsh Office (1988) *National Curriculum Task Group on Assessment and Testing: A Report*. London: DES/WO.

O'Hear, P. and White, J. eds. (1993) *Assessing the National Curriculum*. London: Chapman.

Shorrocks, D. (with L.Frobisher, N.Nelson, L.Turner and A.Waterson) (1993) *Implementing National Curriculum Assessment in the Primary School*. London: Hodder and Stoughton.

REFERENCES

Ball, S. (1990) *Politics and Policy Making in Education*. London: Routledge.

Black, P. (1993) 'The shifting scenery of the National Curriculum', in P. O'Hear and J. White (eds) *Assessing the National Curriculum*. London: Chapman.

Daugherty, R. (1995) *National Curriculum Assessment: A Review of Policy 1987–1994*. London: Falmer.

Dearing, R. (1993) *The National Curriculum and its Assessment: Interim Report*. London: SCAA.

Dearing, R. (1994) *The National Curriculum and its Assessment: Final Report*. London: SCAA.

Department of Education and Science (1977) *Education in Schools: A Consultative Document*. London: HMSO.

Department of Education and Science (1987) *The National Curriculum 5–16: A Consultation Document*. London: DES.

Department of Education and Science (1984) *Records of Achievement: A Statement of Policy*. London: HMSO.

Department of Education and Science/Welsh Office (1987) *National Curriculum Task Group on Assessment and Testing: A Report*. London: DES/WO.

Department of Education and Science/Welsh Office (1988) *National Curriculum Task Group on Assessment and Testing: Three Supplementary Reports*. London: DES/WO.

Department of Education and Science (1989) *National Curriculum: From Policy to Practice*. London: HMSO.

Gipps, C., (ed.) (1992) *Developing Assessment for the National Curriculum*. London: Kogan Page.

Gipps, C. (1993) 'The structure for assessment and recording', in P. O'Hear and J.White, (eds) *Assessing the National Curriculum*. London: Chapman.

Graham, D. and Tytler, D. (1993) *A Lesson for Us All*. London: Routledge.

Harlen, W. (ed.) (1994) *Enhancing Quality in Assessment*. London: Paul Chapman.

Knight, C, (1990) *The Making of Tory Education Policy in Post-War Britain*. London: Falmer.

Lawlor, S., (ed.) (1993) *The Dearing Debate: Assessment and the National Curriculum*. London: Centre for Policy Studies.

Lawton, D. (1992) *Education and Politics in the 1990s: Conflict or Consensus?* London: Falmer.

School Curriculum and Examinations Authority (1995) *Consistency in Teacher Assessment: Exemplification of Standards*. London: SCAA.

School Examinations and Assessment Council (1990) *A Guide to Teacher Assessment: Packs A, B and C*. London: SEAC.

Shorrocks, D. and Nelson, N. (1994) 'The reliability of National Curriculum assessment at Key Stages 1 and 2', in D. Hutchison and I. Schagen (eds) *How Reliable is National Curriculum Assessment?* Slough: NFER.

Simon, B. (1993) 'The Education Reform Act: causative factors', in P. Broadfoot, B. Dockrell, C. Gipps, W. Harlen, and D. Nuttall (eds) (1993) *Policy Issues in National Assessment*. Clevedon, Avon: Multilingual Matters.

CHAPTER 4

Pre-School Provision

Peter Jackson

INTRODUCTION

In a survey of thirty years of pre-school policy from 1963 to 1993, Sonia Jackson (1993) could find no sustained initiative. When even the Plowden Report (1967) balanced its call for expansion with the warning that too much nursery provision could encourage mothers to work full-time regardless of their children's welfare, what hope was there? The White Paper *A Framework for Expansion* (DES, 1972) seemed to offer fresh hope, only to be dashed by Margaret Thatcher's decision to release local authorities from their duty to provide nursery education (Education Act 1980). Again, although in 1989 the House of Commons Select Committee recommended that pre-school education should be made available for all who wanted it, four years later nothing had happened. It was no wonder, said Jackson, that by 1992 a *Times Educational Supplement* editorial (13 November) was pessimistic: 'With public spending ever more squeezed, local authorities in turmoil and government ministers apparently unembarrassable, the chances of improvement look pretty unlikely'.

Few neighbouring continental societies are envious of the UK's record on public educational provision for pre-school children. One can double the thirty years period. In the sixty years following the Hadow Report on nursery and infant education (CCINS, 1933), successive governments resisted demands for a properly coordinated and extensive pre-school system, leaving it up to local authorities to decide what to provide in their areas. Some maintained good provision with what money they had, while others offered little or nothing, leaving it up to self-help groups and commercial establishments to meet demand. In 1995, in the shadow of a general election, policy was at last announced.

The meaning of 'pre-school' needs some clarification. For most of our continental neighbours and the USA, 'school' begins at age six, and there has traditionally been a distinct division between the pre-school curriculum emphasizing care, development and play, and the more formal approach of school 'proper'. In contrast, until recently in the UK, after a patchwork quilt of early childhood experiences, 'school' began at age five with a play- or personal interest-centred curriculum, and this continued with a relatively slow transformation into more formal structures by the age of seven. Thus the British primary school came to exhibit a somewhat different character from continental and American elementary education, representing a gradual change from early informality and child-centredness to later more formal learning.

The effect of the National Curriculum has been to download a more formal structure of learning into the five-to-seven phase Key Stage 1. Moreover, owing to the increased tendency for school admission to date from the beginning of the academic year in which children reach age five, large numbers of children are experiencing at age four more formal structures than they would have found in pre-school. Thus the 'break' from pre-school to formal school, which constitutes a kind of status passage for children in other developed countries, is again avoided in the British system, this time by replacing the child-centred developmental curriculum by the National Curriculum. Summing up, the four-to-seven educational experience in Britain is different from the four-to-seven curriculum in other comparable countries. Here it is characterised by steady transformation rather than abrupt change of level and style: this was true both before and after the advent of the National Curriculum.

Present Provision

The only children for whom local authorities are obliged to provide pre-school education are those identified as having special educational needs; consequently general provision varies considerably across the country, with Wales leading regional provision for three- and four-year olds with about 70 per cent while Scotland provides about 40 per cent.

There are three types of LEA provision:

- *nursery schools,* for children aged between two and five, with their own headteachers, assistant teachers and nursery assistants with NNEB qualifications; the recommended qualified teacher to children ratio is 1 to 22 and general adult ratio 1 to 13.
- *nursery classes,* similar to nursery schools, except that they are integral parts of primary schools.
- *reception classes* in maintained primary schools for those who can get an early admissions place. The recommended staff to children ratio here is 1 to 22.

Most under-fives receive their education in either nursery or reception classes of primary schools. In January 1995, 53 per cent of three- and four-year-olds in England were in maintained nursery and primary schools and a further 4 per cent in independent and special schools (DfEE News 161/95), ranging from pre-preparatory academic schools to alternative systems of education such as Montessori and Steiner.

THE POLICY

The libertarian Right has strongly influenced the direction of national policy over the past sixteen years. Urging the control of money-supply and the reduction in scope and degree of the governmental portfolio, the Right Wing's scepticism about the rhetoric of Downing Street and its cynicism about the ambitions of Whitehall are shared by many people of influence. Chief amongst the groups on the Right is the Centre for Policy Studies which stage-managed the national debate on education.

KEY POINTS

- A Bill (1996) to:
  - give parents of every four-year-old the right to a voucher to secure a pre-school place for their child in the independent or maintained sector
  - provide grants for providing nursery education in the private sector
  - bring pre-school education under the umbrella of the Ofsted inspection scheme.
- A pilot scheme for vouchers, starting 1996, involving four LEAs.

In March 1995, the Centre hosted two public meetings on the Government's pledge to provide nursery education for four-year-olds. The first raised the urgency of nursery education, virtually accusing the Government of dithering pusillanimity; the second considered policy and implementation. The policy group heard presentations of four perspectives: academic, HMI, the independent sector and the Centre for Policy Studies.

Academic

Professor Albert Osborn of Bristol University told the gathering that the American Consortium for Longitudinal Studies had reported revised conclusions from certain experiments which had earlier suggested only modest academic gains for children with pre-school experience over those who had none. Now the surprising statistics were that as those pre-schooled groups had aged into adolescence, they had made much more satisfactory adjustments to society than control groups. Pre-schooled groups were significantly less likely to find themselves in opposition to the law, in need of psychological help or in receipt of welfare. Moreover, these 'positive behaviours' did not fade as the adolescents grew into adulthood.

The academic consensus was that the significant outcome of pre-school education was not so much achievement of academic skills but development in personal organisation and autonomy. Those kinds of pre-school education which emphasized personal responsibility within socially interactive frameworks were those most likely to lead to significant increases in social competence. What should be inferred from all this, maintained Osborn, is that governments would save money later by spending money earlier. There was a real cost-benefit in the universal provision of nursery education.

HMI

The Chief HMI for Primary Education, Chris Woodhead, was not concerned with whether there should be nursery provision: that, was, after all, a Government matter. His concern was the question: supposing there were nursery education for all four-year-olds, what should it be like? His answer was clear, if a little dull: the nursery class should 'acclimatise four-year-olds to reception class work'.

What that meant, he spelt out in more detail. The nursery class should resist the encroachment of the National Curriculum. He had no wish to see its necessary bureaucracy – still less its unnecessary ramifications – stifling the work of the traditional British nursery. On the other hand, it made no sense to ignore the National Curriculum – let alone treat it as some materialistic disease of the spirit. Given that the proposal concerned children of statutory school-age minus one year, it made simple sense that that year should feature the commonsense truths of growing up and getting on together within a context of enquiry which was not purposeless. The National Curriculum, he argued, should indeed inform the thought of teachers as they assisted the development of their children. The problem with teaching and learning in the UK was not that it was too demanding of teachers and pupils but that it was not demanding enough, and though the National Curriculum might only be implicit at the nursery stage, its prospect gave purpose and direction to the children's teaching and learning experiences. In Woodhead's view there should be Government guidance, but it should be of the 'kitemark' variety – the sorts of learning that should take place, the number and qualifications of staff, the staff-pupil ratio, facilities, and so on.

Independent sector

In contrast, Margaret Lochrie for the Pre-School Learning Alliance hoped that a newly funded nursery programme would start afresh. She felt that existing LEA nurseries were needlessly expensive, and nondescript and uniform. Their standard equipment issue, back-up services, child-adult ratios and ideological baggage (e.g. compensatory education implying home deficit) were not only unaffordable, but, in the case of the latter, downright undesirable. Many independent nurseries – including those in her own group – placed far more emphasis than LEA establishments on nurseries as extensions of parental values, as structures where children could find stability and security, and as centres where they could learn the basics of literacy and cooperation. She hoped that the Government would re-think its former policy from first principles.

Centre for Policy Studies

From high and very dry on the Right, Dr Sheila Lawlor maintained that established authorities always favoured systems over users and showed no signs of reversing the trend. The National Curriculum and Ofsted were both statist outcomes of a 'wannabe Reform Act'; the truth was that the country was sinking yet further into bureaucratic monopoly.

The only effective solution was the market: the state should kick-start the process with a vouchers scheme, taking from LEAs not only money but premises and equipment too. Private enterprise could handle things better and less expensively. We should forget about sliding scales for vouchers – sliding scales were socialist, bureaucratic and expensive. We should reject bidding systems from large independent organisations – the university funding system showed that such operations are bureaucratic and inefficient. Leave it to the free market: leave it to demand and supply. As to the value of the voucher, £700 was plenty – why subsidise the well-off or encourage the dump-the-kids brigade by paying more? Eventually, as the invisible hand does its work, the general public would see that we never needed these armies of civil servants and that people are perfectly capable of organising their interacting lives without the assistance – let alone the regulation – of Whitehall.

The outcome

In July 1995, the Education Secretary announced that vouchers for nursery places would be offered to parents of all four-year-olds in the country. The 1996 Bill, however, narrows the scope of the scheme by entitling parents to vouchers only from the term after the child's fourth birthday. Meanwhile, from Spring 1996, a voucher-based scheme will be piloted by four local authorities (the Secretary of State Gillian Shephard was hoping for 10 per cent to volunteer) at a cost of £22 million. Both this and the Bill involve vouchers of £1,100 for parents, funded from cash taken from the LEAs, who retrieve their money for every place a parent 'buys'. (Originally, playgroups were to receive only half this sum, but their campaign to be treated on the same terms as nurseries led to a Government U-turn.)

Those entitled to cash vouchers are independent nurseries and playgroups, and maintained schools and nurseries. They must be able to show inspectors that at the end of three terms they are meeting the standards of content and learning conditions which are at present being set (see below). No extra money is to be given for training staff nor for setting up new nurseries, but there has been one significant concession: in July 1995 the Government announced its intention to dispense with area standards for teaching accommodation and recreation areas, provided that health and safety regulations are still met.

The Government proposals for standards for providers cover the following:

- learning outcomes
- adult-to-child ratios
- premises and equipment
- special educational needs
- inspection
- publication of information for parents
- good practice and training.

As far as learning outcomes are concerned, the School Curriculum and Assessment Authority (1996) has provided proposals to define 'a set of desired outcomes for children's learning by the time they enter compulsory schooling, and to consider the need for guidance on educational activities appropriate to these outcomes, which providers will have to supply'. Learning is divided into six areas. Each has prescribed targets of which the following are examples:

- *Personal and social development*. Children should learn how to work, play, cooperate and be able to undertake activities such as groupwork and taking part in cultural and religious events.
- *Language and literacy*. Children should develop competence in talking and listening and in becoming readers and writers through activities such as listening to stories and being able to write their own names.
- *Mathematics*. Children should learn important aspects of mathematical understanding; for example, they should be able to recognise and use numbers from 1 to 10 and use simple mathematical language.
- *Knowledge and understanding of the world*. Children should develop knowledge and understanding of their environment, other people and features of the natural and man-made world, so developing skills for later learning in history, geography, science and technology. They should be able to do things such as talking about families and friends and using tape recorders and computers.
- *Physical development*. Children should develop physical control, mobility and awareness of space, and manipulative skills in indoor and outdoor environments. Attainment targets include using a range of small and large equipment from balls to climbing apparatus.
- *Creativity*. Children should develop their imagination and their ability to express ideas and feelings in creative ways. They should be able to use a range of materials and suitable tools and resources to represent what they see, hear, touch and feel.

ISSUES FOR DEBATE

1. What is the nature of the effect of pre-school education? Is it primarily academic or primarily developmental?

Professor Osborn's claim that pre-school education improved children's abilities to do well at school seems so unremarkable that most people cannot see why academic researchers have such difficulty demonstrating it. The 1987 Osborn and Millbank study easily showed short-term benefits, as did Jowett and Silva's small-scale project a year earlier. The difficulty however is that of showing that the effects of pre-school are sufficiently longlasting. After a number of years of schooling, can children who attended pre-school be distinguished through academic tests from those who did not?

Osborn's further contention that pre-school education improved the ways individuals coped when schooling was finished seems less intuitive as an idea as well as being rather less robustly supported by research. After the massive American interventionist programme *Operation Headstart* ended in the 1970s, various groups of researchers and workers kept in touch with each other to report their continuing experiences. A leading part in the collating of findings about lasting effects was played by the Consortium for Longitudinal Studies in

Washington, while the findings themselves had a kind of epicentre at Ypsilanti, Michigan where a particular experiment called the Perry Pre-School Project had taken place in the sixties.

The claims are that as the children who experienced pre-school education were tracked, a surprising pattern emerged. They seemed to be making much more satisfactory adjustments to society than control groups. They were significantly more law-abiding, more psychologically stable and less dependent on the state for welfare benefits. Moreover, these 'positive behaviours' did not fade as the adolescents aged into early adulthood. Around these findings a view has formed that the significant outcome of pre-school education is less the achievement of academic skills than the development of social skills.

This is not the place to enter into the details of the argument. There are, as one would expect, both conviction and scepticism in the conclusions of those who have done so. Longitudinal research has its own special problems. Arguments take place over the small size of the research samples, the representativeness of the children, the influence of unaccounted-for factors, the kinds of measures used (e.g. is running away from home a sign of dysfunctionality or of rationality?). Disputants disagree over how such cost-benefit savings can be demonstrated. There is a larger point. If it were demonstrably cost-effective then wouldn't there be a tendency to promote pre-schooling as a means to achieving social conformity rather than educational objectives?

Question for discussion

Should pre-school education be primarily academic or developmental?

---

2. To what extent should independent nurseries be incorporated into the state system?

The answer from HMI seems to be: as long as independent nurseries comply with the state framework and meet its standards, then there is no objection. The prospect of universal nursery education inevitably raises the question of what we are introducing our children to. For Woodhead it should be neither the rushing shallows of national curricula nor the still pools of childhood whimsy; even less should it be strong religion. No doubt all these will be pressed by interested parties, but the DfEE has no desire to become re-embroiled in the religious battles which attended the rise of statutory schooling in this country (and which complicate it still), nor does it welcome re-runs of the progressivist-traditionalist contests of the sixties and seventies.

Nursery education, according to Woodhead, is not simply a convenient extension of home values: it is a set of processes in which children learn commonsense values, consensual attitudes and British culture. The nursery is a place in which teachers' work is purposeful. As guides, they have to know where they are going. We should build from the LEA nursery school service we already have rather than throw all the cards into the air and start from the beginning.

In advocating change and commending the independent sector, Margaret

Lochrie directly challenges Woodhead's views. She draws attention to three powerfully intertwined themes: the cost of local government provision, its ideological content and Government interest in privatisation. First, independent nurseries can, she says, operate profitably at far less than the costs incurred at LEA nursery schools. Second, they are unencumbered by the compensatory ideology which leads LEA institutions to see homes and families as somehow culturally deficient; instead the nurseries in her organisation prefer to work closely with parents and to adapt to home culture. Third, independent nurseries embody the Government's drive for privatisation and the dismantling of state organisations.

Each of these three points has some validity. LEAs have their entrenched stakeholders too in the shape of school keepers, teaching staff and suppliers of materials. To lumber new providers with requirements which in many cases were the outcomes of negotiations within LEAs seems deliberately perverse. Also, if compensatory education with its omnipresent deficit theory – which has taken something of a postmodernist battering since the late eighties – lingers, it does so in the fields of nursery and special needs education. Finally, with respect to privatisation there is a hidden trump: Gillian Shephard, Secretary of State for Education is believed to favour inviting tenders from large groupings of nursery schools rather than allow the Civil Service to extend its empire below the statutory school age. On this matter Party ideology is strong.

Question for discussion

Should the policy to expand opportunity for pre-school education involve the independent sector? If so, should that sector be made to conform to national criteria, such as those listed on p.48?

---

3. The voucher scheme

There is undoubtedly something very appealing about vouchers and indeed the homespun philosophy of the libertarians. The idea that money follows children and that those nurseries which parents favour will prosper has a hands-off-the-tiller simplicity. It also has the implication that the exercise of choice will foster responsibility in parents and contribute to a stronger democracy by emphasizing the autonomy of families.

It is, however, important to acknowledge that it is only a theory – and not just a theory but an experimental, unconfirmed theory. Although Secretary of State Sir Keith Joseph personally backed the idea in the 1980s, he reported regretfully to Parliament that the Kent trials of vouchers had provided no evidence in their favour. Even the USA – the ideological homeland of such a scheme for some thirty years – has just one pre-school voucher experiment at present. The research evidence from the Milwaukee project is that it is inconclusive in its effect: when compared with districts in which a voucher scheme does not operate, there is no significant alteration of pattern as a result of granting vouchers.

Again, as with the proposal that increased spending up front will reduce the final future expenditure, it is difficult to see what evidence would suffice. Social security already dispenses money to fraudulent claimants in a largely unpoliced system. Could a scheme which gave vouchers worth hundreds of pounds to parents of every four-year-old in the country possibly operate without legions of the very bureaucrats Sheila Lawlor is pledged to abolish? Indeed, critics have objected to the fact that more money will be spent on administering the scheme than in providing extra places for pre-school children (*TES*, 10 November 1995).

Dr Lawlor is not at all reluctant to reconsider embedded assumptions. Rather than looking to the Department for Education for progress we should instead, she says, consider it to be serving the interests of the larger bureaucracy – Whitehall – of which it is a part. The National Curriculum made more work for the Civil Service and will make more still if it is extended (even implicitly) to pre-school education. Inspection teams would be wanted next and, before you realised what was happening, that dreadful mistake – Ofsted with its prying and highly paid officials – would be proliferating all over the non-statutory sector. Far from extending the Civil Service empire we should, she maintains, be looking to the stripping of its assets in the form of its nursery teachers' salaries, its LEA nurseries, their materials and even premises. All this would go to fund a much cheaper – but probably more effective – nursery education.

Whatever one might think of her more extreme suggestions, Dr Lawlor's implacable opposition to the extensions of state control does highlight the vexed question of the National Curriculum and its place in the education of young children of school age and earlier. Osborne and Woodhead are on the side of officialdom, Lochrie and Lawlor are opposed. The controversy does seem to have direct relevance to any who are contemplating the launch of a non-standard form of young children's education.

Reaction to the voucher scheme has been mixed. In England private nursery schools educate around 42,000 three- and four-year-olds, with a further 45,000 in mostly private non-statutory day nurseries. The private sector has been understandably quick to comment. Within their general welcome for the scheme the National Private Day Nurseries Association (NPDA), the Association for Advisers for the Under Eights and their Families (AAUEF) and the Pre-school Learning Alliance (PLA) all express conventional worries that well-meaning but financially innocent providers will vie with commercially astute but educationally ignorant entrepreneurs to provide the worst of both worlds. Fears have also surfaced that the scheme is essentially urban-centred: how, critics ask, will providers in rural areas make enough to live on? Nevertheless, there is no doubt that the scheme is good news for the private sector.

The maintained sector regards the scheme with a kind of gloomy asperity. With more than 1200 nursery schools and 5500 nursery classes the LEAs feel they can only lose from the terms of the competition. Julia Bennett of the Association of Metropolitan Authorities commented in *Nursery World* in August 1995 that most of her 68 authorities (out of a total of 116 LEAs) feared that their standards would be undermined by independent providers who would make up in quantity what they lacked in quality. Local authorities are also worried that vouchers could have a rebound effect on provision for three-year-olds. Since only four-year-olds will qualify for the scheme, transferring resources to them could hit existing places for those a year younger.

The Campaign for State Education has commented through their representative Melian Mansfield that, with maintained places currently costing £2500 per year, there will inevitably be cutbacks in the resources for schools. Cynthia James, chair of the British Association for Early Childhood Education (BAECE), and Vicky Hurst, who directs the curriculum guidelines issued by the Early Childhood Education Forum, are similarly pessimistic. Ms Hurst points out that upwards of 80 per cent of four-year-olds are already in infant school reception classes and their vouchers will do nothing to improve teacher-children ratios or ameliorate the formalised curriculum. She believes that 'Key Stage Zero' will in effect be geared to forthcoming tests for five-year-olds and even speculates on the knock-on effect on a 'Key Stage Minus One' (*Nursery World*, 5 October 1995).

Another concern is equality of opportunity. Tricia David (1995) has drawn attention to the fact that pre-school is the place in which children from non-English speaking homes begin public education, where it is essential that bilingual teachers (usually funded under 'Section 11') work alongside early childhood teachers. What will happen to such provision under the new arrangements? Further, what will become of the developing initiatives in combating institutional racism when, as seems inevitable, the complexity and expertise of provision in this highly sensitive area are weakened?

The *TES* (27 October 1995) commented as follows:

> The point to remember about choice and diversity is that they can only come into play if the provision is there in the first place. At present, the supply of nursery places is so patchy, fragmented and ill-matched to need that we have diversity without choice, and no Government commitment to the sort of strategy or funding that would allow genuine choice.

Question for discussion

Is the voucher scheme the right way forward?

THE FUTURE?

It is plain to all who have followed the sequences of events that the Centre for Policy Studies has stage-managed them. It is perhaps instructive to assess the long-term goals behind its initiative. In her pamphlet *Nursery Choices: The Right Way to Pre-school Education* (1994), Sheila Lawlor spells them out. In posing the question: 'Should the priority be to extend the State system or to encourage a variety of provision?', her answer is unequivocal. Any new system should maximise parental responsibility, not minimise it in favour of state authorities. 'Supply side' provision should be opened up by weakening the control of LEAs so that private or voluntary nurseries can transform the system. *That* is the Conservative way – to promote a society based on small units and voluntary associations where parental decisions matter. The issue of nursery education reform is the crucial battleground fought over by those who believe that the state should take over the schooling of the under-fives and those who prefer a sector in which voluntary bodies, charities and a wide variety of provision check state hegemony.

After commenting favourably on the mixed educational economy of France compared to Britain, Dr Lawlor renews her attack on the LEA system. It entrenches, she claims, high costs, poor standards and lack of choice; moreover it is sucking more and more children in to fill up the surplus capacity in the maintained system. The Government's lack of action (until now) amounted to an acquiescence in the face of unchecked creeping statism. The voucher scheme is the only answer for it can be used simultaneously to seed the independent sector and to weaken the state sector: only in this way will the Conservative tradition, pledged to fulfil only the essential obligations of government, be renewed.

Dr Lawlor's argument reminds us that behind the complicated questions of early childhood education, with its disagreements over curricula, testing, pedagogy and funding, lies a massive ideological debate. Between the two most sharply opposing sides there is a chasm. On one side, there is a concentration on macro political philosophy and an impatience with 'minutiae'; on the other, a determination to focus on fine detail and a reluctance to engage with wider questions of the role of the state in modern Britain. No doubt time (and a general election) will see a muddled compromise.

FURTHER READING

Daniels, S. (1995) 'Can pre-school education affect children's achievement in primary school', *Oxford Review of Education*, 21, 163–178.

David, T. (1994) *Educational Provision for our Youngest Children: European Perspectives*. London: Chapman.

House of Commons Select Committee on Education, Science and the Arts (1989) *Educational Provision for the Under Fives*. London: HMSO.

McAuley, H. and Jackson, P. (1992) *Educating Young Children: A Structural Approach*. London: David Fulton.

Office for Standards in Education (1994) *First Class: The Standards and Quality of Education in Reception Classes*. London: HMSO.

Robson, S. and Smedley, S. (eds) (1996) *Early Childhood Education*. London: David Fulton.

Sylva, K., Siraj-Blatchford, I. and Johnson, S. (1992) 'The impact of the UK National Curriculum on pre-school practice: some 'top-down' processes at work', *International Journal of Early Childhood*, 24, 40–53.

REFERENCES

Central Advisory Council for Education (1967) *Children and their Primary Schools*. London: HMSO

Consultative Committee on Infant and Nursery Schools (1933) *Report*. London: HMSO

David, T. (1995) 'Issues in early childhood education', *Journal of Policy Studies*, 10, 325–333

Department of Education and Science (1972) *Education: A Framework for the Future*. London: HMSO.

House of Commons Select Committee on Education, Science and the Arts (1989) *Educational Provision for the Under Fives*. London: HMSO.

Jackson, S. (1993) 'Under fives: thirty years of no progress', *Children and Society*, 7, 64–81.

Jowett, S. and Sylva, K. (1986) 'Does kind of pre-school really matter?', *Educational Research*, 28, 21–31

Lawlor, S. (1994) *Nursery Choices: The Right Way to Pre-School Education*. London: Centre for Policy Studies.

Osborn, A. and Millbank, J. (1987) *The Effects of Early Education*. Oxford: Clarendon.

School Curriculum and Assessment Authority (1996) *Desirable Outcomes*. London: SCAA.

Schweinhart, L., Weikart, D. and Larner, M. (1986) 'Consequences of three pre-school curriculum models through age 15', *Early Education Research Quarterly*, 1, 15–45.

CHAPTER 5

14 – 19

Roger Marples

INTRODUCTION

The education we offer our 14 to 19-year-olds has been a matter of concern and substantial dispute for almost as long as there has been a publicly funded system of education. Since World War II educationalists, industrialists and successive Governments have become increasingly concerned with this phase of education, yet the current arrangements can only be described as a mess, lacking any coherence and sense of direction. For this reason, in 1995 the Secretary of State for Education and Employment asked Sir Ron Dearing, Chairman of the School Curriculum and Assessment Authority, to review the system of provision for 16- to 19-year-olds to try and bring coherence to what is at present fragmented and confusing[1]. The case for reform is very strong indeed. As to whether the system can be reformed in stages with the academic, prevocational and vocational addressed separately, or whether a more radical solution is required, will be for the reader to decide.

The General Certificate of Education, offered from 1951, had originally been designed for the most academically able pupils, with A–levels regarded as both a preparation and means of selection for higher education. But by the mid-1960s, with half of all those staying on in the sixth form either not wishing to study for A–levels or deemed unfit to cope with their demands, pressure was building for reform of the courses and qualifications on offer. It was in response to this task that the Schools Council suggested for post-O level students a two tiered structure, involving around five subjects until the age of 17, leading to a Qualifying Examination (Q–level), followed by three subjects at Further Level (F–level). Such proposals for reform, however, failed to meet with Government approval and were soon forgotten.

Meanwhile a different kind of debate had begun between two factions. On the one hand were a group of right-wing educationalists expressing concern over educational standards in a series of Black Papers published between 1969 and 1975. On the other were those concerned with the sharp rise of youth unemployment in the early 1970s and the apparent failure of schools to provide them with anything more relevant than the traditional academic fare which seemed to be serving them so inadequately. While the former were bemoaning the demise of the grammar school and what they considered to be the outrageously 'progressive' teaching methods supposedly to be found in

[1] Dearing's interim report was published in July, 1995; his final report was in preparation at the time of writing (see p.69).

comprehensive schools, the latter were more successful in terms of attracting the attention of Government. By 1974 the Department of Education and Science was at last addressing the needs of the 40 per cent of school leavers aged 16 who had no further education or vocational training prospects.

Two years later, the Prime Minister, James Callaghan (in a speech at Ruskin College, Oxford) catapulted the debate into the headlines. His principal concerns were the number of school-leavers lacking the basic skills required of them by potential employers and also lacking the wherewithal in terms of technological competence and personal qualities to cope with the rapidly changing social and economic climate. These points were reinforced the following year in a Green Paper, *Education in Schools* (DES, 1977), in which a positive correlation was assumed to exist between the country's relatively poor economic performance and the education system. There followed a major debate (which is still continuing) between those who believe education should directly serve the economic needs of the country and those who are deeply critical of the so-called 'new vocationalism' with which such a view is so often associated.

The 1970s witnessed a substantial rise in the numbers staying on in the sixth form, even though many possessed little more than CSEs (Certificate of Secondary Education), introduced in 1965 for the top 60 per cent of pupils as distinct from GCE (General Certificate of Education) O–level which was aimed at the top 20 per cent. The Keohane Report (DES. 1979) recommended the introduction of a Certificate of Extended Education examination, with compulsory tests of practicality in maths and English as well as vocational studies.

While Keohane was assessing the needs of the less academic pupils, the Further Education Curriculum Review and Development Unit (FEU) was engaged in the same task but with further education college (FE) students in mind. Its report, *A Basis for Choice* (*ABC*) (1979), advocated a prevocational course involving a common core including communication skills, social and economical awareness and working cooperatively, together with vocational courses and work experience. In the autumn of 1980, a DES consultative paper *Examinations 16–18* sided with *ABC* in preference to Keohane, which was a victory for the more hard-nosed vocationalists at the expense of the more 'liberal' educationalists. As a result of pressure from the Schools Council, CSE Boards and teacher unions, however, it was agreed that their interests would be reflected in the contents and validation of a new national prevocational qualification being devised, the Certificate of Pre-Vocational Education (CPVE), soon to be under the joint control of City and Guilds of London Institute (CGLI) and the Business and Technician Education Council (BTEC). The CPVE aimed to assist the transition from school to adult working life by equipping young people with the basic skills, experiences, attitudes, knowledge and personal and social competences required, as well as providing opportunities for progression to continuing education, training and work.

THE POLICY

A–levels and AS–level

With Q–, N– and F–Levels having been consigned to the rubbish bin, the

KEY POINTS

- A-levels regarded as 'the gold standard' and to be preserved
- AS-levels to broaden the curriculum
- Diploma in Vocational Education, NVQs and GNVQs to prepare young people for the world of work as well as higher education
- The plethora of qualifications and and differing structures under review by Dearing
- The TVEI curriculum initiative
- Development of compulsory 'core skills'
- Records of Achievement
- Introduction of vocational pathways from Key Stage 4 onwards
- Diversity of post-16 educational institutions

Government's policy on A–levels has been consistently unambiguous. In both White Papers *Better Schools* (DES, 1985a) and *Education and Training for the 21st Century* (DES/DE, 1991), their status is represented as some kind of academic 'gold standard'. In spite of this, and perhaps even because of this, the problem of how greater breadth might be introduced into post-16 education remains.

In 1987, however, the Government went some way towards addressing the problem by introducing the Advanced Supplementary (AS) examination designed to supplement A–levels. While examined at the same standard as A–levels, AS–levels require only half their content and study time (though there are moves to replace this 'vertical' version by a 'horizontal' one covering the whole syllabus but up to a halfway stage). Although the numbers taking AS–levels have been rather fewer than anticipated (in 1994, 750,000 people were entered for A–levels but only 50,000 for AS–levels), the Government continues to support the idea of two AS–levels together with two A–levels as the norm for the more academically able sixth form student.

Meanwhile the problems associated with A–levels themselves continue to be unaddressed. In many ways they served their function well; but the time has long since passed when their appropriateness for even the most able post-16 students may be regarded as self-evident. Two years is a long time to commit oneself to a course of study in which fewer than 20 per cent may expect to pass in two or more subjects while another 30 per cent will almost certainly fail. In addition, without the appropriate mechanisms for credit transfer, there is little opportunity to transfer from A–level courses to others. These problems were familiar to Kenneth Baker who, as Secretary of State for Education, set up the Higginson Committee to 'recommend the principles that should govern A–level syllabuses and their assessment'. Higginson's report (DES, 1988) recommended that A–levels should be broadened to include five 'leaner' subjects than the more conventional three. Within days, Baker rejected Higginson's proposals on the grounds that they would 'queer the pitch' of the recently introduced AS–levels.

The rejection of Higginson was a wasted opportunity. Since then, AS–levels continue to lag behind A–levels in the credibility stakes, with many students taking them not as a means of broadening the somewhat narrow A–level diet but to increase their prospects of gaining a university place. Moreover, while GCSE, with its opportunities for course-work assessment and criterion-referenced grading, replaced GCE O–level and CSE in 1986, the mismatch between what is expected of 16-year-olds and A–level students is greater than it need be. Since Higginson, the debate on A–levels has continued unabated, with opinion divided between those who wish to see their retention and those who would like to see something different.

However there is a growing consensus that the following aspirations are both realistic and desirable:

- a higher rate of participation in both education and training amongst post-16-year-olds
- parity of esteem for academic and vocational qualifications
- opportunities for credit accumulation and transfer between prevocational, vocational and academic courses together with a modular framework on which this relies
- a wider use of Records of Achievement to provide scope for accreditation during, and not simply on, completion of courses
- the need to re-examine the provision for 16- to 19-year-olds as a whole in the hope of achieving coherence where there is fragmentation and division.

Failure to address these issues will inevitably result in the majority of young people perceiving education as something for other people and withdrawing from the system at the earliest opportunity.

Diploma of Vocational Education

One of the biggest obstacles for the CPVE was its low status image associated with lack of credibility with employers and higher education. In 1990, City and Guilds assumed sole responsibility for it, and the following year decided to replace it with the Diploma of Vocational Education for 14- to 19-year-olds. Similar in some respects to the CPVE, it is hoped that the Diploma will be a positive lead to progression. Whether it will be pursued by pupils deemed non-academic, or what its relationship will be to work done at Key Stage 4 where it might complement rather than compete with the conventional academic courses, remains to be seen.

Technical and Vocational Education Initiative (TVEI)

In October 1982 Mrs Thatcher expressed her concern to the House of Commons about 'existing arrangements for technical and vocational education for young people', and asked the chairman of the Manpower Services Commission and the Education Secretary to develop a pilot scheme in 14 LEAs. By the 1990s there was scarcely a maintained secondary school in the country not involved with TVEI.

TVEI is a curriculum initiative, not a specific course. Its principal objectives are to help young people prepare for the world of work, contribute to the life of the community and learn how to make the necessary adjustments to the changing nature of work. Although it is financed by Government, it is incumbent upon LEAs bidding for funds to demonstrate that they are able to meet a number of criteria, including:

- the promotion of equal opportunities
- the provision of a four-year curriculum with a balance between the general, technical and vocational, designed as a preparation for adult life
- the provision of a vocational component and work experience
- the forging of links between school and future educational and training opportunities
- careers education and guidance.

The scheme was a radical departure from existing curriculum initiatives in that it was to be centrally controlled not by the DES but by the Manpower Services Commission, which was part of the Employment Department. With over £1 billion of extra money, schools were able to appoint TVEI coordinators who developed a very wide range of courses. Although David Young at the MSC intended it to be for those in the middle ability range, it has since widened in scope, and many schools have TVEI schemes with pupils from the full ability range, including A–level students participating in work-related programmes and IT. Schools have found that teacher-pupil relationships have improved as a result of the flexible learning approach, individual action planning and Records of Achievement, while LEAs have been forced to address issues relating to equal opportunities. Teachers have, for the most part, succeeded in avoiding the pitfalls associated with the 'new vocationalism' by devising imaginative courses which are compatible with a genuine liberal education. However, TVEI is currently being phased out, and funding will cease in 1997.

Post-16 education and training

Post-16 education and training in Britain today is both fragmented and stratified. In addition to traditional academic courses, there are numerous other courses and qualifications, many of which are occupationally specific and validated by organisations such as BTEC, CGLI and the RSA. This 'dual track' system is at the root of a number of problems including:

- pressure on 16-year-olds to choose between radically different routes

- unnecessarily early and potentially damaging specialisation
- the question of how parity of esteem between the different routes is to be established and maintained
- problems relating to progression from one track to another.

In addition there are a whole series of problems relating to institutional provision and the enforced competition between them which conspire to frustrate integration. According to Green (1991):

> We now have a hotch-potch of policies and different initiatives aimed at different segments of the age-group and a very muddled institutional framework to deliver them ... There have been no social expectations about what young people between the ages of 16–19 should be doing, and Government policies have not sought to shape any ... Young people reaching the school-leaving age cross a threshold into a kind of limbo-land where ... they are either pupils or students or trainees, but nothing for certain. (p.92)

The fact that almost one-third of the top one-third of the age cohort either fail or withdraw is itself sufficient to merit reform, but there is a widespread feeling amongst educationalists outside the Conservative Party and the Headmasters' Conference that, short of some quite drastic measures to combat early selection into mutually incompatible pathways, the problem of progression will remain, and parity of esteem between the academic and the vocational will continue to be little more that a pipe-dream.

During the 1980s, the Government began to address these issues, albeit in a piecemeal way with no overall strategy. The developments included core skills, GNVQs and Records of Achievement.

Core skills

In a speech to the Association of Colleges in Further and Higher Education in February 1989, the Education Secretary, Kenneth Baker, spoke of the necessity for core skills to be part of the curriculum for all post-16 students. He listed these as: communication (written and oral); numeracy; personal relations (team working and leadership); familiarity with technology (especially IT); familiarity with systems in office and workshop procedures and employment hierarchies; and familiarity with changing work and social contexts. Later in 1989, Baker's successor, John MacGregor, asked the National Curriculum Council (NCC) to devise plans for the inclusion of core skills in all A and AS levels. Its report (NCC, 1990) recommended the following two-part list:

Group one: communication, problem-solving, personal skills
Group two: numeracy, IT, modern languages.

The NCC suggested that the first group should be developed in all post-16 programmes and embedded in every A and AS level syllabus. MacGregor lost no time in accepting the NCC's recommendations, and invited the National Council for Vocational Qualifications (NCVQ) to consult with the FEU and the SEAC on the possibility of including core skills in National Vocational Qualifications

(NVQs), which they duly did.

SEAC, however, expressed concern over the detailed definition of core skills; the problems surrounding them are numerous and have been clearly rehearsed by Lawson (1993). They include:

- difficulties of assessment in post-16 courses, especially when such assessment takes place in a variety of contexts
- the extent to which core skills can be incorporated within syllabuses
- the danger of their becoming a 'phantom curriculum' and being neglected altogether unless staff and resources are identified
- the problem of curriculum overload for post-16 students
- the difficulties associated with definition and transferability of communication, problem solving and personal skills.

To illustrate the last point, communication, after all, is not a mere skill but presupposes some understanding of those with whom one is communicating, and the context and the content of what is being communicated. Problem-solving is also not context-free: if we consider the skills involved in repairing a carburettor with those involved in teaching or advocacy, it is difficult to see how there could be any context-independent problem-solving skills at all. And personal skills is in need of considerable refinement if it is to have any utility.

Meanwhile enthusiasm for core skills continues. The CBI attaches great importance to them, and the National Commission for Education would like to see core skills as a compulsory component of its proposed General Education Diploma. In his Interim Report *Review of the 16–19 Qualifications*, Dearing (1995) has recommended that A–level candidates be encouraged, if not required, 'to show their competence at an appropriate level in the three core skills of communication, number and information technology' (para. 10.13). But while A–levels continue in their present form, there are grounds for doubting that core skills will make a significant impact on bridging the academic/vocational divide.

General National Vocational Qualifications (GNVQs)

The existence of literally hundreds of qualifications, with the inevitable duplication and lack of obvious equivalence, was highlighted in the White Paper *Education and Training for Young People* (DES, 1985b). The Government subsequently set up the National Council for Vocational Qualifications (NCVQ) whose task was to:

- secure comprehensive provision for vocational qualifications
- liaise with validating bodies responsible for qualifications providing entry to, and progression within and from, the system of vocational qualifications into Higher Education and the higher levels of professional qualifications
- design, monitor and adapt as necessary a national framework for vocational qualifications
- identify, specify and implement standards of occupational competence to meet the needs of employees including the self-employed.

Occupational competence was to be recognised in the form of NVQs at five levels from Basic to Professional.

Apart from the obvious dangers of equating the immediate needs of employers with the long term needs of a modern workforce, it would be a mistake to assume that NVQs could make a significant contribution to opportunities for progression as long as they continue to divorce assessment outcomes from general education. The limitations of NVQs were recognised by the Government which, in another White Paper, *Education and Training in the 21st Century*, (DES/DE, 1991) made something of a U-turn by suggesting the creation of more broadly-based, less occupationally specific vocational qualifications known as General NVQs. According to the White Paper, GNVQs should be:

- sufficiently distinctive from occupationally specific NVQs to ensure that there is no confusion between the two
- suitable for use by full-time college and, if appropriate, school students who have limited opportunities to demonstrate competence in the workplace
- of equal standing with academic qualifications at the same level, with which they could be combined.

GNVQs are modular in design and available at three levels – Foundation, Intermediate and Advanced. In contrast to A–levels, with their emphasis on timed written papers, GNVQs focus on criterion-referencing through competence-based assessment.

Unlike NVQs, the award of a GNVQ does not imply that the students can perform competently in an occupation immediately on qualifying, but they will have achieved the general skills, knowledge and understanding which underpin a range of occupations. They are proving to be very popular: about 250,000 people started in the autumn of 1995, and there are proposals to extend them to higher levels.

Records of Achievement (ROA)

Enthusiasm for Records of Achievement goes back at least as far as *ABC*, and it became a condition of TVEI funding that schools provide pupils with Records of Achievement. Because of their obvious function in assisting with transition and progression, the Department issued *Records of Achievement : A Statement of Policy* in 1984, which resulted in grants to finance 20 pilot schemes. In 1991 the National Record of Achievement was established with the aim of recording academic and vocational as well as other achievements not only at school but in FE and throughout working life.

While Records of Achievement are an improvement on the standard school report, it is far from clear that they receive the credibility with employers and HE which they deserve, and it is uncertain how they relate to the National Records of Vocational Achievement obtained within the framework of the NCVQ. While two systems of recording achievement exist side by side, there is little to reassure those who are convinced of the potential of ROA for at least supporting the bridges between the academic and vocational divide.

Key Stage 4

By 1993, it was becoming all too apparent that the curriculum provision for pupils in the 14 to 16 age range allowed too little scope for alternatives other than a strictly academic pathway. The result was that Government was forced into accepting Dearing's recommendations in his report on the National Curriculum and its assessment (Dearing, 1993) that the number of compulsory subjects in Key Stage 4 should be reduced and a high-quality vocational pathway provided.

> Scope for choice of subjects and educational pathways that will enhance motivation for many students who are not getting adequate benefit from school, and make for greater coherence in education from 14 through to 19. (para. 5.52)

GNVQs for 14- to 16-year-olds are being piloted in a selection of schools, and will be monitored by SCAA, NCVQ and Ofsted. Schools will also soon be able to offer one-year 'fat' courses, with half the content of a GCSE, or 'skinny' courses spread over two years.

The institutional framework and the marketplace

The fact that post-16 education and training takes place in a wide variety of institutions – schools, sixth form colleges, FE colleges, tertiary colleges and numerous training agencies – is itself a contributory factor in the difficulties associated with progression. The problem is compounded by the plethora of validating bodies and qualifications available. While organisations such as the Business and Technician Education Council (BTEC), the City and Guilds of London Institute (CGLI) and the Royal Society of Arts (RSA) offer qualifications in conformity with the various NVQ levels, the names or titles attached to such qualifications will differ. On the one hand, the Government expresses concern about the importance of bridging the academic/vocational divide, while on the other it appears to celebrate institutional competition.

Until quite recently, schools attracted most of those staying on post-16; but since 1992 the picture has undergone considerable change, with the majority being catered for by the college sector. If sixth forms and sixth form colleges have traditionally been for the academically most able, FE colleges have tried to offer a wider range of courses, some of which are academic while most are vocational in orientation. Tertiary colleges, although few in number (in 1995 there were only 64 in the entire country) are able to offer a genuinely comprehensive curriculum providing a full range of academic and vocational courses, many of which straddle the academic/vocational divide. Where they exist, they have tended to maintain much closer links with the schools from which the students come, the students are better equipped to find their way through the so-called jungle, with marked improvements in both participation and progression. Their obvious advantages include cost-effective links with the local community and success in breaking down the absurdly divisive nature of post-16 provision.

The Further and Higher Education Act 1992 removed sixth form colleges, FE colleges and tertiary colleges from LEA control, and they are now being funded by the Further Education and Funding Council (FEFC). The result is a system which perpetuates both the wasteful duplication of resources and unnecessary barriers to progression. Institutions whose funding is contingent upon recruitment and retention of students have less incentive to either rationalise in the interests of economies of scale or to provide objective guidance and counselling. The necessity for improvements in respect of the latter are clearly recognised in both the recent White Paper *Competitiveness Forging Ahead* (DTI, 1995), which proposes that all young people between the ages of 11 and 18 should receive professional careers education and guidance, and Ofsted's *Framework of Inspection* (revised 1995).

There is no less a marketplace for those young people who, for whatever reasons, do not remain in full-time education post-16. The White Paper *Education and Training for the 21st Century* (DES, 1985b) proposed that by 1996 every 16- and 17-year-old leaving full-time education should be entitled to a Training Credit to the value of £1000 as a means, according to Michael Howard (then at the Department of Employment) 'of motivating young people to participate more effectively in the training market'. In its 1989 paper, *Towards a Skill Revolution*, the CBI had advocated such credits as part of a 'training market' which saw young people as 'buyers' of vocational training. Those employers who failed to provide training would thereby lose out, and the potential trainee armed with £1000 would find someone else to provide training to at least NVQ Level 2. The credits, launched in 1991, are administered by Training and Enterprise Councils (TECs) which have overall responsibility for the DfEE's budget on work-related further education. Training credits have proved to be less popular than envisaged. This has been largely to do with the timing of their launch, which coincided with the recent recession, as well as their restriction, in the overwhelming majority of cases, to school leavers. Meanwhile the Government's aim of encouraging young people to remain in full-time education fits uncomfortably with the Training Credit Scheme.

ISSUES FOR DEBATE

1. Problems with GNVQs

GNVQs give rise to a number of questions for which there are no clear or obvious answers. The first of these relates to the problem of parity of esteem between A–levels and their 'equivalence'. While the DES White Paper in 1985 spoke of GNVQs as being of 'equal' standard with academic qualifications of the same level, a NCVQ paper (1993) stated that Advanced Level GNVQs had been designed to be of 'comparable' standard to that of A–levels. Separate but equal (or comparable) smacks of a kind of educational apartheid, and it is not at all certain that they do enjoy parity of esteem. As Alison Wolf (1993) says:

> Policy makers may see qualifications and curriculum in terms of upgrading the skills of the workforce as a whole, and recognise the importance of attracting able young people into vocational courses. Individuals see qualifications more in terms of selection – of indicating to future employers and higher education gatekeepers that one is a relatively able, relatively desirable candidate. (p.3)

One of the severest critics of GNVQs, Alan Smithers (1994), bemoans the fact that they have no syllabuses or subject matter, and that they suffer from ambiguity of purpose, falling somewhere between the academic and the vocational and not succeeding in being clearly one or the other. In spite of the efforts of the NCVQ, concerns over quality assurance, grading criteria and external assessment mean that GNVQs are still a long way from enjoying parity of esteem with A–levels, but they appear to be here to stay. Now that the Departments of Education and Employment have become one, we might see further and larger steps towards merging NCVQ and SEAC, with associated improvements in clarity and coherence in the post-16 qualification network.

Question for discussion

What is the solution to the problem of parity of esteem between academic and vocational education?

2. What kind of policy changes would be in the best interests of 14- to 19-year-olds?

Of all the possible alternatives for the future of educational provision for 14- to 19-year-olds, the *status quo* is probably the least satisfactory solution. As we have seen, the present position is one of confusion and incoherence. The need for coherence was recognised in the Crowther Report as long ago as 1959, but successive Governments have failed to grasp the nettle. Unfortunately, there is little agreement on which direction we should go. The interim Dearing Report (1995) posed three models, each of which would allow a mix of academic and vocational studies and lead to a national certificate:

- 'badging' existing qualifications to denote Foundation, Intermediate or Advanced level
- an overarching award to young people who achieve the national target of two A–levels, or their vocational equivalent, plus core skills
- a French-style Baccalaureate award.

There is disagreement about the respective merits of these. Some would like to see a complete break at 14 with two radically different routes after that age, one of which would be largely vocational and one largely, if not entirely, academic. Others would like to see a more comprehensive and unified provision. The merits of each require careful consideration.

A dual track system at 14-plus?

This at least has the advantage of simplicity in that assessment procedures are devised whereby the academic sheep and vocational goats are identified prior to the pursuit of tailor-made and quite separate curricula. But to pretend that selection at 14 would be more capable than the discredited 11-plus of avoiding the dangers of becoming a self-fulfilling prophecy is dangerously naïve. An alternative might be to rely on some form of self-selection. The trouble with this is that it assumes that children of 14 are in the best position to know whether or not they might benefit from further or higher education, and that they are able to see so far into the future that they might dispense with a liberal education with justifiable equanimity.

There is also the problem, as Dearing warned in his interim report (1995), of expecting candidates to mix and match modules for a wider choice of pathways when A–levels, GNVQs and other qualifications are constructed and assessed in different ways.

Problems associated with selection procedures and mixing courses apart, a dual track system would have all kinds of adverse social consequences in terms of social divisiveness and the reduction of equality of opportunity. Even if such fears are unwarranted, the proposal under discussion rests on an assumption which is increasingly open to question – that liberal and vocational education are mutually opposed. Richard Pring (1995) has done more than most to expose the absurdity of this. Firstly, it is to ignore the fact that a good vocational education can itself be liberating. Secondly, it relies on an untenable distinction between theory and practice, as if each is impervious to the other, and that people engaged in practical activities require little or nothing from what theory has to offer, or vice versa. Pring is right to castigate many so-called liberal educationalists who, in concentrating on academic excellence at the expense of so many other qualities, are themselves guilty of a self-fulfilling prophecy. But the alternative is not an equally narrow vocational path 'transforming learning into an acquisition of measurable behaviours, reducing understanding and knowledge to a list of competencies, turning educators into technicians' (p.191).

A radical and comprehensive alternative?

The case for this is very strong indeed. Piecemeal attempts at reform have been plagued by the failure to tackle the stranglehold that A–levels have on the entire system, as well as the continued faith of Government in market-forces which results in a wasteful duplication of institutions and validating bodies. With the recent merger of the Education and Employment departments and the Dearing Review of 16 to 19 qualifications, there are grounds for cautious optimism, but even Dearing's hands are tied when part of his remit includes the maintenance of the rigour of A–levels. During the past five years, organisations such as the CBI, the Secondary Heads' Association, the major political parties, British Petroleum, the Institute for Public Policy Research (IPPR) and the National Commission on Education (NCE) have all contributed to the debate. The most influential by far have been the IPPR's proposals for a British Baccalaureate and the NCE's proposal for a General Education Diploma.

A British Baccalaureate

In highlighting the divisive nature of the English qualifications system with its built-in obstacle race (GCSEs and A–levels) together with its vocational narrowness (NVQs), the IPPR's report (1990) outlines a systematic and persuasive case for a system that is flexible, unified and less fragmented. It spells out a three-stage model, categorised as Foundation, Advanced and Higher. The Foundation stage would be more or less equivalent to GCSE, but would include low-achieving students over the age of 16. The Advanced stage would replace A–levels and all existing vocational awards below HNC, and would lead to an Advanced Diploma or a 'British Baccalaureate'. The Higher stage refers to degree study and higher vocational awards.

The principal aims of the Diploma would be to:

- maximise flexibility of choice
- allow breadth of study within a particular core
- provide the 'foundations of knowledge' necessary for all citizens in a modern democracy, including an understanding of change in the organisation of work and the design and uses of technology
- offer opportunities for specialisation
- encourage students to relate theory to practice through work or community-based experience.

This is the Dearing third model, a 'depth and breadth' option. It is contentious because it introduces the concept of 'domains', four subject groupings (maths and science, humanities, social sciences, modern languages), with students compelled to study 'main' and 'subsidiary' subjects in choosing from more than one domain. While the enthusiasts approve of this provision for specialisation with 'balancing' studies, others do not think that students should be forced into breadth and doubt the wisdom of a qualification attainable by only a minority.

A General Education Diploma

The NCE (1993) criticises the tripartism associated with GCSEs, A- and AS-levels, GNVQs and NVQs, arguing that post–14 education should be planned as a whole, with a unified framework for examinations and qualifications and no sharp break at 16. The Commission proposes a new General Education Diploma to be awarded at two levels – Ordinary (normally for 16-year-olds) and Advanced (normally for 18-year-olds), but with no fixed age limits in either case. Such a diploma would replace existing academic and vocational qualifications. In addition to its dual level status, it would be:

- a grouped award, requiring achievements in a range of subjects including academic technical, practical and vocational studies together with core skills
- a credit-based award, modular in structure, allowing the accumulation of credits over a period, even from separate providers
- a graded award to recognise levels of achievement
- an accredited award, guaranteeing a full curriculum entitlement to all students.

Its credit-based design would provide a flexibility, breadth and coherence in ways not allowed in the present system.

Both proposals are remarkably similar in tenor. A particularly strong feature which they both share is their concern for flexibility in terms of age limits and points of entry and exit. They are detailed in content and models of their kind in providing a commendable basis upon which rational discussion of 14 to 19 provision should proceed.

Question for discussion

What are the respective merits of a 'dual track' system for academic and vocational education and a more comprehensive provision?

THE FUTURE?

The final Dearing Report (1996), consisting of 700 pages and 200 recommendations, was published during the proof stage of this book. The following is a brief summary of the main recommendations; these have been generally accepted by the Government:

Simplification
The present bewildering 'maze' of 16,000 qualifications for 16- to 19-year-olds should be replaced by one simple, slim structure.

Rationalisation
Separate pathways (academic, vocational and applied) should be retained but given equal status and general currency through:

- Four common National Levels – entry, foundation, intermediate and advanced – to facilitate a mixture of academic and vocational courses
- Two over-arching qualifications:
  - A *National Certificate* for a set number of passes at intermediate and advanced levels
  - A Baccalaureate-style *National Diploma* to certify not only the number of passes but also breadth and depth of study at advanced level

  For each qualification, key skills of communication, numeracy and IT should be required components
- Common course elements to enable students to switch between A–level and GNVQ courses
- NCVQ and SCAA to be merged as a single national body for training and education to ensure common arrangements for quality assurance and facilitate mixing and matching of courses
- A reduction in the number of awarding bodies

Standards
- A–level standards should be raised (e.g. through a general review of standards and special papers and assignments for more able students)
- Vocational qualifications should have a greater rigour (e.g. by renaming Advanced GNVQs Applied A–levels and making greater use of external testing)
- AS–levels should be reformulated to represent a full half A–level; there should be new applied AS–levels and an AS–level in key skills
- The National Record of Achievement should be revamped and relaunched

Training
- Particular urgency is needed to address the needs of the fifth of all school-leavers who currently end up with no employment, training or education. Disaffected 14-year-olds should be allowed to start vocational courses in the workplace or at college
- Youth training should be relaunched with a system of National Traineeships to reward achievement in key skills and lead to qualifications such as GNVQs and GCSEs

FURTHER READING

Higham, J. (1996) *The Emerging 16–19 Curriculum: Policy and Provision*. London: David Fulton.
Hitchcock, G. (1988) *Education and Training 14–18*. Harlow: Longman.
Macfarlane, E. (1993) *Education 16–19 in Transition*. London: Routledge.
Pring, R. (1995) *Closing the Gap: Liberal Education and Vocational Preparation*. London: Hodder & Stoughton.
Richardson, W., Woodhouse, J. and Finegold, D. (eds) (1993) *The Reform of Post–16 Education and Training in England and Wales*. Harlow: Longman.
Whiteside, T. and Everton, T. (eds) (1992) *16–19: Changes in Education and Training*. London: David Fulton.

REFERENCES

Confederation of British Industry (1989) *Towards a Skill Revolution*. London: CBI.
Dearing, R. (1994) *The National Curriculum and its Assessment*. London: School Curriculum and Assessment Authority.
Dearing, R. (1995) *Review of 16–19 Qualifications Framework: Interim Report*. London: School Curriculum and Assessment Authority.
Department of Education and Science (1977) *Education in Schools: A Consultative Document*. London: HMSO
Department of Education and Science (1979) *Proposals for a Certificate of Extended Education* (Keohane Report). London: HMSO.
Department of Education and Science (1980) *Examinations 16–18: A Consultative Paper*. London: HMSO.
Department of Education and Science (1984) *Records of Achievement: A Statement of Policy*. London: HMSO.
Department of Education and Science (1985a) *Better Schools*. London: HMSO.
Department of Education and Science (1985b) *Education and Training for Young People*. London: HMSO.
Department of Education and Science (1988) *Advancing 'A' Levels* (The Higginson Report). London: HMSO.
Department of Education and Science/Department of Employment (1991) *Education and Training in the 21st Century*. London: HMSO.
Department for Education (1994) *Competitiveness: Helping Businesses to Win*. London: HMSO.
Department of Trade and Industry (1995) *Competitiveness: Forging Ahead*. London: HMSO.
Further Education Unit (1979) *A Basis for Choice*. London: FEU.
Finegold, D., Ewart, K., Miliband, D., Raffe, D., Spours., K. and Young, M. (1990) *A British Baccalaureate: Ending the Division between Education and Training*. London: IPPR.
Green, A. (1991) 'Comprehensive education and training: possibilities and prospects', in C. Chitty, (ed) *Post–16 Education: Studies in Access and Achievement*. London: Kogan Page.
Halsall, R. and Crockett, M. (eds) (1996) *Education and Training 14–19: Chaos or Coherence?* London: David Fulton.
Lawson, D. (21993) 'Curriculum policy development since the Great Debate', in H. Tomlinson, (ed.) *Education and Training 14–19: Continuity and Diversity in the Curriculum*. Harlow: Longman.
National Commission on Education(1993) *Learning to Succeed*. London: Heinemann.
National Council for Vocational Qualifications (1993) *Information and Notes on GNVQs*. London: NCVQ.
National Curriculum Council (1990) *Core Skills to 19: A response to the Secretary of State*. London: NCC.
Ofsted (1995) *Framework of Inspection* (rev. ed.) London: Ofsted.
Smithers, A. (1994) *All Our Futures*. Manchester: Manchester University Press.,
Wolf, A. (ed.) (1993) *Parity of Esteem: Can Vocational Courses Ever Achieve High Status?* London: University of London Institute of Education.

Part II

EQUAL EDUCATIONAL OPPORTUNITIES

CHAPTER 6

Special Educational Needs

Derek Shaw

INTRODUCTION

A child with special educational needs (SEN) is one who has a learning difficulty which requires special educational provision. A weakness of the term is its catch-all nature. In its daftest form this leads some to claim that *all* children have special needs. Used like this, 'SEN' does no more than assert that children need some degree of individual provision and so does not contribute to the debate. Setting aside such a view, it remains true that the term refers to individuals and groups whose disabilities or circumstances are very different from each other. The corollary is that the term refers to different groups at different times.

The first distinction to be borne in mind is contained within the Warnock Report (DES, 1978), which was the culmination of an enquiry into the education of handicapped children and young people. The report suggested that 'up to one in five children at some time during their school career will require some form of special education' (DES, 1978, para 3.17). This observation is the source of the widely quoted assertion that '20 per cent of children have SEN'. The figure reflects a broad continuum spanning those whose disabilities are profound, permanent and multiple as well as those whose disabilities are transitory and will, if promptly and effectively met, cease to exist. The report acknowledged a distinction between those for whom special separate provision had traditionally been made and those who had generally been taught in ordinary schools. It estimated the first category, those taught in ordinary schools, accounted for around two per cent of all children, and consequently the latter were estimated as amounting to 18 per cent of the school population. 'The two per cent', 'the 18 per cent' and 'the 20 per cent' have since become common terms.

Special needs arise from a variety of circumstances and take a variety of forms. Causes may be medical, physical, intellectual, psychological, or social; or they may arise from factors that lie within the learning situation. Similar, or even the same, circumstances will affect individuals in different ways. Appropriate adjustments to contexts may take many forms. The differing meanings of the legislation for differing groups – and not just individuals – should always be in the forefront of our minds when discussing the effects of change. Innovation may suit some interests much better than others.

THE POLICY

KEY POINTS
Education Act 1981 • The concept of a continuum of need • Identification and individual staged assessment • Statements of SEN for children who need special resources • Integration/inclusive education *Education Reform Act 1988* • The impact on SEN of the National Curriculum, its assessment, delegated funding and open enrolment *Education* Act 1993 • Extension of parental rights • Time limits to speed up the statementing process • Code of Practice

Education Act 1981

When the 1981 Education Act was placed on the Statute Book, it signalled a significant break with the established tradition of special education in the United Kingdom. It attempted to alter approaches to the education of 'special' children by replacing the notion of 'handicap' that had informed policy since the Education Act of 1944. In its place the new concept of 'special educational need' (SEN) would be the guide to:

- identifying the obstacles to a child's learning
- selecting the most effective teaching approaches
- placing the child in the most beneficial educational setting.

This represented the enactment of the proposals of the Warnock Committee (see Introduction).

A continuum of need

The Act refers to children with *special educational needs*. This term was intended to encompass both those with more severe disabilities, who were being taught in special schools, and those who were receiving 'remedial' education in ordinary schools. The effects of children's disabilities had been recognised in the Education Act 1944, but the focus at that time had been upon children's 'handicaps'. The new term intended to emphasise the significance of appropriate provision rather than the child's shortcomings, and to end the sharp distinction between two groups of children – the handicapped (the 'two per cent') and the non-handicapped.

The Act states that 'a child has a "special educational need" if he or she has a *learning difficulty* which calls for *special educational provision*' (Sect.1.1). The two keys terms are then defined:

A child has a *learning difficulty* if:

> (a) he has a significantly greater difficulty in learning than the majority of children of his age; or
> (b) he has a disability which either prevents or hinders him from making use of educational facilities of a kind generally provided in schools within the area of the local authority concerned, for children of his age. (Sect.1.2)

Special educational provision is defined as:

> provision which is additional to, or otherwise different from, the educational provision made generally for children of his age in schools maintained by the local education authority concerned. (Sect. 1.3)

Note how these definitions raise problems of relativity between LEAs. The division in the Act between those who would and would not require some additional resourcing has re-affirmed the 'special' nature of some children's needs when compared to others. This has made the concept of the 'continuum of need' difficult to sustain in the perceptions of teachers, especially as the Act concentrates on 'the two per cent' and has little to say about those who have become known as 'the 18 per cent'.

Identification and individual assessment

The Act places strong emphasis on the assessment of each child's learning abilities and the obstacles to his/her learning. For those children (the '18 per cent') who have traditionally been the concern of the ordinary school, assessment is a matter involving the child's class teacher and other teachers in the school. If the school comes to believe that it cannot, without outside help, successfully plan a child's learning, then other professionals become involved. Additionally, emphasis is placed on early identification to minimise the cumulative effects of the learning disability going unacknowledged. The Act envisages that at all times parents will be involved in, and informed of, matters concerning their child's progress.

Staged assessment leading to a Statement of Special Educational Need

The 1981 Act provides for assessment to be undertaken, progressively, in a series of five stages. It is envisaged that the first three stages will involve a level of expertise sufficient to meet the needs of the great majority of children with SEN

– the '18 per cent'. Their learning needs will be met by the mainstream school, which will adjust its teaching and learning strategies to accommodate the child, arranging additional teaching or support if necessary. For those children for whom the mainstream school cannot, without additional resources, meet the child's needs, then the fourth stage provides for a multi-disciplinary assessment to be undertaken. This means that, in addition to the evidence from the school and the child's parents, the LEA must seek advice from medical, psychological and social services. If the LEA then deems it necessary, it can elect to issue a Statement of Special Educational Need. This document contains the following:

- an account of the child's SEN
- an outline of the provision necessary to meet the child's SEN
- the type of school in which the child's needs will be met and, perhaps, the name of a particular school
- an account of any non-educational needs which might, for example, be provided by the health services
- any non-educational provision to meet such needs.

The LEA may or may not find that a statement of need is merited. Parents have a right of appeal (formerly to a local appeals committee, now, under the 1993 Act, to an independent tribunal) if they feel that the LEA's proposals are inappropriate.

Integration/inclusive education

The issue of where children with SEN should be educated has taken a very prominent place in some discussions. When a child has been deemed to require special provision, the 1981 Act places a duty on LEAs to secure that the child is educated in an ordinary school, subject to the following conditions:

- that the parents views have been considered; and,
- the placement will be compatible with

   1. the child receiving the special educational provision that he or she requires;
   2. the provision of efficient education of the children with whom the child will be educated; and
   3. the efficient use of resources.

This part of the Act has also been subject to wide-ranging criticism and we shall discuss it in greater detail later.

Education Reform Act 1988

The Education Reform Act which set up the National Curriculum made no mention of special educational needs, but some of the principal provisions of the Act provoked a great outcry amongst the special needs lobby, which alleged that its provisions conflicted with the principles that had informed the 1981 Act.

Education Act 1993

The most recent legislation, the Education Act 1993, followed on the heels of the White Paper *Choice and Diversity: A New Framework for Schools* (DfE, 1992a) and the consultation paper *Special Educational Needs: Access to the System* (DfE, 1992b). As far as special educational needs is concerned, the Act attempted to meet some of the criticisms of the earlier arrangements:

- It extended parental rights by creating a new independent tribunal to hear appeals
- It attempted to speed up the statementing process by setting time limits for each stage
- It required the Secretary of State to issue a Code of Practice giving practical guidance to LEAs and schools on their responsibilities to children with SEN.

The Department for Education also published a number of Circulars, including the *Organisation of Special Educational Provision* (DfE 1994a) and a package of six Circulars, known collectively as *Pupils with Problems* (DfE 1994b).

The Code of Practice

The most notable outcome of the Act, from the point of view of schools, was the publication of the *Code of Practice on the Identification and Assessment of Special Educational Needs*. This re-affirmed and consolidated earlier arrangements, but attempted, in addition, to respond to some of the criticisms that had been levelled at current practice. Schools, LEAs, health authorities and social service departments now have a statutory duty to 'have regard to the Code' (DfE, 1994c, p.ii).

Part 1 of the Code sets out its fundamental principles. These are:

- the concept of a continuum of need
- maximum access to the National Curriculum for children with SEN
- most children with SEN will be educated alongside their peers in ordinary schools
- the LEA may be involved in meeting the needs of pre-school children
- partnership between children, their parents, schools, LEAs and other agencies is the key to purposeful assessment and provision.

In essence this is a re-statement of the Warnock principles.

Part 2 of the Code defines the operation of three school-based stages of assessment in considerable detail. Clearly this is recognition of earlier criticism and is intended to diminish the gulf between children with statements and those without. Great emphasis is placed on the role and responsibility of the school's Special Educational Needs Co-ordinator. These efforts aimed to ensure that greater recognition of the needs of children with SEN were universally welcomed, but, as Fish and Evans (1995) remark, 'The resource implications – in terms of class teacher and SEN Co-ordinator time required to carry out procedures, to prepare evidence, to write reports and to work with parents in schools of different sizes and types – are not recognised' (p.20). This part of the

Code also places a responsibility on the governors of a school to 'do their best to secure that the necessary provision is made for any pupil who has special educational needs' (para 2.6).

The Code then goes on to offer criteria for informing the decision to award (or not) a statement of need and to supply guidance on annual reviews of statements. For the first time, statutory time limits for statementing are set out. Also included is advice on assessments and statements for children under five.

ISSUES FOR DEBATE

1. Does the concept of special educational needs help or hinder children with disabilities?

As we have seen, the term 'special educational needs' took centre-stage in the Warnock Report. Soon after its adoption, Mary Warnock herself wrote a piece reflecting on the value of the term. She argued:

> There was a kind of simplicity in the concept which made it attractive; and it was useful in so far as it at least departed from the medical model based on diagnosis of defects, and turned attention to a service model, based on delivering the goods. And it might have worn better, this smart little number, if it hadn't been for the recession. (1982, p. 57)

It is clear that the intentions of the committee were humanitarian. Although the committee acknowledged that the system of disability categories in place since 1944 had afforded recognition for some children and ensured that they were provided for, it was anxious to move away from categories, arguing that:

- categories label and stigmatise children
- categories leave some children with disabilities unrecognised (because these children do not 'fit') and therefore unresourced
- categories assume commonalities and do not recognise individual needs
- categories fail to recognise multiple disability.

What, then, was the effect of the new concept? First of all, it did not abolish categories because, as Pumfrey and Mittler (1989) point out, 'In essence new categories were created by the 1981 Education Act: either the child had or did not have, SEN. If it was decided that such needs existed, a statement of SEN was, or was not prepared. Not to have SEN is also to be labelled' (p.29).

Secondly, by extending the concept of SEN to embrace 'the 18 per cent' as well as 'the two per cent', competition for the available resources has been heightened between qualifying groups. By claiming to address the educational needs of 20 per cent of pupils rather than two per cent, 'the potential for dissatisfaction among parents (and voters) is some tenfold greater' (p.30).

Thirdly, as with much of the legislation in this area, the changes were introduced without additional finance. The rhetoric surrounding the Act induced increased expectations amongst both parents and teachers, leading Pumfrey and Mittler to comment 'For a government or society to will the end but not provide the means, is futile and dishonest' (p.30).

It was no doubt for these kinds of reasons that Mary Warnock (1992) has since retracted her earlier justification of the concept of SEN quoted above:

> The idea of a continuum of ability and disability, with only those at the very end identified by a 'statement' was too vague. It was all very well as an ideal; indeed it may have been beneficial in that it may have made children with disabilities seem less of a race apart. But as a basis for legislation, especially at a time when LEAs were increasingly short of money, it was disastrous. (p.3)

Question for discussion

Has the concept of SEN outlived its usefulness?

---

2. Problems with statementing

We have seen that the operation of the 1981 Act provided for some children to be awarded a 'statement of special need' and the accompanying additional resources. On this matter, too, Mary Warnock has reflected critically:

> The whole concept of 'statementing' for only a few children, with the rest supposedly having their needs met according to what individual schools can provide, must be radically rethought. And this is the more urgent as schools become increasingly competitive over examination results and have to manage their own finances. (Warnock, 1992)

Implicit in Warnock's claim is a concern for those who do not have statements and who must, therefore, be provided for from within a school's normal budget. This restates the difficulties with establishing what level of need qualifies for additional resources, and what level of resourcing is 'ordinary'. The problems this raises for LEAs have been pinpointed by the Audit Commission and HMI (1992):

> LEAs have no guidelines as to the level of need with which a school should ordinarily be expected to cope, or the level of resource the school is expected to provide before referring the child to the LEA. This lack of definition in the Act makes it very difficult for LEAs to budget, because there is no firm basis on which to assess how many pupils will require extra help from the LEA and what the amount of the help will be. (para 17)

The problem being identified is concerned with the financial resources made available for children with SEN. Whatever the amount of resources, whether or not it is in some sense 'enough', the responsibility of LEAs and others is to ensure that the distribution of funds is equitable: 'LEAs have this open-ended commitment at a time when the Education Reform Act has curtailed their flexibility to deploy resources by prescribing the way in which the schools' budget should be allocated' (para 19). As a consequence, parents can see that children with similar needs to their own may be treated more favourably by other LEAs. 'The lack of definition of the client group and of the respective responsibilities of schools and LEAs leads to inconsistencies in practice between LEAs' (para 20). From its own survey of cases, the Audit Commission noted that:

- pupils with widely differing levels of need had been issued with statements
- schools had been able to point out children without a statement with greater needs than those with a statement
- LEAs had admitted that factors which had been influential included 'the level of determination of the school or parent and whether the parent was represented by a lawyer or voluntary organisation' (para 22).

If it is true that determined parents can be more successful than others, regardless of the merits of the case, then it is hardly surprising that 'a new spirit of litigation has taken over relations between parents and local authorities' (Warnock, 1993). Warnock offers the opinion that 'The more people are encouraged to believe in the Parents' Charter the more they will wish to sue local authorities for not giving them their rights'. She adds: 'This adversarial attitude adopted by parents, and, perforce, local authorities is damaging to the child, and damaging to the trust between authorities and parents, without which no special provision will succeed'.

Ironically, this distressing view arises from attempts to ensure that parents' views are adequately heard in the decision-making process, and certainly there is evidence that this has not always been the case (see, for example, Evans *et al.*, 1989; House of Commons, 1993). The Government has been committed to improving parental rights, on this occasion, with unforeseen difficulties. Warnock associates this with a further matter:

> The greater the number of children with statements, the more it comes to be assumed that those children with SEN who are in mainstream schools and who have no statements are all right ... Such considerations lead me to believe that statementing ought to be abolished.

Warnock's principal difficulty seems to lie with ensuring provision for those with the most severe needs whilst preserving the continuum. The following says it: 'The problem is how to resource a continuum of need. Clearly it is administratively much easier to identify, categorise and 'pigeon-hole' pupils for resource purposes' (Lunt and Evans, 1994, p.39).

It is quite clear that the DfEE is well aware of this problem. Whilst retaining the procedure for statementing, the Code of Practice places a firm responsibility on schools to plan appropriate provision for children who are judged to have SEN but to be at Stages 1 to 3 and so reduce the need for statementing. However, the actual level of resourcing against which schools must operate continues to be controversial, despite the statement in the following excerpt from the Code.

> The decision not to issue a statement may be disappointing to parents and seen as denial of additional resources for their child. Parents may appeal to the Tribunal over a decision not to issue a statement. The LEA should ensure that parents are aware that resources are available within all maintained schools to meet the majority of special needs of their pupils and that parents fully understand the school-based stages of assessment and the monitoring and review arrangements which will ensure that their child's needs are met by the school, with external support if necessary, in an appropriate way. (DfE, 1994c para 4.17)

Question for discussion

Should statementing be abolished?

3. Inclusive education v. separate schools

Much writing about special needs in recent years has focused on the claim that separate provision for children with SEN is inappropriate:

> These three rights or principles – the right to education, the right to equality of educational opportunity and the right to participate in society – add up to a powerful case for integration. Accepting them means accepting that every child has the right to attend an ordinary school and to receive there an appropriate education delivered as part of the school's normal pattern of educational provision. (Hegarty, 1993, p. 65)

Indeed, some authorities have moved to close special schools in their areas. An account of the guiding principles associated with this policy decision is offered by Corbett (1994):

> Inclusive education can be seen as one step on from integration: more assertive, life-enhancing and visionary. It also seeks to forge links with other social justice issues, thus avoiding the construction of a hierarchy of oppression, in which those who champion a particular disadvantaged group claim priority over others. (p. 75)

It is interesting to set these views against those of Vladimir Lubovskii, in a speech to a Child Care Conference in London in 1988. At that time, Lubovskii was the Director of the Research Institute for Defectology of the Academy of Pedagogic Sciences of the USSR.

> The concept of integration in no means contradicts the concept of differentiation. Our differentiation regards integration as the final goal of special education: the school leaver must be fully integrated in productive activity. The most effective way of achieving this integration is to educate people in a special school. (1988, p.6)

The language of the speech is a little odd to Western ears, but his message finds resonances. Chapman (1994), the head of a large special school, argues that there are children whose needs are such that they can only be met within separate provision. And when Warnock appeared before the House of Commons Education Committee in 1993 and was asked a question about integration, she told the Committee: 'I believe it would be an absolute disaster if the number of special schools was reduced radically' (H.C. Parliamentary Papers 1992-93, Paper 287, para.45).

Some writers have seen an over-emphasis on integration, or inclusion, claiming that it is driven as Chapman has it 'by zealots'. The arguments that are developed are not against children with disabilities being in mainstream schools, but ask, rather, what is in the interests of the children themselves and what evidence suggests that the children benefit. Hegarty (1993) discusses the problems of collecting evidence in this area and reviews some of the available data himself. He concludes that the evidence produces no clear balance of advantage for or against integration.

In an article entitled 'The Primacy of Pedagogy', Aubrey (1993) complains that 'research has focused predominantly on the educational setting or place of receiving the educational provision rather than upon the quality of the actual teaching received' (p. 14). Her argument is that the focus on the location distracts from what she claims is the significant factor affecting the child's learning – the nature of the teaching that the child receives. Expanding on what she claims is the more legitimate research goal, she asks 'Are there teaching principles *unique* to special needs pupils or do the *same* educational principles which apply to effective teaching and schooling for ordinary children apply equally to special children?' (p. 14).

In answer to this, Norwich (1990) criticises those who try to represent the issue as one about doubting that there is much expertise involved in special needs teaching. This line of argument, he says, is intended to undermine the claim that special educational provision is necessary – that special children can only be taught by special educators with special skills:

> Different teachers have opted to work with different age groups, perhaps with different areas of the curriculum and/or with children with exceptional learning characteristics. By doing so they learn specific skills ... which are not immediately transferable without relevant training experience. (p. 123)

The final quote in this section is pragmatic, but provides food for thought:

> The vast majority of special educational resources are based in separate special schools where pupils will receive considerably enhanced funding by a factor of four to eight. The easiest and administratively most straightforward way to gain access to these resources is to place a child in a special school. This 'guarantees' the additional expenditure. Furthermore, so long as considerable resources are 'earmarked' and based in separate schools, it may make more sense economically to place children there, since the special provision 'plant' is being financed and staffed, and placement of pupils there may result in economies of scale and more economic use of expensive facilities. (Lunt and Evans, 1994, p. 44–5)

Question for discussion

Some LEAs are trying to place more emphasis on mainstreaming for children with SEN. Is this policy an appropriate one in principle? If so, what conditions would make its implementation acceptable?

---

4. The impact of the Education Reform Act 1988 and the Education Act 1993

It is important to appreciate that much of what is to be said about the 1988 Act and special educational needs is concerned with the Act as a whole. The elements interlock. It is together that they have such a formidable set of consequences; their separation below is for convenience.

The National Curriculum and its assessment

There has been some ambivalence amongst special educators about the desirability of a prescribed curriculum for children with SEN. However, the same group remain committed to ensuring the right of those with SEN to the maximum participation possible in the education service. Accordingly, the SEN lobby campaigned for the 1988 Act to state unequivocally that access to the National Curriculum was a right for children with SEN. The Department was not persuaded, but shortly after the Act had been passed, it issued *National Curriculum: From Policy to Practice* (DES, 1989) which contained the important sentence, 'All pupils share the same statutory entitlement to a broad and balanced curriculum, including access to the National Curriculum' (para 8.1).

However, problems remained concerning the structure of the National Curriculum, the focus of its content, the system of levels and, not least, the arrangements for assessment. Three issues in relation to SEN assessment predominate:

1. The extent to which the assessment system will consign the '18 per cent' to failure.
2. The extent to which the performance of the '18 per cent' will lead schools to consider them 'undesirable' because of their depressing effect on a school's profile in the 'league table'.
3. The insensitivity of a system designed for the majority of school pupils to the changes in performance of children with moderate, severe and profound learning difficulties or disabilities.

The model of the National Curriculum devised by the Task Group on Assessment and Testing (TGAT) envisaged a progression through a series of levels. The common characteristics of children with learning difficulties is that their progress is markedly slower than that of their peers. Teachers of these children, who in ordinary circumstances face a continuing struggle to boost confidence, share a general anxiety that the results of these assessments, being continuously within the lower levels, may serve to undermine enthusiasm and motivation.

The second matter concerns the publication of the results of National Curriculum assessment, which was trumpeted by the Government as a mechanism that would encourage schools to raise standards. Few in the special needs lobby believed that the spotlight of public opinion would transform the attainments of children with SEN. This move was accompanied by a rhetoric of good schools flourishing and poor schools being told to become 'better' or face closure. A simple logic was promoted: good results would attract pupils' parents; these schools would recruit well; finance would follow recruitment. Therefore, the school's interest is best served by removing those who depress the profile of achievement, who do not enhance the school's image and may, thereby, inhibit recruitment. The spectre of being unwanted pupils looms over children with SEN.

The third matter bears mainly on special schools. Children whose achievements are most different from their peers are commonly recognised as having severe impairments. Whether in ordinary or in special schools, different criteria are applied when recognising progress. One view is that the National Curriculum is irrelevant to these children's needs. Many children will have needs that are not met by the National Curriculum, and may conflict with it. Much special education has been informed by the concept of the individually constructed developmental curriculum. At the same time, special needs campaigners are wary of children with severe disabilities being declared ineducable. An alternative view therefore accepts the desirability of the common educational agenda, but queries whether an assessment system that cannot detect the incremental changes in achievement that mark the progress of those who may remain working 'within Level 1' is satisfactory.

Delegated funding, open enrolment and 'opting out'

The requirement that LEAs should delegate funding to individual schools led to a widespread concern that this would be against the interests of children with SEN. Essentially, the view is that children's SENs are relatively expensive to meet and will take up more than their 'fair share' of resources. The argument is rather more complex, since LEAs are required to devise formulae that will govern the distribution of funds to schools. The law requires that the greater part of this allocation should be related to the number of children that the school succeeds in recruiting. However, LEAs are permitted to build an element within the formula to reflect the number of children with SEN on a school's roll. At this point it is clear that the 'attractiveness' of children with SEN may hinge upon the size of the element of funding that is attached to them: what is their 'worth'? They could be a valued source of additional funds, but they could also be cost liabilities. This form of funding is distinct from monies allocated, by way of statements of need, to support individual children. In this latter case the funds are 'attached to the child' and have a specific purpose, for example the employment of a classroom helper for a specified number of hours. The most sceptical (or cynical) query how much more attractive it may be to spend on those pupils whose performance will reflect creditably in 'league tables' and thus encourage other parents to send their children to a 'successful' school. If this view is uncomplimentary to the teaching profession, it is seen as reflecting the pressures which bear on heads and governors in an education system which is market-driven.

There is another perspective connected with delegated funding, and this applies to both LEA schools and those which have opted for grant-maintained status. The 1980s saw a continuing development in LEA-based 'learning support teams'. They grew out of the remedial services and child guidance clinics that were already in place and provided a valuable extra service to schools. But the effect of decentralised funding has been to deprive LEAs of central resources and to compromise their ability to maintain these teams as an authority-wide resource. The government's view is that the funds continue to be available – and in the most appropriate place, that is in the school where the need must be met. The difficulty is most strongly felt in small primary schools where the transferred funds do not achieve a critical mass. LEAs have adopted a number of approaches, of which the 'agency' model seems the most popular. In this, as the name suggests, the LEA has an 'honest broker' relationship with its schools to whom it offers various services; but the LEA will only employ the support staff if the schools elect to 'buy in', and it remains the decision of the individual school whether it chooses to become a client of the service. An approach that may complement or replace such an arrangement is the practice of 'clustering' whereby a group of schools combine their resources in search of the critical mass referred to above.

The Code of Practice

Through the Code of Practice which the 1993 Act now requires, a framework governing special educational provision is set out. In general this endorses existing arrangements, confirming the Warnock concept of special educational needs and the role of statementing in meeting these needs. The emphasis now is placed on improving the administration of these arrangements rather than upon revising them. In general, the Code has been welcomed among professionals. However, because it places additional responsibilities on schools and school-based professionals, discharging the responsibilities laid down in the Code requires more than goodwill: it requires trained personnel.

> Although there has been a programme to train SEN co-ordinators for some years, the new legislation, together with the Code, comprise a complex series of changes for which governors, senior staff and co-ordinators will need further training. Above all the independence of schools and the uncertainty about support services, or the ability to pay for them, will require the further development of SEN co-ordinator skills. The financing of training from within school budgets will again be related to school priorities. As the Audit Commission/HMI Report (1992) pointed out, incentives are necessary if schools are to take special education responsibilities seriously, and at present such incentives do not exist. (Fish and Evans, 1995, p.58-59)

As regards the effects of LMS and GMS on the provision of special education, Fish and Evans have a similarly bleak message:

> It is hard to avoid the conclusion that a policy designed to enhance parental choice and the independence of individual schools has made it more difficult to ensure that there is an adequate range of special educational facilities and support services. (p.71)

Readers may recall the comment early in this chapter from Pumfrey and Mittler (1989) about society willing 'the end but not the means'. It is a matter for some regret that six years later, in connection with the latest legislation, Fish and Evans (1995) are moved to write:

> The resource implications of the school-based assessment and provision expected by the new framework have not yet been seriously considered. At the time the legislation was passed, it was said to be 'resource neutral'. There appears to be an unrealistic assumption that adequate resources exist and that all that is required is good management. (p. 23)

Question for discussion

Do you agree with those who argue that the 1988 Act has worked against the interests of children with SEN? What changes would you propose in the curricular and funding arrangements?

THE FUTURE?

At root, two fundamental difficulties inform debates in this area. Firstly, how much funding is the Government willing, or able, to direct to meeting children's special educational needs? Secondly, is devolution of responsibilities (and finance) consistent with the forms of provision that will enable children to receive appropriate, high quality education? In neither case does there appear any immediate likelihood of change in present trends. There seems to be a continued reliance on a committed, hard-working and under-recognised group of professionals. One is left wondering how long they will be prepared to continue in this way.

FURTHER READING

Bibby, P. and Lunt, I. (1995) *Working for Children: Securing Provision for Children with Special Educational Needs*. London: David Fulton.

Department for Education (1994) *Code of Practice on the Identification and Assessment of Special Educational Needs*. London: Department for Education.

Fish, J. and Evans, J. (1995) *Managing Special Education: Codes, Charters and Competition*. Buckingham: Open University Press.

Norwich, B. (1990) *Reappraising Special Needs Education*. London: Cassell.

Riddell, S. and Brown, S. (eds) (1994) *Special Educational Needs Policy in the 1990s: Warnock in the Market Place*. London: Routledge.

Visser, J. and Upton, G. (eds.) (1993) *Special Education in Britain after Warnock*. London: David Fulton.

REFERENCES

Aubery, C. (1993) 'The primacy of pedagogy', *Special Children*, No. 70, 14–17.

Audit Commission/HMI (1992) *Getting in on the Act*. London: HMSO.

Chapman, N. (1994) 'Caught in the crossfire: the future of special schools', *British Journal of Special Education*, 21, 60–63.

Corbett, J. (1994) 'Challenges in a competitive culture: a policy for inclusive education in Newham', in S. Riddell and S. Brown (eds) *Special Educational Needs Policy in the 1990s*. London: Routledge.

Dearing, R. (1994) *The National Curriculum and its Assessment: Final Report*. London: SCAA.

Department of Education and Science (1978) *Special Educational Needs* (Warnock Report). London: HMSO.

Department of Education and Science (1989) *National Curriculum: From Policy to Practice*. London: DES.

Department for Education (1992a) *Choice and Diversity: A New Framework for Schools*. London: DfE.

Department for Education (1992b) *Special Educational Needs: Access to the System* (consultation paper). London: DfE.

Department for Education (1994a) *The Organisation of Special Educational Provision*. (Circular 6/94) London: DfE.

Department for Education (1994b) *Pupils with Problems* (Circulars 8–13). London: DfE.

Department for Education (1994c) *Code of Practice on the Identification and Assessment of Special Educational Needs*. London: DfE.

Evans, J., Everard, B., Friend, J., Glaser, A., Norwich, B. and Welton, J. (1989) *Decision-Making for SEN: An Inter-Service Resource Pack*. London: University of London, Institute of Education.

Fish, J. and Evans, J. (1995) *Managing Special Education: Codes, Charters and Competition*. Buckingham: Open University Press.

Hegarty, S. (1993) *Meeting Special Needs in Ordinary Schools*. London: Cassell.

House of Commons (1993) *Meeting Special Educational Needs: Statements of Needs and Provision* (Third Report of the Education Committee). London: HMSO.

Lubovskii, V. (1988) 'Against integration', *Special Children*, 23, 6–7.

Lunt, I. and Evans, J. (1994) 'Dilemmas in special educational needs: some effects of Local Management of Schools', in S. Riddell and S. Brown (eds) *Special Educational Needs Policy in the 1990s*. London: Routledge.

Norwich, B. (1990) *Reappraising Special Needs Education*. London: Cassell

Pumfrey, P. and Mittler, P. (1989) 'Peeling off the label', *TES*, 13 October, 29–30.

Riddell, S. and Brown, S. (eds) (1994) *Special Educational Needs Policy in the 1990s*. London: Routledge.

Warnock, M. (1982) 'Children with special educational needs: integration revisited', *Education Today*, 32, 56–62.

Warnock, M. (1992) 'Special case in need of reform', *Observer*, 18 October, Schools Report, p. 3.

Warnock, M. (1993) 'Foreword' in J. Visser and G. Upton (eds). *Special Education in Britain after Warnock*. London: David Fulton.

CHAPTER 7

Race

Augustine Basini

INTRODUCTION

Taylor's (1987) optimism, following the publication of the Swann report (1985), that multicultural education especially in white schools would be 'dramatically increased', has not been sustained. When the Prime Minister, John Major, can state that 'Primary teachers should learn how to teach children to read, not waste their time on the politics of equality of gender, race and class' (quoted in Chitty and Simon, 1993, p.144), the prospect for equal opportunities, and multicultural education in particular, is bleak. Where competition is the prevailing ideological ethic, then the very notion of equality can be discredited.

The 1988 Education Reform Act ignored the important conclusions of *Education for All*, the 800-page report of the Swann Committee on the Education of Children from Ethnic Minority Groups published three years earlier. As Tomlinson (1989, p.461) pointed out:

> The Education Reform Act became law in July 1988 and, despite the presence in the education system of over half a million children and young people perceived as racially or ethnically different to a white norm, there was no mention in the Act of race, ethnicity or even multicultural education.

In spite of this, the National Curriculum does provide opportunities for teachers to promote anti–racist and multicultural initiatives, and during Ofsted inspections schools must show evidence of their arrangements for implementing equality of opportunity.

THE POLICY

The legal context

The 1976 Race Relations Act was a response to the racism in our society. It:

- made it unlawful to discriminate against anyone on the grounds of race
- defined racial discrimination in four ways – direct, indirect, segregation and victimisation
- established the Commission for Racial Equality (CRE) with the responsibility to monitor the Act and see that it is being implemented
- placed a duty on LEAs to eliminate unlawful discrimination.

Discrimination on grounds of race includes schools admissions, staff

KEY POINTS

- Racial discrimination is illegal (Race Relations Act 1976)
- The development of local multicultural educational policies
- The Swann Report's recommendations on combating racism
- Racial equality opportunities in the National Curriculum
- The Ofsted framework for inspecting schools and equal opportunities
- Promotion of racial equality in the Children Act 1989

appointments, careers advice, access to facilities and awards of discretionary grants. The following definitions are based on explanations given by Siraj–Blatchford (1994, p.132):

Direct racial discrimination consists of treating a person less favourably on racial grounds (i.e. a person's race, colour, nationality, citizenship, ethnic or national origin) – for example, refusing to employ someone because they are black. Whether intentional or not, this is illegal.

Indirect racial discrimination refers to practices, procedures, requirements or conditions which have an adverse effect on a racial group – for example, recruitment by word of mouth so that information on a vacancy is given only to potential applicants who are white.

Segregation refers to unlawful treatment by separating children or adults on racial grounds.

Victimisation refers to discriminating against persons because they have previously complained against racial discrimination.

Section 71 of the Race Relations Act placed responsibilities on LEAs to eliminate unlawful racial discrimination and to promote equality of opportunity and good relations between persons of different racial groups. The CRE has successfully taken cases of unlawful discrimination to court. As Leicester (1991) points out 'There are legal, as well as moral reasons for governing bodies (and others) to promote equal opportunities in their school' (p.11). Even so, some cases have been unsuccessful (see Chapter 10).

The development of local authority multicultural educational policies

The Inner London Education Authority was one of the first LEAs to develop an equal opportunities policy on race. While different writers have put their own interpretation on the development of authorities' responses, there seems to be general agreement that the main perspectives can be identified as a shift from promoting policies of assimilation and integration to policies focusing on cultural diversity and then, more recently, to policies of equality, social justice and anti-racism. The main features of each, together with a brief evaluation, can be summarised as follows:

Assimilation/Integration (1950s and 1960s)
A belief that:
- race relations are good
- curricula should at all times reflect British traditions
- 'all children are children' – the 'colour blind' approach.

Dangers of this perspective:
- Black communities are defined as 'the problem'
- It is racist, involving the notion of white cultural superiority
- It discriminates against black people, requiring them to ignore their own cultural identity
- It reflects an inaccurate view of Britain's position in world society, and therefore miseducates everyone, white as well as black.

Cultural Diversity and Multicultural Education (1970s)
A belief that:
- multicultural aspects should be taught in schools
- racism given a low profile
- multicultural education will promote a 'positive self-image' amongst black people
- other tongues should be valued positively.

Weaknesses of this perspective:
- It ignores socio–economic position of black people and institutional discrimination
- It assumes that racism is held by few people, and ignores structural racism in education and in society
- It sees Black culture as homogeneous and static, ignoring power relationships between white and black people.

Equality, Social Justice, Anti–Racism (1980s)
A belief in:
- the central and pervasive influence of racism
- the importance of the black perspective
- all pupils learning about such concepts as the rule of law, rights and responsibilities, and such topics as the peaceful resolution of conflict and the role of the police
- removing discrimination in educational establishments
- continuous monitoring of policies and provision by LEAs and schools.

Comments:
- This perspective may seem threatening and uncomfortable to many white people, but it must not be avoided for fear of a backlash.
- Arguments against racism and for racial equality need continual emphasis because racism:
  is contrary to natural justice
  prevents learning
  gives a false view of identity and history
  is against the law.

[Adapted from Inner London Education Authority (1983) *Race, Sex and Class: 3. A policy for Equality: Race*. Full text also produced in Cohen and Cohen (1986, pp.23–43).]

Leeds City Council, in justifying their anti–racist policy in 1987, noted the inadequacies of the policies of 'assimilation', 'multi–racialism' and 'multi–culturalism', that is the first two models explained above:

> The implications of all these models is that the existence of the black people and their culture is the problem ... In fact, the real response to race and education should be based on equality – with central attention being given to racism and to measures to unlearn and dismantle racism. (quoted in Todd, 1991, p.45)

Education for All (The Swann Report)

In March 1979, Shirley Williams, Secretary of State for Education in the last Labour government, set up a Committee of Inquiry into the education of children from ethnic minority groups under the chairmanship of Anthony Rampton. This committee began its work against a background of concern expressed since the 1960s, mainly by African Caribbean and Asian communities, about the poor performance of their children in schools. Coard (1971) further enhanced this concern with the publication of a controversial pamphlet provocatively entitled *How the West Indian Child is Made Educationally Sub–normal in the British School System*.

The interim Rampton report, insensitively entitled *West Indian Children in Our Schools*, was published in 1981. Soon afterwards, the Chairman was replaced by Lord Swann. The final report of the Committee, more appropriately entitled *Education for All*, was published in 1985. The main findings (DES, 1985) were as follows:

- Racism in schools and society is the major underlying cause of West Indian children achieving poor educational standards.
- Negative attitudes of teachers and inappropriate curriculum are also important factors in underachievement.
- There are widely differing attitudes and expectations of the education system among West Indian parents .

Shirley Williams asserted that

> Lord Swann's report, *Education for All*, is the boldest, most comprehensive statement on the subject of multicultural education so far produced in Britain. It is uncompromising in its argument that multicultural education must be the basis of every child's schooling, not only those in minority groups. It is frank in admitting that racial prejudice and discrimination add an extra dimension of deprivation to the prospects of those already adversely affected by poor socio-economic status.
> (quoted in Foreword to Verma, 1989)

Swann acknowledged that Britain is a multi–racial and multi–cultural society, and this affects all schools and pupils. His approach was pluralism, and the watchword 'diversity within unity'. He redefined the 'problem' as educating *all* children from whatever ethnic group, arguing that multi–cultural understanding had to 'permeate all aspects of a school's work' and that it was 'necessary to combat racism, to attack inherited myths and stereotypes. ... Only in this way can schools begin to offer anything approaching the *equality of opportunity* for all pupils which it must be our aspiration of the education system to provide. (DES,

1985, p.769) (emphasis in original).

Not all commentators were as enthusiastic and sanguine as Shirley Williams about the value of the Swann report as will be briefly indicated later.

Racial equality opportunities in the National Curriculum

Although the Education Reform Act made no specific provisions on race, the Education Secretary Kenneth Baker (1987, p.8) claimed that it would 'open doors of opportunity for all children'. From the start, the National Curriculum Council (1988, p.4) stated that it would 'be taking account of ethnic and cultural diversity and ensuring that the curriculum provides equal opportunities for all pupils, regardless of ethnic origin or gender'. Also the School Examination and Assessment Council stressed that in the development of SATs (standard assessment tasks) every effort would be made to avoid race, culture or gender bias (Gregory, 1994). Moreover, the Department of Education's Circular 5/89 explained how it was 'intended that the curriculum should reflect the culturally diverse society to which pupils belong and of which they will become adult members' (para. 17), while a copy of *From Policy to Practice* (DES 1989), sent to every teacher in the country, stated that the National Curriculum would 'certainly need to include ... coverage across the curriculum of gender and multicultural issues' (para. 3.8). The DES Circular 16/89 advocated the collection of ethnically-based data to help achieve equality of opportunity for ethnic minority pupils, suggesting that a school was better equipped to offer each child suitable education if the basic facts about his or her cultural identity were known. It also warned against any practice, however unintentional, that put ethnic minority children at a disadvantage.

During 1990 and 1991, the NCC issued a series of guidance documents stressing that multicultural education was relevant for all pupils and should permeate all aspects of the curriculum; that schools should actively promote cultural diversity and address problems of racial prejudice; and that bilingualism should be considered a positive asset and a rich resource in the context of the National Curriculum (NCC 1990a, b; 1991a, b).

In July 1992 the Government published the most important education White Paper since 1987, *Choice and Diversity*. Although it had nothing specifically to say about equal racial opportunities, it did stress that 'It is the responsibility of the Government and the education service to provide pupils everywhere with the same opportunities. The reality all too often is that some pupils are deprived of that right'. (DES, 1992, para. 11.1).

These examples from policy papers illustrate the intention of the policy makers to promote equal racial opportunities. Whether the reality has matched the rhetoric will be considered later.

The Ofsted framework for inspecting schools

Every Ofsted report is expected to include an evaluation of the school's policy and practice for equality of opportunity. The most recent edition of the Ofsted

Handbook (1995) contains a number of specific references to ethnicity and race. The framework for inspection makes clear that:

> Throughout the inspection, the requirements of the schedule should be applied in relation to *all* the pupils in the school. Inspectors must ensure that the full range of age, gender, attainment, special educational need, ethnicity and background is taken into account, including the provision for, and attainment of, pupils for whom English is an additional language. (p.10, original emphasis)

The inspection schedule referred to includes the requirement to ascertain whether 'the attainment and progress of minority pupils is comparable with others in the school' (p.54); and in reporting the strengths and weaknesses in the planning and content of the curriculum, ethnicity must be taken into account (p.74). Judgements on the quality of relationships in the school must:

- include 'the degree of racial harmony, where applicable' (p.60)
- take account of pupils' 'recognition and increasing understanding of the diversity of beliefs, attitudes and social and cultural traditions' (p.63)
- be based on observational evidence of 'the ways in which pupils, including those from ethnic groups, relate to one another' (p.62)

The Children Act 1989 and racial equality

Siraj–Blatchford (1994) states that:

> The Children Act is the first piece of childcare legislation which makes specific reference to racial equality, and because the legislation cuts across local authority departments and day care services for under–eights its potential to promote greater racial equality is considerable. (p.135)

The Act gives local authorities the obligation and opportunity to promote and improve 'race' equality aspects in their services for the young. In pre–school provision and early years education, local authorities are expected to train staff and ensure that all ethnic groups have full and equal opportunity to participate in caring for and educating young children.

ISSUES FOR DEBATE

1. Why is the term 'race relations' controversial?

As the Runnymede Trust (1993) explains, words have different meanings for different groups and also their use changes over time. The term 'race relations' is a case in point, and there is little agreement about its use. The controversy is centred on the dubious concept of race.

> The term 'race' principally arose out of 'pseudo scientific' doctrines of the nineteenth century advanced in Britain and Europe, which attempted to develop elaborate racial classification and even theories of history on the supposedly 'scientific' assumptions that human beings were naturally divided into discrete 'races', each with distinctive physical features ... [which] were used as a basis for explaining or inferring human behaviour or actions ... and asserting that 'white' races were superior. (Wright, 1992, pp.1–2).

In Britain today 'race' is not a viable biological concept. As Banton and Harwood (1975) state 'As a way of categorising people, race is a delusion, ... lacks scientific validity and is moulded by political pressures rather than from evidence of biology' (quoted in Richardson and Lambert, 1985).

'Race' is consequently placed in quotation marks by many writers. Gillborn (1995) is sympathetic to the view of Allen (1994) who criticises the practice of using quotation marks and sees 'little use in it' unless they are used for all terms which are socially constructed and contested. However, Gillborn judges that, for the present, 'the dangers inherent in the common-sense notions of "race" warrant inverted commas around the term' (p.195).

'Race' has been used to describe socio-cultural characteristics such as language, religion, life style, customs and values. However, as Wright (1992) correctly points out, in these contexts the term 'ethnic' or 'ethnic relations' would be more appropriate and accurate in place of the more commonly used term 'race relations'. In arguing that 'race' is a social construct and can be built into a social system to promote a particular ideology such as superiority, Figueroa (1991) asserts that '"race", racism and ethnicism can be sustained and even constructed or "reconstructed" through schooling and more widely in the education system' (p.6). Gillborn (1995) too argues that 'far from being a fixed, natural system of genetic difference, "race" operates on a system of socially constructed and enforced categories, constantly recreated and modified through human interaction' (p.3).

The Inner London Education Authority (1983) considered it necessary to offer definitions of the terms it used in its race policy statements. *Afro-Caribbean* , they said, refers to people whose origins are in Africa or the Caribbean (the preferred term in the books published in the last two years is 'African–Caribbean'); *Asian* refers to people whose origins are in the Indian Subcontinent; *Black* refers to both African–Caribbean and Asian people.

> The term black emphasises the common experience which both people have of being victims of racism. Other groups, who together with black communities are usually referred to as 'ethnic minorities', also suffer varying degrees of prejudice and discrimination. ... Some white ethnic groups, such as the Irish and Jews, experience prejudice and discrimination. We do not wish to use the term 'immigrant' and 'coloured': 'immigrant' is now frequently inaccurate and has pejorative overtones; 'coloured' is an unacceptable euphemism to many black people'. (ILEA,1983,p.4)

As education should be about giving respect to each person, it is important to refer to people using the terminology they themselves find most acceptable. As this terminology may change over time it is necessary to make sure that the words used are accurate and appropriate.

Questions for discussion

1. Do you see any problems arising from the definitions suggested in this section? Would they be acceptable to everyone?
2. Is the concept of 'race' important?

---

2. What are the statistics and demography of ethnic groups?

To be able to participate intelligently in the debate concerning equal opportunities in education with specific reference to ethnic minority groups, it is imperative to know the facts. As Todd (1991) points out

> 'The numbers game' is a phrase which has been used to refer to particular forms of debate about community change: forms of debate which implicitly carry moral dimensions and assumptions of the relative worth of different types of people. (p.3)

In his discussion of the 1965 White Paper *Immigration from the Commonwealth,* Moore (1975) argued that 'The question of numbers became central to the black immigration debate. Once the debate is about numbers there are no issues of principle to be discussed, only how many?' (p.27).

Just prior to becoming Prime Minister in 1979, Margaret Thatcher remarked on television how a committee on immigration had reported that

> by the end of the century there would be four million people of the New Commonwealth and Pakistan here. Now I think that's an awful lot and I think that people are really rather afraid that the country might be swamped by people with a different culture. And you know the British character has done so much for democracy, for law and done so much throughout the world that if there is any fear that it might be swamped, people are going to react and be rather hostile to those coming in. (quoted in Hardy and Vieler–Porter, 1992, p.104).

Such statements are hardly helpful to developing good race relations.

What, then, are the statistics about ethnic groups in Britain? The Central Office of Information (1991) gives the following figures:

White groups:	51,470,000
All ethnic minority groups:	2,577,000

The 2.6 million members of ethnic minority groups in Great Britain are 4.7 per cent of the population. Forty-three per cent (over 1 million) live in Greater London and 28 per cent Greater Manchester, the West Midlands, West Yorkshire and the other metropolitan counties.

Most areas of Britain have between 0 per cent and 2.4 per cent of the ethnic minority population. These include Wales and the Border Counties, the West Country, Essex and East Anglia, North Yorkshire, Cumbria, the North East and Scotland (Skellington and Morris, 1992, p. 45).

It is important to reiterate the warning given by Skellington and Morris (1992) who had some reservations about including a section on demographic trends for fear it might be misused to 'reinforce stereotypes or exacerbate a sense of "otherness" between ethnic groups' (p.36). However, on balance they felt that it would leave the reader better informed. That is also the purpose here.

Questions for discussion

1. Why is it important to know the facts about numbers of ethnic minority groups? What are the dangers of concentrating on numbers?
2. Given that most ethnic minority groups live in conurbations, what are the implications, if any, for educational policy on 'race'?

---

3. Does recent educational policy promote racial equality?

There have been many concerns expressed that national policies since 1988 will not promote racial equality. As Epstein (1993) points out, many teachers argued that the time-consuming and demanding requirements of the pre-Dearing National Curriculum would not allow for equal opportunity initiatives. Whitty notes how the Hillgate Group (1987) proposed attainment targets in history that 'ensure a solid foundation in British and European history and ... no concessions to the philosophy of the global curriculum currently advocated by multi–culturalists' (Whitty, 1990, p.20). This narrow perspective has been promoted by Dr Nick Tate, the chief executive for the School Curriculum and Assessment Authority. In a speech to headteachers in 1995, he said it was a mistake to respond to cultural diversity with 'some kind of watered down multi-culturalism'. He advocated the teaching of the majority culture, with the emphasis on the English language, English history, literature, heritage, and the study of Christianity which are 'at the heart of our common culture and our national identity' (quoted in the *Guardian*, 19 July 1995, p.3). Dr Tate seems to be harking back to an imaginary golden age of Victorian values. As John Sutton, General Secretary of the Secondary Heads Association stated, there is already a feeling that the National Curriculum leans too heavily towards English culture and history. The danger, as Blenkin and Kelly (1994) argue, is that black children may see the schooling being offered them as predominantly designed for pupils from a white, Anglo–Saxon culture.

Sarup (1991) expresses three concerns about the National Curriculum and its relation to the black children. First, the power of local education authorities to determine policy has been weakened, and consequently they may quietly drop anti-racist education policies. Secondly, there is the prospect of 'white flight' from racially mixed schools, as white parents exercise their new 'parental choice'. This could lead to schools segregated along racial and class lines with the majority of black pupils confined to 'sink' schools in the inner city. This view is endorsed by Whitty (1991), who argues that, in the UK, 'current reforms would seem to relate to a version of post–modernity that emphasises "distinction" and "hierarchy" within a fragmented social order, rather than one that positively celebrates "difference" and "heterogeneity", (p.20), and that this would have particular consequences for the predominantly working class and black populations that inhabit inner cities. Feintuck (1994) also makes the point that 'without protection against racial segregation provided in the USA in relation to charter and magnet schools, the potential for selection leading to 'all–white' GM schools is very real' (p.119). Sarup's third point is that testing will stress the 'product' as opposed to the 'process' of education. Indeed, an HMI report (Ofsted, 1992) has stated that the majority of bilingual children are being disadvantaged because of the demanding linguistic content of the instructions and the cultural contexts of some of the tasks.

Another example that illustrates how policy issues concerning race have been removed from the agenda is the fate of the Multicultural Task Group, set up in July 1989 and officially abandoned in January 1991 even though £49,000 had been set aside by the National Curriculum Council to publish multicultural guidance materials (Tomlinson, 1993). As Graham (1993) points out, the NCC were asked by many for separate guidance on multicultural education, but ministers and civil servants made it clear that this was a 'no–go area' (p.132).

More recent developments have further undermined the status of 'race' as a policy issue. Gillborn (1995) argues that:

> While the dominant discourse has remained constant, during the late 1980s and early 1990s the role of 'race', and related issues of 'racial' and ethnic equality, has been reconstructed ... [so as to] marginalise 'race' issues and effectively deny 'race' a legitimate place on the [education] policy agenda. (pp.32–33)

During the passage of the Bill which lead to the 1993 Education Act, the CRE/Runnymede Trust (15 February, 1993) published a position paper entitled *Choice, Diversity and Equality*. The following ten proposals were made:

1. The principle of equality of access and opportunity should be set out in the Education Bill.
2. Anti–discrimination legislation should ensure that the new funding authorities should be subject to the Race Relations Act.
3. The new School Curriculum and Assessment Authority should be required to take account of the ethnic and cultural diversity of British society and of the importance of the curriculum in promoting equal opportunity for all pupils
4. Dangers of a two–tier system should be averted by ensuring that there is equitable researching and funding lest ethnic minority pupils be disproportionately disadvantaged.
5. Formal guidance should be given to schools, local authorities and funding authorities on how they can ensure that their admissions procedures and criteria are not against the letter and the spirit of the Race Relations Act.
6. Formal guidance should be given to schools in order to prevent the use of sanctions, particularly exclusions, from being unlawfully discriminatory.
7. The multi–faith nature of British society should be firmly anchored and reflected in the planning and development of religious education and collective worship, both locally and nationally.
8. Membership and staffing of the new bodies should reflect the multi–racial nature of British society.
9. Ethic minority parents and communities must be fully consulted about educational policy affecting them, and be involved in decision–making processes.
10. All aspects of the education system should be rigorously monitored to identify potentially discriminatory effects on ethnic minority communities.

If these proposals were implemented the prospects for improving racial equality in schools would be more optimistic.

Question for discussion

Are the CRE/Runnymede Trust (1993) proposals 'pie in the sky'?

---

4. Why do some groups from ethnic minority groups underachieve in schools?

Ever since Coard (1971) published his provocative pamphlet stating that black children in British schools labour under three crucial handicaps – low expectation of the pupils, low motivation because the pupils feel there is no point in trying, and low expectation of the teachers towards black pupils – there has been a great deal of research and a large number of official reports on the subject. Klein (1993) argues that there seems to be some consensus that *as a group* white children have achieved better than children from ethnic minority groups. There is less agreement as to why this disparity occurs and how it can be overcome. It is essential to appreciate, however, that there are huge variations in all groups, and some ethnic minority children achieve to a high level.

Gipps and Stobart (1990) suggest that research indicates how the performance gap between students of British background and ethnic minority students is much less significant (indeed in some cases reversed) relative to the mid–1970s, and they confirm the views of black British students that differences are due to the effectiveness of the school, with many tests being culturally biased. As Klein (1993) argues, 'There is no single causal factor in underachievement, and this certainly holds true for black underachievement' (p.5).

None the less, as Sarup (1991) and Figueroa (1991, 1993) point out, racism in school and society is still prevalent. In a critical analysis of the Swann report, Troyna and Carrington (1990) argue that the Swann Committee continued to avoid the question of how the education system might respond to racist impulses in society, and that Swann would not accept the notion of institutionalised racism, identifying it mainly in terms of individual prejudice. As Figueroa (1993) argues, 'The situation of Caribbean–heritage pupils in the British education system needs to be seen in terms of inequality and not simply in terms of "underachievement"' (p.212). This would lead to questioning national policies, discrimination and institutional processes, and racism.

The IQ and race debate has been discredited. In Annex D of the Swann report, Mackintosh and Mascie–Taylor show that there is no reliable evidence that indicates race to be a determinant of IQ. None the less, readers should be aware that every few years the issue resurfaces. In 1994, the cover of *Newsweek* (24 October) proclaimed: 'IQ : Is It Destiny? A hard look at a controversial new book on Race, Class and Success.' The furore, which was reported in most of the press, was the publication of Murray and Herrnstein's *The Bell Curve: Intelligence and Class Structure in American Life*. The authors argue that, on average, white Americans are a full 15 IQ points more intelligent than black Americans. It is easy to get impatient and irritated by this old unsustainable debate, but as Ferguson, under the heading 'The one taboo that should never be broken', argues, 'The latest theories about racial inferiority may sound like neutral academic research, but in the real world they will be enthusiastically embraced by those with an unpleasant racist agenda' (*Sunday Times*, October 1994).

To conclude on an optimistic yet worrying piece of research, under the heading 'Young black pupils top of class in the 3 Rs: Five-year-olds cause school rethink', the *Sunday Times*, 4 December 1994, reported:

> A study by Birmingham education authority of more than 6,000 five-year-olds shatters the belief that Afro–Caribbean children are trapped in underachievement and low aspiration almost from birth. The study found that black children are outperforming pupils of all other races at the age of five in the most important skills of reading, writing and arithmetic. They maintain their lead until at least Key Stage One at seven. This evidence suggests the value placed on a good education by many black families. The findings have raised fears that many black children are being failed by the education system. There is evidence to suggest that black pupils generally are up to four times more likely to be suspended from secondary school and are least likely to get five or more GCSE passes at grades A to C. By 16, Afro–Caribbean pupils are among the least successful ethnic groups. Some senior educationists blame the decline on low expectations of the schools, stereotypical views and prejudice. (p. 5)

Question for discussion

What are the explanations given for the underachievement of black pupils? Can the explanations be sustained?

THE FUTURE?

There is no room for complacency concerning future policy to promote racial equality. There is plenty of evidence that racism is still rife in Britain. There needs to be more local democracy restored to the LEAs so that equal opportunities policies can be promoted and monitored. The time released by the revised National Curriculum should allow schools to promote multi-cultural anti–racist education, and not only in schools where there are large numbers of children from ethnic minorities.

In a diverse society, there needs to be a change in the current government education policy that promotes a single culture and a single religion. Equality of respect should be built into national, local and institutional polices and future proposals that affect schooling. The implementation of the CRE/Runnymede Trust proposals listed above would be a big step forward in developing and promoting equal opportunities for ethnic minorities.

The best that can be hoped for is very guarded optimism that the professionalism and good will of the teachers will see all their pupils performing to their full potential. As Tomlinson (1993) asserts, 'It is possible for a multicultural dimension to be incorporated into the National Curriculum even though official action has sought to exclude or minimise such a dimension' (p.27). Or, as Gillborn (1995) found in his research, progress, 'though painful, slow and uncertain – is not in vain' (p.193).

FURTHER READING

Fyfe, A. and Figueroa, P. (eds) (1993) *Education for Cultural Diversity: The Challenge for a New Era*. London: Routledge.

Gill, D,. Mayor, B. and Blair, M. (eds) (1992), *Racism and Education: Structures and Strategies*. London: Sage.

Gillborn, D. (1995) *Racism and Antiracism in Real Schools*. Buckingham: Open University Press. (Part I deals clearly with 'race', research and policy. Part II, entitled '"Race" and educational practice', reports on Gillborn's research on antiracist change in secondary schools.)

Klein, G. (1993) *Education Towards Race Equality*. London: Cassell.

Siraj-Blatchford, I. (1994) *The Early Years: Laying the Foundations for Racial Equality*. Stoke-on-Trent: Trentham Books.

Wright, C. (1992) *Race Relations in the Primary School*. London: David Fulton. (Based on Wright's research into four inner city primary schools.)

REFERENCES

Allen, S. (1994), 'Review of D. Morgan and M.Stanley (eds) *Debates in Sociology*', *Sociology*, 28(1), 301–4.

Baker, K. (1987) Speech to annual Conservative Party conference, Blackpool, 7 October.

Banton, M. and Harwood, J. (1975) *The Race Concept*. Newton Abbott: David and Charles.

Blenkin, G. M. and Kelly, A. V. (eds) (1994) *The National Curriculum and Early Learning: An Evaluation*. London: Chapman.

Central Office of Information (1993) *Aspects of Britain: Immigration and Nationality*. London: HMSO.

Chitty, C. and Simon, B (1993) *Education Answers Back: Critical Responses to Government Policy*. London: Lawrence and Wishart.

Coard, B. (1971) *How the West Indian Child is Made Educationally Sub-normal in the British School System*. London: New Beacon Books.

Cohen, L. and Cohen, A. (eds) (1986) *Multicultural Education: A Source Book for Teachers*. London: Harper & Row.

Commission for Racial Equality/Runnymede Trust (1993). *Choice, Diversity and Equality: A Position Paper on the Education Bill*. London: CRE.

Department of Education and Science (1985) *Education for All*. (The Swann Report). London: HMSO.

Department of Education and Science (1989) *From Policy to Practice*. London: HMSO.

Department of Education and Science (1992) *Choice and Diversity* (White Paper). London: HMSO.

Epstein, D. (1993) *Changing Classroom Cultures: Anti–Racism, Politics and Schools*. Stoke-on-Trent. Trentham.

Feintuck, F. (1994) *Accountability and Choice in Schooling*. Buckingham: Open University Press.

Figueroa, P. (1991) *Education and the Social Construction of 'Race'*. London: Routledge.

Figueroa, P. (1993) 'Caribbean-heritage pupils in Britain: educational performance and inequality', in A. Fyfe, and P. Figueroa (eds) *Education for Cultural Diversity: The Challenge for a New Era*. London: Routledge.

Gillborn, D. (1995) *Racism and Antiracism in Real Schools*. Buckingham: Open University Press.

Gipps, C. and Stobart, G. (1990) *Assessment : A Teacher's Guide to Issues*. London: Hodder and Stoughton.

Graham, D. (1993) *A Lesson for Us All: The Making of the National Curriculum*. London: Routledge.

Gregory, E. (1994) 'The National Curriculum and non–native speakers of English', in G. Blenkin, and V. Kelly. (eds) *The National Curriculum and Early Learning: An Evaluation*. London: Chapman.

Hardy, J. and Vieler–Porter, C. (1992) 'Race, schooling and the 1988 Education Reform Act', in D. Gill, B. Mayor and M. Blair (eds) (1992) *Racism and Education Reform: Structures and Strategies*. London: Sage.

Hillgate Group (1987) *The Reform of British Education*. London: Claridge Press.

Inner London Education Authority (1983), *Race, Sex and Class: 3. A Policy for Equality: Race*. London: ILEA.

Klein, G. (1993) *Education Towards Race Equality*. London: Cassell.

Leicester, M. (1991) *Equal Opportunities in Schools: Social Class, Sexuality, Race, Gender and Special Needs*. Harlow: Longman.

Mackintosh, N. and Mascie-Taylor, C. (1985) 'The IQ question', in Annex D of Department of Education and Science *Education for All* (The Swann Report). London: HMSO.

Moore, R. (1975) *Racism and Black Resistance in Britain*. London: Pluto Press.

National Curriculum Council (1988) *Introducing the National Curriculum Council*. London: NCC.

National Curriculum Council (1990a) *Curriculum Guidance 3: The Whole Curriculum*. York: NCC.

National Curriculum Council (1990b) *Guidance on Education for Citizenship*. York: NCC

National Curriculum Council (1991a) *Newsletter*, February. York: NCC.

National Curriculum Council (1991b) *Circular No.11: Linguistic Diversity and the National Curriculum*. York: NCC.

Ofsted (1992) *Assessment, Recording and Reporting*. London: HMSO.

Ofsted (1995) *The OFSTED Handbook*. London: HMSO.

Richardson, J. and Lambert, J. (1985) 'The sociology of race', in M. Haralambos (ed.) *Sociology: New Directions*. Ormskirk: Causeway Press.

Runnymede Trust (1993) *Equality Assurance in Schools: Quality, Identity, Society*. Stoke-on-Trent: Trentham Books.

Sarup, M. (1991) *Education and the Ideologies of Racism*. Stoke-on-Trent: Trentham Books.

Siraj-Blatchford, I. (1994) *The Early Years: Laying the Foundations for Racial Equality*. Stoke-on-Trent, Trentham Books.

Skellington, R. and Morris, P. (1992) *'Race' in Britain Today*. London: Sage.

Taylor, W. H. (1987) 'Ethnicity, diversity and schooling in the "White Highlands"', in M. Golby, (ed.) *Perspectives on the National Curriculum, No. 32*. Exeter: School of Education, University of Exeter.

Todd, R. (1991) *Education in a Multicultural Society*. London: Cassell.

Tomlinson, S. (1989) 'Education and training', *New Community*, 15 (3), 461–9.

Tomlinson, S. (1990) *Multicultural Education in White Schools*. London: Batsford.

Tomlinson, S. (1993) 'The Multicultural Task Group: the group that never was' in A. King and M. Reiss (eds) *The Multicultural Dimension of the National Curriculum*. London: Falmer.

Troyna, B. and Carrington, B. (1990) *Education, Racism and Reform*. London: Routledge.

Verma, G. K. (ed.) (1989) *Education for All*. London: Falmer.

Whitty, G. (1990) 'The New Right and the National Curriculum: state control or market forces?', in B. Moon (ed.) (1990) *New Curriculum – National Curriculum*. Buckingham: Open University Press.

Whitty, G. (1991) ' Making sense of urban education after Thatcher', in S. Ball (ed.) *Education Reform: A Critical and Post-structural Approach*. Buckingham: Open University Press.

Wright, C. (1992) *Race Relations in the Primary School*. London: David Fulton.

CHAPTER 8

Gender

Elaine Sillitoe

INTRODUCTION

As has been increasingly recognised over recent years the relationship between gender and education is complex. However, recent examination results are leading to fundamental questioning, almost to the issues being turned on their head. Concern is now being expressed about the under-achievement of boys compared with girls, although the results of both boys' and girls' have improved. Indeed, some critics fear there is a danger of the push for equality for girls being overwhelmed by attention being focused on how to raise boys' standards. There is also the question of what is being learnt through the 'hidden curriculum', since this influences both subject choices and behaviour. It can be argued that, in this respect, girls are still disadvantaged.

The history of schooling for both the middle- and working-classes has been marked by gender differentiation. Among the middle-classes girls' education was influenced by the domestic ideology which developed from 1780 to 1850, the period in which industrialisation separated home and work. The woman's role was that of 'ladylike homemaker'.as wife and mother (Purvis 1991): she was to supervise the running of the household and provide an emotional haven for the husband. She did not need an intellectual education. Although there was little differentiation in the limited education received by the working-classes in the early nineteenth century (Silver and Silver, 1974), differentiation soon became marked.

The middle-class domestic ideology also influenced attitudes to working-class girls, whose role was that of the 'good woman' who would have practical household skills. They would learn to be 'good' servants and later 'good' wives. Female subservience to males underlay both concepts. The dominant Church of England National Society and the nonconformist British and Foreign Schools Society both provided the 3Rs and religious instruction, but the girls also did needlework. Although the Revised Code of 1862 made attendance and success in the 3-Rs the only basis for the notorious payments by results, girls still had to do plain needlework. From 1867 extra grants were paid for a wide range of subjects, such as geography and social sciences, but few girls studied these. Instead, there was increased emphasis on domestic subjects. Domestic economy was made compulsory for girls in 1878, and in the 1880s there were also grants for such subjects as laundrywork, dressmaking and elementary hygiene. The boys did more mathematics and also technical drawing. Thus, although boys and girls were at the same schools, they received a differentiated curriculum, which, despite feminist successes, continued into the twentieth century. The Board of Education (1923) affirmed an equal but different approach, and, although it considered that the curriculum had become too academic for both sexes, it was especially concerned about this in relation to girls, for whom training for the duties of motherhood and work in the home was regarded as paramount.

This tension between femininity and academic education was also a theme in the development of even the more academic schools for middle-class girls from the mid-nineteenth century, although for most their education 'tended to stress ornamental knowledge that might attract and impress a suitor' (Purvis, 1991, p.64). They studied music, drawing, possibly a language, although some other subjects would have been introduced but not very systematically. The academic schools, which wanted to provide wider opportunities for middle-class girls, still had to combine an academic curriculum with teaching girls to be 'ladylike'; parents would not want to see their daughters become unmarriageable. Thus the prospectus of the North London Collegiate School, founded by Miss Buss, emphasised the influence 'of the Female Character upon Society', which meant that the better educated future mothers were, the more successful they would be in teaching their own children. This helped to diffuse hostility whilst sending pupils on to higher education. Access here was the result of another long and determined struggle, and girls proceeded despite medical warnings that intellectual effort would affect their fertility. Academic opportunities gradually became greater as single women increasingly followed careers.

Theoretically, gender differentiated expectations in the curriculum ended with the 1944 Education Act, which established secondary education for all based on 'age, ability and aptitude'. In practice, however, assumptions about gender roles continued to shape policy decisions. Both the Crowther Report in 1959, discussing the education of 15- to 18-year-olds, and the Newsom Report in 1963, dealing with average and below-average 13- to 16-year-olds, stated that later secondary schooling should reflect girls' 'natural interests' and their future in marriage and domesticity.

THE POLICY

KEY POINTS

- Sex Discrimination Act 1975
- Little Government support for gender equality in the early and mid 1980s, with the exception of TVEI
- Initiatives of LEAs and committed individuals and groups
- The mixed impact of the Education Reform Act and subsequent legislation on gender equality

The passing of the Sex Discrimination Act 1975, influenced by the growth of the women's movement, seemed to mark a significant shift in official attitudes. Sex discrimination was made unlawful in admissions to schools, the appointment of teachers (except for girls-only schools), access to the curriculum and other opportunities provided by schools. Although it has been difficult to bring cases under the Act, the legislation has had a significant impact in giving legal official backing for those trying to further gender equality in the face of indifference or hostility.

During the early and mid-1980s, the Government took no clear lead in encouraging gender equality. Its contribution was virtually limited to the Technical and Vocational Education Initiative (TVEI), funded by the Manpower Services Commission with the intention of improving vocational training for 14- to 18-year-olds in order to improve Britain's market position and widen the availability of skills. To qualify for TVEI funding, schools had to meet the criterion of equal opportunities. Opportunities were to be available to young people of both sexes, who were to be educated together on courses within each project, with care taken to avoid sex stereotyping (MSC, 1984).

Nevertheless, TVEI courses did tend to be stereotyped, with students' choices reflecting the gendered division of labour. Although the MSC did not withdraw funding even when equal opportunities were not being provided, the criterion made some schools question their approach in relation to gender, while TVEI conferences allowed the sharing of ideas about furthering gender equality. Also, some local authorities used part of their TVEI funding for in-service courses on equality and on equal opportunities posts.

The needs of the economy also resulted in leading companies giving financial support to attract girls into science, technology and engineering. Their purpose was market-driven, but the implementation of the various initiatives was carried out by feminists. The Engineering Council and Equal Opportunities Commission ran a Women into Science and Engineering Campaign (WISE). For primary schools, a booklet was produced for staff, who were encouraged to use examples which would be familiar to girls, to ensure that girls had hands-on experience and to consider girls-only groups until girls became more confident. For secondary schools, the project encouraged girls to continue with physical sciences and technical craft subjects when option choices were made, but its efforts to make interaction more 'gender fair' ran into opposition from many (mostly male) teachers who did not accept that they were sex-stereotyping. However, the project and its suggestions received wide publicity and probably influenced individual teachers and departments. Another example was the Women into Information Technology campaign. Approaches included girls-only workshops, workshops for teachers, and suggestions for software that did not reinforce aggressiveness and appealed to girls as well as boys.

The early and mid-1980s was also a period of considerable research by feminists into influences on girls in schools. Some of it was funded and carried out by professional researchers; in other cases teachers as researchers were used in the hope that their findings would influence others in their school (Millman, 1987). The concerns raised led to some local authorities taking a leading role in furthering equal opportunities, sometimes on a wide front (as in the London Borough of Brent), sometimes in relationship to a particular aspect: for instance, Sheffield LEA carried out a one-year project on careers education and gender stereotyping.

The most far-reaching and effective programme was initiated by the Inner London Education Authority (ILEA), which was abolished under the Education Reform Act 1988. ILEA produced documentation on a policy for equality (race, sex and class), encouraged the development of whole-school equality policies, provided in-service training on equality issues, and appointed advisers to give support for equal opportunities within schools. The effectiveness of these measures is suggested by the findings of Kelly *et al.* (1987): in their study of teacher attitudes towards gender, ILEA teachers emerged as the most feminist. ILEA's last analysis of examination results before it was abolished showed that girls in mixed schools were doing as well as those in all girls' schools, which was different from earlier results (*TES*, 9 March 1990). ILEA's claim that this was due to its strong policy of promoting equal opportunities could well be right; but, of course, it is impossible to gauge whether this was a one-year abnormality or whether it could have become a consistent trend. The results do, however, suggest that a positive official approach to equal opportunities can be effective, and that mixed schools do not necessarily depress girls' attainment – an important point as for the foreseeable future the overwhelming majority of girls in state schools will continue to attend mixed schools.

The educational landscape was fundamentally altered by the passing of the Education Reform Act 1988. As described in earlier chapters, the Act introduced a centrally-prescribed curriculum (the National Curriculum) which was to be 'broad and balanced'. As a result, option choices were delayed. Although the post-Dearing reforms have increased opportunities for options at 14-plus, both boys and girls must still study science (including physics, chemistry and biology) until 16. Previously, girls had often dropped physics and chemistry at 14 and thus cut themselves off from a wide range of future careers. A modern language, often previously avoided by boys, also has to be studied until 16, and Technology (which includes 'girls' subjects' such as cooking and 'boys'' craft subjects) is now also compulsory. However, the original proposal that all should do 20 per cent science at Key Stage 4 was dropped. Pupils can either do a single or double science, but are unlikely to continue with science at A–level if they take the single one. Across the curriculum, schools are obliged to ensure equal opportunities, and national tests are supposed to do the same.

The 1988 Act altered the balance of power in education, with central government acquiring increased powers, schools gaining increased autonomy through Local Management of Schools, and local authorities losing all control over schools that became grant-maintained. These measures effectively reduced the power of local authorities to influence equal opportunities policies. The 1993 Education Act has further reduced the power of local authorities as they now have to work with the Funding Agency for Schools if grant-maintained schools in the area teach more than 10 per cent of pupils.

The Further and Higher Education Act 1992 has also weakened local authorities' influence. Vocational and academic courses at local further education colleges are now funded through the centralised Further Education Funding Council, whilst remaining FE courses and most adult education are paid for out of the LEA general budget. With pressures on this budget, costs of adult education have often risen and might be full-cost. Coats (1994) argues that this will reduce many women's educational opportunities; women-only provision like the New Opportunities for Women programme has built up women's confidence and encouraged them to enrol for access courses and enter higher education. This confidence-building is especially important for women who have been out of paid employment due to family responsibilities. They often have limited financial resources and might not be able to afford the fees now, so will lose out again on educational opportunities.

A national policy which should support gender opportunities, however, is embedded in the framework for Ofsted inspections, which requires inspectors to ensure that schools provide equal opportunities (Ofsted, 1995).

ISSUES FOR DEBATE

1. Have the changes in the control of education been beneficial for equality of opportunity?

The changes can be viewed from differing feminist perspectives. The main ones in the 1980s were liberal feminist and radical feminist. Liberal feminists concentrated on giving girls (and boys) equal opportunities to develop all their potential within the existing system. Radical feminism was based on a concept of 'patriarchy' (male domination of females), with equality only achievable through fundamental restructuring of society. In practice, though, the emphasis for feminist teachers was on practical measures for change and led, according to Weiner (1987), to two differing approaches in relation to education, namely equal opportunities and anti-sexist. Equal opportunities proponents concentrated on working for improvements within the system, for example, developing girls' potential by furthering access to all subjects, making teaching materials less sexist and reforming school organisation to make it less sexist. The anti-sexist approach demanded much more fundamental change to undermine male dominance both in terms of the school structure and the curriculum content. However, Asker (1986) has argued that in practice there is much overlap, and there has therefore not been the division and subsequent loss of confidence amongst teachers in relation to gender that perhaps resulted from the multicultural/anti-racist debate. There has also been increased awareness of differences amongst girls (Jones, 1993); girls' experiences will be influenced by class and race as well as gender, but the way girls interpret their experiences results in a more complex picture (Riddell, 1992).

Central government's support for gender equality has been weak. It is true that John Major supported the Opportunity 2000 initiative, whereby leading businesses have pledged to greatly increase the number of women in top management by the year 2000. However, he has not made efforts to encourage the promotion of women in the education field. His insistence that the proportion of GCSE assessment by examination be increased was thought at the time to disadvantage girls as they put more effort into their course work, but this view has now been questioned by Janette Elwood in relation to both English and mathematics (*TES*, 24 November 1995). Professor Armstrong has claimed that the pressure from John Major and Ian Sproat, Minister for Sport, to revive competitive team games in schools might be counter-productive as far as girls are concerned as they prefer more individual or social physical activity (*TES*, 15 September 1995).

The increased autonomy of schools plus the diminishing powers of LEAs means that equality will depend on the commitment and energy of individual governing bodies and school staffs. The great demands that have been made of teachers by the need to introduce the subject programmes of study, together with the loss of morale by the undermining of their autonomy in curriculum matters, will have sapped the energy of many, who feel they cannot undertake further commitments. Moreover, in-service work has concentrated on implementing the statutory demands of the National Curriculum and therefore external stimulation for equality efforts has been lacking.

Individual schools now have considerable financial responsibilities under LMS, and this has resulted in 'senior appointments increasingly being seen as 'men's business'', (Riley, 1994, p.27). When women are in managerial positions in schools they are likely to have pastoral responsibilities. Moreover women continue to be under-represented in headships. Although 81 per cent of nursery and primary teachers are women, only 57 per cent of headteachers in that sector are women; the equivalent figures for secondary schools are 49 per cent and 30 per cent (Central Statistical Office, 1995). School management is not providing positive role models for girls.

Question for discussion

Should the Government take a stronger lead in promoting gender equality in education?

---

2. Has the National Curriculum increased gender equality?

The National Curriculum introduced a common curriculum which had been a feminist demand (Weiner, 1994). This keeps options open for both girls and boys and prevents girls making gendered choices of lower-status subjects at 14 (with lower work prospects) when they are more vulnerable to peer pressure. The requirement that all take science (physics, chemistry and biology) until 16 is an important development for girls, as previously many had excluded themselves from many career opportunities by dropping physics and chemistry at 14. However, recent analysis of balanced science examination statistics shows that about 50 per cent of girls take the single science module, not the double one or separate sciences. This does not completely exclude them from continuing with the physical sciences at A–level, but makes it very unlikely. Current trends are not promising. (Possible reasons for this are discussed in Issue 3, the 'hidden curriculum'.) The experience of balanced science and technology programmes of study from five years of age might alter girls' perceptions. For instance, the 1993 SATs results in Wales showed girls ahead of boys in both mathematics and science. However, although the results of the Assessment of Performance Unit, before it was disbanded, showed that girls at 11 were as good in the science tests as boys, this was not the case in certain topics such as gears and levers (an important base for physics at secondary school), which would often have been part of boys' experience outside school but not of most girls and would have probably not been taught in primary school. The necessary foundations being laid in the primary curriculum might therefore have the long-term effect of increasing girls' representation in the double module and at A–level; however, this will also be influenced by what is taught and how.

The common curriculum is the one aspect of the National Curriculum that is positive in terms of gender and equality. Equality (including the gender dimension) is a cross-curriculum theme, but it has no statutory status and could easily be 'lost' when following the very tightly-prescribed subject curriculum. In the National Curriculum documentation studied by Burton and Weiner (1990), equal opportunities did not appear in the statements of attainment targets nor the programmes of study. The authors point out that although the Mathematics Consultation Report recognised the need for non-statutory guidance to include gender equality, this did not materialise in the non-statutory guidance on mathematics. The post-Dearing National Curriculum documents retain practical applications of mathematics at all stages and might increase girls' motivation. Evidence from Holland (Volman *et al.*, 1995) suggests that a mathematics curriculum that is relevant to everyday life does increase the number of girls choosing it. (Ironically, shortly after the Dutch introduced this, entry to higher mathematics and science courses was limited to those who had studied the alternative curriculum!) This evidence reinforces the importance of a common and girl-friendly curriculum if girls are to be persuaded to continue with the subject at A–level.

It would appear, however, that the content of the science curriculum has became less girl-friendly since the Dearing slimdown and the loss of the communication profile. Another setback has been the drawing up of the English literature list for Key Stages 3 and 4. The new documentation gives examples of the differing categories of literature but has been strongly criticised for the paucity of examples of women writers and poets in the period 1900 onwards. This is an important issue since the examples given in official guidance are likely to influence teachers' choices and to increase the 'invisibility of women' (Spender, 1982), leading to girls feeling that they are less important. There are therefore reservations about the overt curriculum and its influence on girls' motivation and self-esteem.

Question for discussion

What changes, if any, to promote gender opportunities would you like to see in the official guidance on the National Curriculum?

---

3. What are the ongoing influences of the 'hidden' curriculum?

It has also been claimed that factors in the 'hidden curriculum', identified by feminist research, have not been confronted. One is the content of the books used in schools and the messages they convey. Research in the 1970s (e.g. Lobban 1975) demonstrated how stereotyped parental roles and boys dominated reading schemes and children's fiction. Northam (1987) showed that females appeared less frequently in mathematics books, and as children went through schooling, examples became increasingly male-orientated with girls doing the recording not the problem-solving.

What is the current situation? HMI (1989) found that in all but one of 17 schools visited, books written by women writers or with central female characters were under-represented. Given the financial constraints on budgets since that finding and the need for schools to spend their money on books to implement the National Curriculum, it is unlikely that the situation has changed significantly.

Has the material developed for implementing the National Curriculum given more visibility to women? Osler (1994) studied 36 textbooks published in 1991–92 which related to three out of the five core study units in history at Key Stage 3. She found that, although the experiences of men and women were required to be taught in the National Curriculum, photographs of men outnumbered those of women, the proportion varying from about twice to 26 times as many. As Osler points out, sketches and reconstructions would have been commissioned by the authors, so the opportunity was there to provide a better gender balance. She did find some examples of women performing a wider range of jobs than might have been expected, some examples of women's writings, and some questioning of the paucity of sources on women's lives in earlier periods – which does at least question women's visibility. But she concludes that rather narrow aspects of women's experiences still predominate in a large proportion of cases, and that textbooks still have a long way to go to achieve a gender balance. Without providing supplementary resources, she says, teachers could include very little reference to women's lives.

One improvement that Osler noted is that gender neutral terms (e.g. not just 'he') were used when appropriate. This is not quibbling. Lafrance (1991) cites research indicating that children think of men when 'he' alone is used – again marginalising women. This improvement was also noted in Connolly's (1993) review of 13 geography textbooks for Key Stage 3. Again, the illustrations concentrated on men: 51 per cent of photographs were of males or with males as the focus, compared to 21 per cent of women or women dominant; similar figures were found for commissioned drawings. In noting that two-thirds of illustrations did not include people and that geography is chosen by more boys than girls, Connolly argues that the human dimension needs to be emphasised more to make it girl-friendly. A more positive finding was the inclusion of a wide range of roles for women (e.g. in science), but the caring role of men was neglected.

The National Curriculum Council (1990) drew attention to the fact that both girls and boys are likely to have responsibility for home and work. Yet the evidence suggests that boys and girls come to school at five with stereotyped gender roles (Smithers and Zientek, 1990). With the significant male youth unemployment rate, it is important to provide males with a wider range of adult roles.

Boys and girls also learn their comparative importance through the way teachers interact with them. Studies consistently show that boys demand teacher attention and dominate mixed classrooms. The extent of that domination is well illustrated by Spender's (1982) experiences in teaching. She was concentrating on giving the girls attention, but the maximum she managed to give them was 42 per cent; however, the boys complained that she was giving the girls too much time! Clarricoates (1987) found that in the primary schools she studied lesson material was chosen with the boys in mind to avoid discipline problems, teachers feeling the girls would accept whatever was taught. Girls will interpret these classroom experiences and realise their subordinate status. In secondary schools, too, the teachers are 'controlled' by the boys with the result that the girls are not given time to develop their answers or to ask questions. According to Mahony's (1985) research, boys' reactions of looking bored, fidgeting, and calling out ('Turn it off', 'Pull the plug out') resulted in teachers cutting off girls because of the threat of discipline problems.

Boys dominate the physical space and grab the best equipment, making it difficult for girls to do the required work (Mahony, 1985; Riley, 1994). Sexual harassment is an everyday aspect of this social control. Boys sometimes use derogatory terms such as 'slag', which Lees (1986) points out is difficult for the girls *per se* and also because it is irrational. They can also make very explicit remarks about girls' physical appearance and even do some 'touching up' (Wolpe, 1988). The result is that girls tend to keep a low profile – not helpful to their all-round development.

Jordan (1995) argues that it is a minority of boys who are discipline problems, but the conforming boys, whom the more disruptive might consider wimps, define themselves as masculine by being 'not female' and showing contempt for girls. It is clear that new definitions of masculinity are needed so that girls are not caught in the crossfire between the two male groups.

Question for discussion

In the light of the above discussion on gender equality, examine the text and illustrations of some books commonly used in schools and compare your findings with the research cited.

---

4. Are girls still disadvantaged?

Recent examination results show that instead of falling behind boys at secondary school, as previously, girls have now overtaken them. GCSE results are about level in mathematics and science, but girls are ahead in geography and history and even further ahead in French and English. This has been put down to girls' conscientiousness compared with showing intellectual bite, but girls are now also slightly ahead at A–level, in terms of number of passes; however, girls with higher GCSE scores are not matching boys in grades at A– and AS–levels

(DfEE, 1996). Also, girls are learning more than subjects at school, and as the above sections have shown they *are* disadvantaged in their all-round development. (There might well be different messages in single sex schools, but most girls do not attend them, not least because of the scarcity of places.)

Moreover, girls are still under-represented in physics at A–level. Science teachers may now be more inclined to use girl-friendly examples, but girls might still be aware of underlying attitudes. Studies (Pratt *et al.*, 1984; Kelly *et al.*, 1987) have found that teachers of the physical sciences and crafts have more stereotyped views than teachers of other subjects, and this might influence girls' choices. Given the under-representation of girls at A–level and the fact that girls are not making a significant impact in scientific fields, many decisions which are important for society are largely uninfluenced by females. Furthermore, career advice is often still stereotyped: Evetts' study (1993) of female engineers showed that the 'official' career advisors had not encouraged non-traditional choices, though individual teachers had been more supportive.

Nevertheless progress has been made. For example, over half the medical students are now women, nearly half newly qualified chartered accountants are women and half of Abbey National branch managers are women. Fifteen per cent of directors in Opportunity 2000 companies are now women, though the proportion in all companies is only three per cent. There *are* more opportunities for women and more role models, *but* women's average earnings are still under 75 per cent of men's, and a quarter of women are in part-time jobs, which are predominantly poorly paid. For most women, labour prospects are still limited. Moreover, recent successful sexual harassment claims at industrial tribunals (a woman pilot, a carpenter, a fire fighter) reflect that men in traditionally male areas of work can use this method to exclude women.

However, it might well be that girls and young women in school today will be considering longer-term work prospects. Women overall are delaying having children (the average age for a first baby is now 27), and many young women claim that they are not going to have children. Moreover, pupils today are aware of the impact of the increased divorce rate, either through their own or their friends' experiences. The realisation that the family income might depend on the mother after divorce (or if the husband is unemployed) will influence many girls' educational goals. However, there is a danger that girls might face a backlash as concerns about boys' underachievement are addressed. There is also the danger that fears of alienated young unemployed men and the growth of suicides amongst young men might refocus all attention on the boys.

Question for discussion

Should schools try to widen boys' concepts of masculinity?

THE FUTURE?

There is unlikely to be any official pressure to further girls' opportunities. However, there have been equality initiatives even in the recent unhelpful climate. Dissemination of information about these could well stimulate other teachers, including senior management whose support is often a crucial factor. Ruddock (1994) and Frith and Mahony (1994) would be useful sources. The period of stability in relation to the National Curriculum front might free time and energy for equality programmes, but these are likely to be patchy. Boys need to be encouraged to reach their potential, but not at girls' expense.

Unless there is an expansion in the economy, more competition between women and men in the market place is an inevitable concomitant of equality. However, it must be remembered that white middle-class males are still high achievers and are likely to dominate positions of power in the foreseeable future.

FURTHER READING

Frith, R. and Mahony, P. (eds) (1994) *Promoting Quality and Equality in Schools: Empowering Teachers through Change*. London: David Fulton.

Osler, A. (1994) 'Still hidden from history? the representation of women in recently published history textbooks', *Oxford Review of Education*, 20, 219–235.

Rudduck, J. (1994) *Developing a Gender Policy in Secondary Schools*. Buckingham: Open University Press.

Weiner, G.(1994) *Feminisms in Education: An Introduction* (Chapter 6). Buckingham: Open University Press.

Gender and Education. Articles in this journal are provocative, challenging and informative. Essential reading in order to stay abreast of current issues.

REFERENCES

Asker, S. (1986) 'What feminists want from education', in A. Hartnett and M. Naish, (eds) *Education and Society Today*. Lewes: Falmer.

Board of Education (1923) *Report of the Consultative Committee on the Differentiation of the Curriculum for Boys and Girls*. London: HMSO.

Burton, L. and Weiner, G. (1990) 'Social justice and the National Curriculum', *Research Papers in Education*, 5, 203–228.

Central Statistical Office (1995) *Social Focus on Women*. London: HMSO.

Clarricoates, K. (1987) 'Dinosaurs in the classroom: the "hidden curriculum" in primary schools', in M. Arnot and G. Weiner (eds) *Gender and the Politics of Schooling*. London: Unwin Hyman.

Coats, M. (1994) *Women's Education*. Milton Keynes: Open University Press.

Connolly, J. (1993) 'Gender balanced geography: have we got it right yet?', *Teaching Geography*, April, 61–4.

Crowther Report (1959) *Report of the Central Advisory Council for Education 15–18*. London: HMSO.

Department for Education and Employment (1996) *Statistical Bulletin No. 2*. London: HMSO.

Evetts, J. (1993) 'Women in engineering: educational concomitants of a non-traditional career choice', *Gender and Education*, 5, 176–78.

Frith, R. and Mahony, P. (eds) (1994) *Promoting Quality and Equality in Schools: Empowering Teachers through Change*. London: David Fulton.

HM Inspectorate (1989) *Reading Policy and Practice at Ages 5–14*. London: DES.

Jones, A. (1993) 'Becoming a "girl": post-structuralist suggestions for educational research', *Gender and Education*, 5, 157–166.

Jordan, E. (1995) 'Fighting boys and fantasy play: the construction of masculinity in the early years of school', *Gender and Education*, 7, 59–86.

Kelly, A., Baldry, A., Bolton, E., Edwards, S., Emery, J., Levin, C., Smith, S. and Wills, M. (1987) 'Traditionalists and trendies: teachers' attitudes to educational issues', in G. Weiner and M. Arnot (eds) (1987) *Gender under Scrutiny*. London: Hutchinson.

Lafrance, M. (1991) 'School for scandal: different educational experiences for females and males', *Gender and Education*, 3, 3–11.

Lees, S. (1986) *Losing Out*. London: Hutchinson.

Lobban, G.(1975) 'Sex roles in reading schemes', *Educational Review*, 27, 202–210.

Mahony, P. (1985) *Schools for the Boys*. London: Hutchinson.

Manpower Services Commission (1984) *TVEI Review*. Sheffield: MSC.

Millman, V. (1987) 'Teacher as researcher: a new tradition for research on gender', in G. Weiner and M. Arnot (eds) *Gender under Scrutiny: New Inquiries in Education*. London: Unwin Hyman.

Newsom Report (1963) *Half Our Future*. London: HMSO.

Northam, J. (1987) 'Girls and boys in primary maths', in G. Weiner and M. Arnot (eds) *Gender under Scrutiny: New Inquiries in Education*. London: Unwin Hyman.

Office for Standards in Education (1995) *Framework for Inspection*. London: HMSO.

Osler, A. (1994) 'Still hidden from history? the representation of women in recently published history textbooks', *Oxford Review of Education*, 20, 219–235.

Pratt, J., Seale, C. and Bloomfield, J. (1984) *Option Choices: A Question of Equal Opportunity*. Slough: NFER/Nelson.

Purvis, J. (1991) *A History of Women's Education in England*. Milton Keynes: Open University Press.

Riddell, S. (1992) *Gender and the Politics of the Curriculum*. London,Routledge.

Riley, K. (1994) *Quality and Equality*. London: Cassell.

Rudduck, J. (1994) *Developing a Gender Policy in Secondary Schools*. Buckingham: Open University Press.

Silver, P. and Silver, H. (1974) *The Education of the Poor*. London: Routledge and Kegan Paul.

Smithers, A and Zientek, P. (1990) *Gender, Primary Schools and the National Curriculum*. London: NASUWT and the Engineering Council.

Spender, D.(1982) *Invisible Women: The Schooling Scandal*. London: Writers and Readers Co-operative.

Volman, M., van Eck, E. and ten Dam, G. (1995) 'Girls in science and technology: the development of a discourse', *Gender and Education*, 7, 283–292.

Weiner, G. (1994) *Feminisms in Education: An Introduction*. Buckingham: Open University Press.

Weiner, G. and Arnot, M. (1987) 'Teachers and gender politics', in M. Arnot and G. Weiner (eds) *Gender and the Politics of Schooling*. London: Unwin Hyman.

Wolpe, A. (1988) *Within School Walls: The role of Discipline, Sexuality and the Curriculum*. London: Routledge.

Part III

DIVERSITY AND CHOICE

CHAPTER 9

Diversity

Peter Jackson

INTRODUCTION

The announcement in 1992 of a White Paper on 'diversity' in education brought mixed reaction. While for some the word promised further liberation from the authoritarian effects of the 1944 Education Act, for others it confirmed fears neatly expressed by Andy Green two years earlier: 'It would be a sad irony if the country which was last to create a national education system, and which never quite completed the job, should be the first to dismantle it' (1990, p. 316). In the face of these reactions, it is worthwhile to consider the notion of diversity.

It implies variety, difference and plurality and has recently been associated with business and finance. Businesses extend their activities into various disparate fields in order to minimise risks and increase the chances of profit. Finance houses maintain different portfolios of investment for the same reasons. Diversity seems an appropriate aim for a Government intent on encouraging schools to develop as businesses rather than remain as outreaches of a Welfare State.

Since the National Curriculum is binding on all state schools, curricular uniformity is a prime candidate for diversification. Could the government be contemplating relaxing the National Curriculum, allowing more variation in what schools may offer? Then there is the centrality of Christian worship. Could the government be considering accommodating the Muslim and other religious communities on the same terms as the Christian? Was it contemplating removing the religious dimension altogether? And what of special needs? What would diversification mean in this sphere – a return to segregation?

General arguments on diversity

Whatever particular changes are mooted, the general argument for diversity is clear. All things change and policy should acknowledge and accommodate that fact. Moreover, since the Government proclaims its commitment to parental choices and points out that choice between similar things is hardly choice at all, then what is now similar should be encouraged to become different. And there is an important side-benefit: the freedom to diversify allows schools to respond more effectively to local circumstances.

And as the general argument *for* is obvious, so is its counter. Diversity is not self-evidently a virtue. It may be 'unnatural' for things to remain uniform, but for various reasons it can be preferable that they do. Deterioration is a category of change, just as is improvement. As for parental choice, diversity can lead to confusion or difficulties of comparison, whereas uniformity can preserve standards for comparison. To the extent that parents have common goals for their children, their choice of schools is better exercised on measured differences of degree rather than kind. A side-benefit is that uniformity is more manageable. Organising schools, training teachers, assessing pupils, trialling experiments, distributing money – these all benefit in terms of efficiency and fairness from uniformity.

If general arguments balance, it is customary to look for comparative evidence. The Government pores obsessively over France and Germany: what does it learn? When Germany was partitioned between the Allied Powers after World War II, the British Sector was organised according to ministerial circulars (following the 1944 Education Act) which encouraged, though did not prescribe, three types of school. Whereas the key element – the technical school – was ignored in the UK, in Germany it was a priority. Since then the German system has retained its tripartite character and enriched it by funding schools which in the UK would be independent. The comprehensive systems which the Russians and the Americans introduced to their respective sectors are not typical of modern Germany. Of course, as Figure 9.1 shows, attainment is far higher in Germany than in the UK. The comparison with Germany would seem to support diversification.

But France does at least as well and, like the UK, is overwhelmingly comprehensive. In Scotland 9 per cent, in Wales 9 per cent and in England about 86 per cent of schools are comprehensive, having changed over the course of some thirty years – in both urban and rural authorities – from the bipartite rump of Grammar and Secondary Modern. So, leaving aside Northern Ireland which retains a bipartite system, the UK system has similarities with France. What distinguishes France from the UK are the high standards its schools achieve, its lack of a significant independent sector, and a justice and equality of funding for schools which is unknown here. Opponents of diversity want more uniformity, not less; they want inequality reduced.

THE POLICY

The language of the White Paper *Choice and Diversity* (DfE, 1992) is not modest:

> The previous decade focused on the raising of standards. Now this White Paper carries this great programme of reform further forward. (p. iii)
>
> Growing diversity in education will be one of the features of the 1990s. (p. 43)

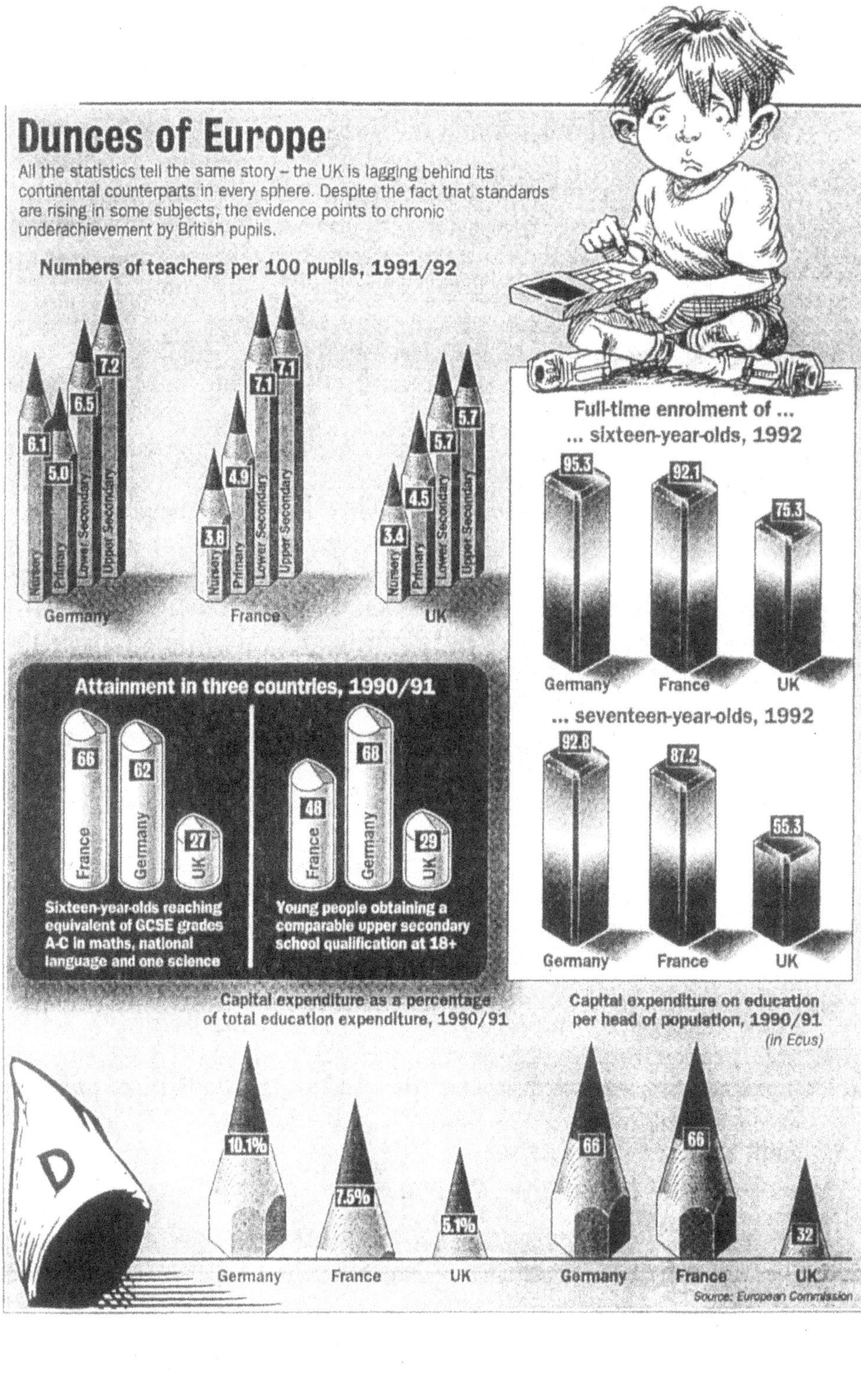
Dunces of Europe
All the statistics tell the same story – the UK is lagging behind its continental counterparts in every sphere. Despite the fact that standards are rising in some subjects, the evidence points to chronic underachievement by British pupils.
Numbers of teachers per 100 pupils, 1991/92
6.1
5.0
6.5
7.2
Nursery
Primary
Lower Secondary
Upper Secondary
Germany
3.8
4.9
7.1
7.1
Nursery
Primary
Lower Secondary
Upper Secondary
France
3.4
4.5
5.7
5.7
Nursery
Primary
Lower Secondary
Upper Secondary
UK
Attainment in three countries, 1990/91
66
France
62
Germany
27
UK
Sixteen-year-olds reaching equivalent of GCSE grades A-C in maths, national language and one science
48
France
68
Germany
29
UK
Young people obtaining a comparable upper secondary school qualification at 18+
Full-time enrolment of ...
... sixteen-year-olds, 1992
95.3
92.1
75.3
Germany
France
UK
... seventeen-year-olds, 1992
92.8
87.2
55.3
Germany
France
UK
Capital expenditure as a percentage of total education expenditure, 1990/91
10.1%
7.5%
5.1%
Germany
France
UK
Capital expenditure on education per head of population, 1990/91
(in Ecus)
66
66
32
Germany
France
UK
D
Source: European Commission

KEY POINTS

- A 'rich and diverse system of state-funded education', subject to Government controls
- Transition to GM-status made easier and seen as the main route to diversity
- Curricular specialism, specialist schools, technology, business sponsorship and vocational courses all encouraged

There would be a 'new and evolutionary framework for the organisation of state-funded schools' which would allow 'a rich and diverse system of state-funded education' under the controls provided by the Government. The controls were the National Curriculum, the school assessment and examination process, Ofsted, local governing bodies, financial sourcing from the centre and Education Associations for failing schools. The undeclared claim was that the UK's basic pattern – non-selective primaries and secondaries, all ruled by local education authorities – exerted conformist pressure and had done so for well over thirty years. The 'liberating measures' of the 1988 Act – opting out, Local Management of Schools, publication of results and parental choice – offered opportunities for diversification which were augmented by the White Paper.

But which was the prime objective – the development of school distinctiveness, or the demise of the local education authorities? The latter were, after all, clearly targeted in the 1988 Education Reform Act and nothing since then indicated that the Government had changed its mind. It is possible that 'diversity' was simply a new slogan advertising the same policy – strip LEAs bare of power. Certainly while the achievement of grant-maintained (GM) status is seen as the chief route to diversification, the suspicion must linger that the undermining of LEAs is the Government's priority.

The take-up of GM status has, on any reckoning, been meagre – less than four per cent of all UK mainstream schools in 1994–95 (*DfE News*, 284/95, Table 1). With the reductions in extra funding previously enjoyed, there is little likelihood of sudden change. What of the voluntary sector? Because less than four per cent of the 7269 church schools have opted out (*TES*, 15 September 1995), the Government proposed in 1995 that diversity would be achieved by a 'fast track' whereby such schools dispense with parental ballots; but the idea was condemned with such vehemence by the churches, who regarded it as discriminatory and divisive, that it was dropped. It seems clear that the weakening of LEAs and the consequent centralisation of powers in the Funding Agency for Schools remain the Government's objective. Sadly, it has ignored the opportunity to argue its case for abolition of LEAs.

The urgency of establishing a technical and vocational curriculum for a country which abandoned it at the turn of the century is another motivation for the White Paper. For the whole of the century the UK has stumbled along, doing little for the 75 per cent of youngsters who don't want to or can't take advantage of the post–16 academic education which is virtually all that has been on offer. In the wake of the White Paper *Education and Training for the 21st Century* (DfE, 1991), the 1992 document could not duck the problem of a systematic technological education, and it would not cease its continued siege of the LEAs.

The declared thrust of the policy in the 1992 White Paper is that schools should become more distinctive through:

- *specialising in one or more curriculum areas* by allocating more time in the formal curriculum; developing extra-curricular activities; adopting a more flexible diurnal or annual timetable
- *attracting sponsorship from business and industry:* a category of sponsor-governor would be permitted in voluntary-aided and grant-maintained schools
- *developing technology as the key bridging course* spanning academic and technical aspects of education
- *prioritising the vocational aspects of technology:* this is considered of first importance for a country widely understood as having failed to develop technical education
- *enhancing the status of vocational courses* in order to achieve parity of esteem with academic courses.

The kind of schools emphasising technology, as distinguished by the 1992 White Paper, are:

- *City Technology Colleges (CTCs)*
  These are institutions (only 15 so far) set up in partnership with business in major cities. They promote curricula with strong emphasis on technology and science, supported by the widespread use of information technology.
- *Technology Schools*
  As a controlled experiment a number of schools, drawn from both GM and LEA sectors are equipped with technological facilities. They will be monitored for their progress in developing technology.
- *Technology Colleges*
  Like Technology Schools, these emphasise technology in the curriculum, and like City Technology Colleges they are linked to business through sponsors. Unlike CTCs, they may be developed anywhere in the country. 'Technology' is interpreted liberally as an approach to their special emphasis which may range from Business Studies Colleges to Creative Arts Colleges, as well as Technology Colleges.

Schools can apply for such official designation in different ways:

- Grant-maintained schools can apply directly to the Secretary of State for Technology College status.
- Voluntary-aided schools can apply to become Technology Colleges. Additionally, they may apply for GM status and will not be obliged to pay their present 15 per cent contribution to capital and external repair costs; they keep

their safeguards over their ethos by maintaining a majority of their foundation governors on the governing body.

- Special schools can also apply for GM status which can include uprating to 'specialist' (sponsorship-bearing) special schools.
- LEA-maintained schools have first to apply for GM status before being eligible for Technology College status.

So, GM schools are closer to special status than LEA schools, and voluntary-aided schools are given financial incentives and favoured representation on governing bodies if they opt out. The White Paper made various proposals for easing the transition to GM status, and some of these featured in the 1993 Act. A new GM school can now be set up by the Funding Agency or by any group of 'promoters' (e.g. a religious group), and independent schools can 'opt in' to GM status. If the 1996 Bill becomes law, GM schools will be able to mortgage land, buildings and other assets to raise private money for developments. The White Paper proposals are also heavily biased towards technology. This reflects the 1991 White Paper *Education and Training for the 21st Century* which called for renewed efforts to bridge the academic-technical divide in British education and to raise the standard and esteem of technology.

ISSUES FOR DEBATE

1. Diversification of the academic curriculum

The 1992 White Paper supports the diversification of the academic curriculum, but its recommendations are somewhat insubstantial. It is difficult to see how they could be otherwise, given the demands of the National Curriculum. A writer from the Centre for Policy Studies (influential on libertarian conservative thinking) tackles this in *An Entitlement to Knowledge: Agenda for the New Schools Authority*. The Government's reformist philosophy, Anthony O'Hear (1993) argues, exhibits a necessary tension between two forces: the liberating tendencies which encourage parental choice and responsibility, competition and differentiation; and the regulatory policies which guard against bad schools, incompetence and unprofessional conduct. Chief among these are the National Curriculum and national testing.

Because reform carries dangers, some regulation is, he feels, necessary, but the Government was heavy-handed in imposing a National Curriculum of such size, complexity and bureaucracy. It should simply specify the essential content to which any child in the country should be introduced. It was a mistake to inflate it with four non-statutary cross-curricular themes, to lumber primary school teachers with hundreds of separate statements of attainment, and to retain a subject-specific assessment programme. All these hamstring schools and teachers in doing what they are best at. He warns that the School Curriculum and Assessment Authority has the potential to become 'an instrument of dread conformity'.

While O'Hear claims that the National Curriculum leaves no room for specialisation, David Hargreaves (1991) concludes that the National Curriculum is too ponderous even to do the job it was designed for. Arguing pre-Dearing, he maintains that coherence – making sense of the learning for pupils – is simply unattainable. For secondary school teachers coherence was a special problem between subjects; for primary school teachers the problem was located within subjects. The cross-curricular themes simply broke the camel's back.

Even after the Dearing revision of the National Curriculum it is hard to see what room schools have for diversifying the academic curriculum. There is an air of desperation about the White Paper's advice to stretch the timetable to create extra curricular space.

Question for discussion

Should the Government's regulatory policies be eased in order to improve the chances for curriculum diversity?

---

2. Diversification of the non-academic curriculum

'Non-academic" is not a satisfactory descriptor of the vocational curriculum, but then neither is 'vocational'. The former implies that theory is non-existent or low-level while the latter denies vocationalism to scholars, scientists and historians. In the absence of a better word, 'non-academic' shall stand for those programmes of study which are not squarely based on the Secondary Regulations Curriculum laid down in the first decade of this century and virtually duplicated in the present National Curriculum. The diversification of the non-academic curriculum is an issue for comment since the White Paper is plainly technology-oriented. Will the encouragement of technology work?

Peter Pilkington (1991) hopes that it will but believes that it won't. Using historical and comparative arguments to substantiate his position, he picks out the 1902 Act as the turning point in state education in this country. Near the end of the century some city elementary schools developed higher grade classes, often in partnership with established industries. Striking to our eyes is their technological and vocational character and their intermingling of work and school. The 1902 Act killed that initiative stone dead, established the new secondary education on the foundation grammar school curriculum, and effectively closed off all but professional employment from education. Eventually comprehensive schools embraced the grammar school curriculum and vocational education was reduced to a series of initiatives.

Contrast this, says Pilkington, with the position in France and Germany whose vocational qualifications – the Baccalauréat Professionel and the Berufsschulabschluss – are as well known in Europe as GCSEs in England and Wales. He points out that French schooling is common up to the age of 16 when two routes are opened: the Lycée, where students take the traditional Baccalauréat and the Lycée Professionel where they take one of the many varieties of Baccalauréat Professionel. German schooling is tripartite, rather than comprehensive. About 38 per cent attend the Hauptschulen (roughly, the UK secondary modern), 27 per cent the Gymnasien (Grammar) and 5 per cent the

Comprehenzen. The gap is filled by the Realschulen (29 per cent) which is an intermediate school, to which pupils from Hauptschulen can transfer, and from which pupils gain a leaving certificate qualifying them for entry to vocational schools or technical colleges, or to higher stages of the Gymnasien. In the German system, up to 60 per cent of young people between 15 and 18 take advantage of vocational training organised in schools and part-time colleges. In 1988 well over two million were in part-time or full time vocational schools.

Despairing of the gradualist approach which usually passes for change in the UK system, with initiative after initiative retreating into obscurity as soon as funding is withdrawn, Pilkington argues against bridging the gap between academic and non-academic post–16 school programmes. Instead, he proposes separate paths at age 16 into Academic or Technical Colleges, each with entirely separate ranges of public examinations. The Government should use the device of weighted vouchers to get the system started, he argues. The lamentable alternative, joint academic and vocational courses, would not only make it more difficult to move to distinctly different systems later, but would also have the effect of weakening the A-levels (the one clear success of the UK system) while doing nothing for parity of esteem for the technical. For Pilkington, the proposals in the White Paper simply do not go far enough either in theory or in practice.

One might agree with Pilkington's insistence on the need for radical reform, without quite seeing how to bring about his particular solution. How can the in-built and endemic ad hockery of the UK 'system' be dealt with by the in-built and endemic ad hockery of our parliamentary legislation? The UK has always – ever since 1870 anyway – pursued a policy of development only on the shoulders of what already existed. Thus, as Andy Green (1994) has pointed out, voluntarism is at the heart of the UK system. This amounts to an unbridgeable gulf between ourselves and the French.

'System' is an honorary title in the UK for the results of an endless do-it-yourself job, adding a bit here and a bit there, never throwing anything away in case it might come in handy, never turning down help from a know-all neighbour no matter how incompetent. It is a system of a sort, at least in the sense of being as unmistakably British as a stuttering, long-calcified Edwardian central heating system. The proposals of the White Paper on technology come from the same odd-jobbing philosophy and amount to little more than a bag of spanners.

Question for discussion

How persuasive do you find Pilkington's proposals?

---

3. Diversification of ability

The thrust of the Labour Party's 1995 document *Diversity and Excellence* (1995a) is for the replacement of the Funding Agency for Schools by LEAs. It wants to restore them as the main organs of administration. The document insists that the old conception of LEAs as controllers of education must give way to the idea of LEAs as facilitators. They would, for example, channel 90 per cent of each school budget directly to schools and be responsible for all their capital spending, except in the case of aided schools which would have different arrangements. There would be three kinds of schools: *Community* (formerly LEA), *Aided* (formerly voluntary-controlled or voluntary-aided) and *Foundation* (formerly grant-maintained). The document exhibits two characteristic Labour concerns:

- democratic representation (no quangos) through LEAs which will become the administrative authority for GM schools as well as 'community schools' (see Chapter 11)
- prohibition of selection by tests at 11-plus.

The prohibition of selection at 11-plus looks unambiguous and might reassure socialists who felt that Labour was shedding its educational skin. However, what could it mean ? With Key Stage 2 assessment providing information on pupils' academic ability and with the diagnostic tests which many schools already set, schools will have more information than the 11-plus tests were ever able to provide. Again, with increasing diversification among schools, aptitude (or what parents think their children would be good at) will be an increasingly significant factor. Finally, the emphasis on home-school cooperation, with contracts of duties, responsibilities and rights (which many schools are negotiating with parents) will inevitably grow in importance.

All these developments underline the differences between the present day and the time when the 11-plus was *the* selector. What is crucial is whether there is an overarching power to distribute places. Does the Labour Party still believe that LEAs should control the ability profile in schools? That is a very considerable power, one which seems totally at odds with parental choice and with 'New Labour' philosophy. Far from giving back powers to the LEAs, New Labour might even be forced to re-consider its policy of LEA-as-facilitator. After all, if 'facilitation' is all that is needed, why bother with an Authority at all? If schools want to cooperate, why not let them?

Dennis Lawton (1994) warns that 'uniformity' is code for the comprehensive system. The sub-text to the White Paper is, he maintains, 'rid the country of the comprehensive system'. The point is supported by David Miliband (1991). A programme for diversification is scarcely needed, he argues, for schools high in the academic league tables will attract more pupils than they can take, and their selection procedures will favour the higher achievers so that the league table position will be enhanced. Such schools will widen the gap between themselves and their competitors. In no time a pattern will emerge which would be similar to the pre-comprehensive school pattern. There would be no need for even a formal 11-plus examination.

But the underlying reality is surely that diversity of ability really cannot be avoided within a system based on parental choice, and it would be quite unacceptable to return powers to authorities to dole out groups of pupils to schools in different bands, as happened under the old system. The idea, entertainingly floated by Geoffrey Walford (1994), that we might use random selection has only limited appeal. Popular with the more venal television companies, it has few academic supporters outside the Centre for Policy Studies.

The spectre of an abilitocracy on the lines of Michael Young's satire *The Rise of the Meritocracy* is probably best exorcised by the thickening-up of the league table statistics whereby 'value-added' information is added to the statistics so that the public can judge which schools are making most difference to their pupils. The signs are that this will be taken up (see Chapter 15). Perhaps of more importance however, in the long run, will be the growth in prominence of variables other than academic performance.

To sum up this short consideration of 'diversification by ability', there is no evidence from *Choice and Diversity* that the Government is intent on bringing back selection of the old 11-plus sort. On the other hand, it is obvious that selection goes hand-in-hand with parental choice; and, since choice is a declared aim of the document, selection is on the agenda. Over-subscribed schools too will need admissions policies. What this means is that they have to declare their criteria. To rule out the ability of pupils as a criterion for educational selection is to carry social engineering to an absurd degree. While race and colour as criteria are quite properly excluded for all schools, and sex is a conceptual criterion for single-sex schools (as is creed for religious foundations), ability is a reasonable criterion for all places of learning.

Question for discussion

'To forbid schools to use academic standards as a criterion for selection is as muddle-headed as to forbid parents to use the academic standard of a school as one of their criteria.' Do you agree?

---

4. Society and diversity

In his 1994 paper 'Postmodernism and state education', Andy Green maintains that the postmodernist supporters of diversity and choice share with the neo-liberal marketeers certain perceptions: Government keeps governing everything; it exhausts initiative with delay; it clones its institutions by its prescriptions; it wastes money through management by civil servants and politicians; it makes contracts with powerful interest groups; and it avoids accountability by the use of quangos.

But whereas the libertarian Right maintains that choice and diversity will raise standards and promote efficiency and that is why educational provision must change, the postmodernist holds it must change because society has left the old certainties behind, along with so-called homogeneous classes. Today's society is heterogeneous and fragmented – and none the worse for it. Diversification and plurality are ideas whose time has come.

From this viewpoint the 'comprehensive schools' issue is an irrelevance. The battles were fought long ago, 'in a different country'. To the general public – and especially the school-students and their parents – state schools are just schools. They may differ from each other in local esteem but they share far more with each other than comprehensive-schoolness. They are all compulsory, custodial, rule-bound institutions, staffed almost exclusively by state-paid teachers who routinely reward and penalise pupils who all follow the same broad programme within, on the whole, rather poor working conditions.

The public wants diversity and plurality because it is itself diverse and plural. It rejects the labels of homogeneity which politicians and moralists pin on it. The main criterion for choice of school is not its academic effectiveness, it is its suitability for particular pupils (which can include academic effectiveness). Many social groups believe that state schools ignore or reject their culture. If they lack the means to buy more tailored education, they have to take it off-the-peg even when it is ill-fitting. It is no wonder that close-knit cultural communities want change so badly. Diversity, following those old catchwords 'assimilation' and 'integration' has been promised and delayed for so long that the public can be forgiven for wondering whether the term, now it has arrived with party political approval, really does herald plurality or simply more of the same.

Postmodernism is a name for a general unease about the whole collection of ways in which things have been done up till now. 'Unease' because it suggests a lack of specificity – something one cannot quite define – a sort of mood, a feeling that change is inevitable and cannot be put off much longer. Above all, a sea-change for everyone, not just for an intellectual minority. At the beginning of the 1980s this feeling was distinguishable as two propositions about the recent past: the differences between opposing positions mattered less than the assumptions the antagonists held in common; and these assumptions must be reviewed, challenged and, if necessary, disposed of.

In many fields, postmodernism has been operationalised in the scrutiny and rejection of past ways of thinking, and earlier radicals – such as Illich, Holt and Spring – have been re-discovered. Even a former Secretary of State for Education, Sir Keith Joseph, in an interview just before he died, gave voice to a misgiving that strikes a postmodernist chord:

> I wish we'd taken a different route in 1870 ... If we could move back to 1870, I would take a different route. We've got compulsory education, which is a responsibility of hideous importance, and we tyrannise children to do that which they don't want, and we don't produce results. (quoted in Ball, 1990, p.62)

Although the sentiment was lost to sight in the rhetoric of Joseph's successor Kenneth Baker (with his enthusiasm for standards, competencies, accountability and the 'entitlement curriculum'), its spirit survived in the Centre for Policy Studies which Joseph himself helped to establish. The White Paper is, in the last analysis, a deal between the ideas of the libertarian Right and the Civil Service, with the latter very much the dominant partner.

Geoff Whitty (1992) has shrewdly pointed out that, although the language of heterogeneity, fragmentation and variety, which so characterises postmodernist thinking, is to be found also in the discourse of the New Right, it would be an error to conflate the two groups. The New Right believes in the power of demand-led free and open markets to raise standards, whereas the postmodernist maintains that state schooling contains deeply embedded vested interests and social engineering assumptions which are indefensible and incurable.

For Andy Green, whose 1990 observation opened this chapter, it is the postmodernist who is most in tune with the times. His 1994 analysis of this educational condition suggests that influential opinion is questioning and rejecting state systems. True, in Continental Europe, Government support for them is strong, and in the USA the President's *Goals 2000: Educate America Act: A Strategy for Re-inventing Our Schools* (issued in 1993) calls for a commanding role for the federal government in areas of curriculum and standards. But Green quotes Jay Scribner and colleagues (1994) who claim that the blurring of divisions between public and private – so evident during the Reagan and Bush administrations – continue under the Democratic presidency. For Green, the UK Government still uses the rhetoric of national policy and national responsibility but in reality is determinedly abandoning both. The paradox is that, while Green and others think that the increasing heterogeneity and fragmentation of society are good reasons for establishing a properly purposeful state system of education, postmodernists believe they are grounds for the dismantling of such systems.

Question for discussion

Should a diversification of schooling be welcomed on the grounds that today's society is heterogeneous and fragmented?

THE FUTURE?

The main political parties have much educational policy in common. Of course, it is the Conservatives who have done the work. Time and again Labour have objected to particular measures and then come to agree with them. One could not say there was a consensus, but there is not the chasm which many forecast back in 1988.

Because society is diversifying, the tentative, modest reforms of the White Paper probably will take hold. Schools will use the opportunities for greater diversification to develop more distinct identities. The National Curriculum will be reduced still further, giving schools more freedoms to develop. The Church of England is part of the Establishment, perhaps inextricably so, but the time for curbing its power cannot be far off. For the first time since Henry VIII, Anglican churchgoers are outnumbered by Roman Catholics. It cannot be long before Anglican churchgoing slips to third place behind Muslims. British society is far more variegated than the present Government admits.

School information, including 'value-added' information, will increase. Governance by quangos must reduce: it is indefensible that so much power, patronage and money is dispensed so cavalierly by government. Perhaps representative regional bodies will take over as an alternative to both unrepresentative quangos and too-numerous LEAs.

The move to greater diversification will require another regulatory body – a Teachers Professional and Ethical Council (much as the Labour Party (1995b) have proposed) which will be necessary to safeguard standards of conduct and practice. Relatedly, the easy, careless way many parents accept the least inconvenient schooling for their children must change. Handing over children to other adults, even if they are professionals, is a matter of parental responsibility which should be acknowledged more widely. The Council would show that, in a society whose risks are becoming daily more evident, teachers are attending to their responsibilities as privileged guides for children.

Finally, schools must change. The stimulation of postmodernist thought – whether through the provocative deconstruction of David Hargreaves' *The Mosaic of Learning* (1994) or the work of Aronowitz and Giroux (1991) – can bring many benefits. Though it might sound paradoxical, a strong well-ordered state sector can withstand and benefit from a fringe of less mainstream institutions rather in the way that ordered trading estates can draw nourishment, symbiotically, from souk-like markets that spring up on their outskirts.

FURTHER READING

Allder, M. (1993) 'The meaning of "school ethos"', *Westminster Studies In Education*, 16, 59–69.

Ball, S. (1993) 'Education markets, choice and social class: the market as a class strategy in the UK and the USA', *British Journal of Sociology of Education*, 14, 3–19.

Fletcher, J. (1995) 'Policy-making in DES/DfE via consensus and contention', *Oxford Review of Education*, 21, 133–148.

Hargreaves, A. (1994) 'Restructuring restructuring: postmodernity and the prospects for educational change', *Journal of Education Policy*, 9, 47–66.

Hustler, D., Brighouse, T. and Rudduck, J. (eds) (1995) *Heeding Heads: Secondary Heads and Educational Commentators in Dialogue*. London: David Fulton. An interactive exploration of how recent education policy changes have shaped headteachers' perceptions of their mission in a climate apparently designed to bring about a high degree of standardisation and conformity.

Rust, V. (1991) 'Post-modernism and its comparative education implications', *Comparative Education Review*, 35, 610–626.

REFERENCES

Aronowitz, S. and Giroux, H. (1991) *Postmodern Education: Politics, Culture and Social Criticism*. Minneapolis: University of Minnesota Press.

Ball, S. (1990) *Politics and Policy Making in Education: Explorations in Policy Sociology*. London: Routledge.

DfE (1991) *Education And Training For The 21st Century*. London: HMSO.

DfE (1992) *Choice and Diversity: A New Framework for Schools*. London: HMSO.

Green, A. (1990) *Education and State Formation: The Rise of Education Systems in England, France and the USA*. London: Macmillan.

Green, A. (1994) 'Postmodernism and state education', *Journal of Education Policy*, 9, 67–83.

Hargreaves, D. (1991) 'Coherence and manageability: reflections on the National Curriculum and cross-curricular provision', *Curriculum Journal*, 1, 31–41.

Hargreaves, D. (1994) *The Mosaic of Learning*. London: Macmillan.

Labour Party (1995a) *Diversity and Excellence: A New Partnership for Schools*. London: Labour Party.

Labour Party (1995b) *Excellence for Everyone*. London: Labour Party.

Lawton, D. (1994) *The Tory Mind on Education*, 1979–1994. London: Falmer.

O'Hear, A. (1993) *An Entitlement to Knowledge: Agenda for the New Schools Authority*. London: Centre for Policy Studies.

Miliband, D. (1991) *Markets, Politics and Education: Beyond the Education Reform Act*. London: Institute for Public Policy Research.

Pilkington, P. (1991) *End Egalitarian Delusion: Different Education for Different Talents*. London: Centre for Policy Studies.

Scribner, J., Reyes, P. and Fusarelli, L. (1994) 'Educational politics and policy: and the game goes on', *Journal of Education Policy*, 9, 205–26.

Walford, G. (1994) 'A return to selection?', *Westminster Studies in Education*, 17, 19–30.

Whitty, G. (1992) 'Education, economy and national culture', in R. Bocock and K. Thompson (eds) *Social and Cultural Forms Of Modernity*. Buckingham: Open University Press.

CHAPTER 10

School Choice

Jim Docking

INTRODUCTION

It is often suggested that the policy to promote school choice is inextricably linked with the policy to promote a diversity of schools, the subject of the previous chapter. Diversity, it is contended, is both a prerequisite for, and a consequence of, school choice. However, although the Government's policy to promote diversity is partly to increase the scope for parental choice, the Government also encourages choice between similar kinds of schools. In this chapter we are concerned with the policy that parents should be allowed to choose between all types of school available, similar as well as dissimilar, and we shall focus mainly on choice of secondary school within the maintained system.

The Universal Declaration of Human Rights asserts that 'parents have a prior right to choose the kind of education that shall be given to their children' (para 26.3), while Article 2 of the Protocol to the European Convention for the Protection of Human Rights and Fundamental Freedoms establishes that the State shall respect the right of parents to ensure that their child is educated 'in conformity with their own religious and philosophical convictions'. Most of the current debate about school choice in this country, however, is about the appropriateness of regarding schools as 'providers' competing for custom among 'consumers' in an education 'market' and changing their 'product' accordingly.

Phillip Brown (1994) argues that school choice represents a 'third wave' in the development of education. The 'first wave' consisted of the rise of mass schooling for the working classes in the late nineteenth century; the 'second wave' marked the provision of education based on individual merit and achievement; the emerging 'third wave' is characterised by

> the move towards a system whereby the education a child receives must conform to the wealth and wishes of parents rather than the abilities and efforts of pupils. In other words, we have witnessed a shift away from the 'ideology of meritocracy' to what I will call the 'ideology of parentocracy'. (p. 51)

Brown sees 'parentocracy' as a reaction to the egalitarian ideals of universal locally-controlled comprehensive education and policies of equality of opportunity, which the Right alleges has failed to raise standards. Although the state lays down national curricular requirements, it is schools and parents, he argues, who are given the main responsibility for improving standards: schools will try to raise levels of achievement to attract custom, while parents who are dissatisfied with one school can turn to another. Consequently,

> Selection will now be determined by the free play of market forces, and because the state is no longer responsible for overseeing selection, inequalities in educational outcome, at least in official accounts, cannot be blamed on the state. Such inequalities (the Right prefer the term 'diversity') will be viewed as the legitimate expression of parental preferences, differences in innate capacities, and a healthy 'diversity' of educational experience. (p. 64)

School choice is now firmly embedded in education policies not only in Britain but in many other industrialised nations. However, as an international report prepared for the OECD (1994) has shown, it does not always work the same way as in this country. In Australia, for example, the choice is mainly between public and private schools (70 per cent of which are Catholic), with private schools accounting for over a quarter of all enrolments and receiving subsidies from the Government and states. The Netherlands goes a crucial step further in giving equal funding to public and private schools (the latter accounting for as much as two-thirds of pupil enrolment) in the belief that parents should have access to the type of school they desire – even to the extent of new schools being created to reflect belief systems so far unprovided for in the locality. In the USA, where school choice policies are becoming more prevalent, there is often a greater diversity of schools, particularly in states where there is no compulsory curriculum.

THE POLICY

KEY POINTS

- The right of parents to state a preference for the school they want their child to attend
- School choice extended to special education
- 'Open enrolment', the duty of schools to admit pupils up to their physical capacity, linked to school funding
- 'Assisted places' in independent schools
- The promotion of a diversity of schools to expand the scope for choice
- Information to help parents choose schools
- Coordinated admission policies among groups of LEA and GM schools encouraged

Statutory provision for school choice was introduced in the 1944 Education Act, which laid down that 'pupils are to be educated in accordance with the wishes of their parents' (Sect. 76). However, this clause was not intended to open the doors to unfettered school choice but to allow parents to opt for church schools, which were being brought into the state system (Stillman, 1986). In any case, LEAs were able to reject parents' preferences on grounds of 'unreasonable public expenditure', though parents could also appeal to the Secretary of State on the grounds that the LEA had acted 'unreasonably' (as they still can).

In the period up to 1980, there was much discussion by both the main political parties about extending parental choice. The Conservative Party in opposition was particularly attracted to this policy because of its electoral appeal in shifting the balance of power away from local authorities and towards parents. Under this pressure, the Labour Government in 1978 introduced a bill to strengthen parents' choice, but failed to get it through Parliament before the general election the following year was won by the Conservative Party. The Education Act of 1980, however, was similar in many respects to the 1978 Bill. It:

- gave parents the explicit right to express a preference for the school they wished their child to attend, even if the school was not in the authority where they lived[1];
- reversed the burden of proof in favour of parents: now the LEA had to show why a parent's preference should not be satisfied;
- required local authorities and voluntary-aided schools to publish annually their rules of admission, including the criteria for deciding which children should be given priority when the school was over-subscribed;
- enabled the Secretary of State to require schools to publish information to help parents make their choice;
- required both LEA and voluntary-aided schools to set up independent appeal committees (although the LEA enjoyed a majority among the members) whose decision would be binding. The Ombudsman was also given powers to investigate complaints of maladministration in an authority's management of school choice (a facility extended to voluntary-aided and grant-maintained schools in the Education Act 1993).

The 1980 Act also extended parental choice into the private sector, albeit marginally, by making it possible for children to obtain an 'assisted place' at an independent school. Over 30,000 pupils, representing five per cent of those in independent schools, now receive such assistance, which costs £104m a year. The Government has announced plans to double the number of places and extend them to under–10s, even though the scheme is undersubscribed by about 4,000 places (*TES*, 1 December 1995).

In spite of these innovations, the wishes of many parents were to be frustrated by a qualifying provision in the Act, which preserved the right of a local authority to resist a parental preference where this would 'prejudice the provision of efficient education or the efficient use of resources'. Now, through a policy of 'open enrolment' under the Education Reform Act 1988, local authorities and voluntary-aided schools are no longer allowed to refuse a parent's preference on grounds of educational efficiency or economy, unless the capacity of the school had been exceeded. Where demand for places exceeds

[1] In 1989, the Court of Appeal held that it was unlawful, under the 1980 Act, for the London Borough of Greenwich to give its own residents priority in school admissions

those available, the LEA's or school's admissions criteria come into operation. 'Acceptable' criteria include having a brother or sister who has attended the school, proximity of the school to home, and attending a named 'feeder' primary school; 'unacceptable' criteria include discrimination on grounds of race, special needs, behaviour, or religious belief (unless a church school). As explained in the previous chapter, the 1988 Act also increased the diversity of schools, from which at least some parents could choose, by bringing in grant-maintained schools and city technical colleges. These set their own admissions criteria, subject to agreement with the Secretary of State. Gone now is the ubiquitous neighbourhood school and attempts by local authorities to balance the intake between schools.

Parents were given more assistance in making choices under the 1992 Schools Act, which gave the public greater access to information about schools. As a result, LEAs are now required to produce league tables of examination results and other performance indicators (see Chapter 15). The same Act set up a more comprehensive and regular system of school inspection under the new Office for Standards in Education, whose reports must be published, adding further to the information parents can use in choosing between schools (see Chapter 14).

In a move to get its message into every home, the Government issued the first Parent's Charter in 1991. However, the heading 'Using Your Right to Choose' was widely criticised on the grounds that, in fact, all parents can do is to state a preference. The corresponding heading in the revised Charter (DfE, 1994), circulated to all households including those without children, was simply 'A School Place for Your Child', but the emphasis on parents' rights in the matter of choice was retained:

> You can say which school you would prefer your child to go to. ... *As a general rule, you now have a right to a place in the school you want unless all the places at the school have been given to pupils who have a stronger claim to a place at that school.*
> (pp.9–10, original emphasis)

With the advent of 'opting out', parents were able to apply for places at GM schools whilst also expressing a preference among LEA schools. This duplication caused delay and uncertainty, a matter somewhat redressed in the Education Act 1993 which encourages groups of GM and LEA schools to coordinate their admission arrangements, with or without the LEA's agreement. The Secretary of State can impose his own scheme if local ones prove unsatisfactory, and any agreement – voluntary or imposed – takes precedence over the LEA's duty to comply with parental preferences.

The same Act has extended school choice rights to parents of children who have statements of special educational need – though for LEA special schools the authority can override parents' wishes if the school is deemed unsuitable for the child, prejudices the 'efficient' education of other pupils, or would lead to an inefficient use of resources. In the case of GM schools, although the LEA has general responsibility for special needs in the area, it has no right to nullify parents' choices, according to a DfEE ruling in January 1996.

In the dynamics of a true market, unpopular schools would close, releasing resources for the popular schools to expand in response to parental demand. Political considerations often prevent schools with surplus places closing, but recently the Government has shown some willingness to channel extra resources into the more popular schools.

School choice is now a major component of Government policy. The motive has been largely two-fold: first, to establish diversity of educational opportunity by reversing the policies of the 1960s which supported universal locally-controlled comprehensive education; secondly, to improve school effectiveness and reinstate more formal teaching methods by breaking up the dominance of the education 'establishment' by compelling schools to respond to the views of parents. Although the measures have commanded much support, the policy – or at least its effects – has not been without its critics, as we shall see in the next section.

ISSUES FOR DEBATE

1. Is school choice necessarily in the interests of freedom and democracy?

This question centres on the argument that choice and accountability to the consumers are essential prerequisites of any democratic system. Market provision and parental choice in education represent 'true democracy', so it is said, because the consumer 'votes' each time a choice is made, while school choice increases school accountability because, as schools compete for custom, they find it necessary to provide the kind of information that parents want rather than to just satisfy their professional criteria.

In a spirited defence of parental school choice, Brenda Almond (1994) has insisted that the 'fundamental question', concerns 'the legitimate boundaries of state power'. First of all, she argues, a state monopoly of education carries dangers of totalitarianism, while parental choice dissipates power by guaranteeing educational variety. Almond acknowledges that parents can be hypocritical or inconsistent in the reasons they give for making a choice; that some make choices based on ignorance or prejudice and for their own good rather than the child's; and that others make choices which are in the interests of their own child at the expense of others. None the less, she sees parental choice as the over-riding factor since it helps to preserve 'the freedom of the individual, toleration and the right to be different':

> For governments and experts can be mistaken too, and in their case the potential damage that error can produce is on a vastly larger scale. This is the heart of the argument against educational monopolies, whether of experts or of governments, or of experts working for governments. It is an argument for damage limitation, and at the same time an argument for social freedom in the widest possible sense. (p.76)

In contrast, Pat White (1994) suggests that there is a tension between a policy which promotes school choice and one which develops education for citizenship – which is also a prerequisite for freedom and democracy. She is not against all forms of parental choice; for instance, she supports choice which suits the child's personality or which offers something special in the curriculum. Nor does she rule out private education as long as it provides an agreed common civic education and does not cater only for a certain group, such as the rich, or those from a particular ethnic or religious background. Her fear, however, is that relatively unfettered school choice is socially divisive, threatening to suppress the conversation between social, religious and ethnic groups and serving to emphasise the differences between groups of people rather than the common bonds between citizens. In attacking the claim that parental choice nurtures democracy by allowing a diversity of schools and therefore a diversity of ways of life and practices, she insists that the interests of democracy require school choice policy to be balanced by one which helps children come to value the ideals that members of the society have in common ...

> Educational institutions need to embody in their practices both a recognition of the diversity and the bonds of mutuality connecting citizens. For toleration requires trust and the building of relationships of trust between groups is a delicate matter. ... This seems to indicate a need for common schools, run on democratic lines, where people grow to respect and trust each other and are concerned not merely to live and let live but that others should flourish. With the result that compromise is not regretted but welcomed as a way of accommodating others' concerns. (p.88)

There is no doubt that many parents go out of their way to place their children in 'segregated' schools such as those which have strong links with religious bodies or which attract particular racial and class groups (see Issues 2 and 3). Some have even gone further than this: not content with choosing between what is already on offer, they have set up schools which meet their requirements, as Walford (1994) has shown in his account of the development of evangelical New Christian schools. The question is whether White is right in assuming that such separatism could undermine the development of dispositions and skills which are in the interests of citizenship and democracy.

Question for discussion

Do you agree with the argument that school choice, in so far as it could support separate educational provision for distinctive groups of children, should be resisted on the grounds that it threatens the cohesion of society?

---

2. Does school choice really empower parents?

Government policy is that parents should be able to choose the school they want for their children. In reality, however, the implementation of the policy works better for some than for others.

First of all, the scope for choice is clearly more limited in some localities than others. For families who live in rural areas or small towns, there will obviously be less diversity of schools than for those living in metropolitan areas. In these circumstances, it makes no sense to say that parents can 'choose' between, say, a mixed and single sex school, or a comprehensive and a city technical college. This kind of problem can occur even in large towns, according to a survey among 323 parents in a 'relatively prosperous, non-industrial city' (Brain and Klein, 1994).

Secondly, there is very little choice in terms of curriculum emphasis or teaching style. Recent research for the Parental and School Choice Interaction Study (PASCI) at the Open University (Glatter *et al.*, 1995) has shown that, on the whole, the only choice parents have is between selective, comprehensive and church schools. These researchers suggest that, to improve parents' scope for choice, there will need to be changes in national policy, including more encouragement for schools to innovate (which means less National Curriculum). The aforementioned OECD study (1994) points out that school choice is always going to create problems in satisfying parental preferences as long the exercise is characterised largely in terms of the competition between schools of dissimilar status but offering similar curricula rather than in increasing diversity in terms of curriculum opportunities and teaching style:

> Ultimately the only way in which more choices can be satisfied is if preferences are more evenly spread. Schools that differ by pedagogical style or subject balance are more likely to be chosen evenly than if they differ by social or academic status. Demand pressures are rarely enough on their own to create such diversity. Initiatives to diversify educational supply may therefore be needed to create a genuine set of choices. Under a uniform model of schooling, choice is more likely to reinforce educational hierarchies than to improve educational opportunities or overall quality. (OECD, 1994, p.8)

Thirdly, some schools overtly or covertly set up restrictions so that the school rather than the parent makes the choice. Overtly, this will occur with selective and church schools, and the Department now allows all maintained secondary schools to select up to ten per cent of their intake on the basis of aptitude in art, drama, music, sport or technology (DfE, 1993). Covertly (although it is illegal) some oversubscribed schools are said to be effectively selecting whom they want to teach, at least to the extent that children with behaviour problems or special needs stand less chance of being admitted. In January 1996, the Education Secretary announced proposals to allow all schools to select up to 15 per cent of their intake on the basis not only of aptitude in a particular subject but also general or specific ability, possibly making use of interviews, thus effectively reducing the scope for parent choice.

Fourthly, many parents have been frustrated in finding that they cannot place their child in the school of their first choice. The Department recorded 46,000 appeals in 1993–94 (*TES*, 20 December 1996), a rise of 120 per cent since 1989–90, and a recent survey by the National Foundation for Educational Research (Jowett, 1995), found that appeals were rising in eight of the ten authorities studied. This research also shows how some parents, depending on the approach adopted, find the appeals procedure threatening and intimidating, suggesting a need for more customer-friendly arrangements.

Fifthly, school choice is more realistic for certain social groups. In so far as the law facilitates school choice for some, so it effectively reduces it for others. On the basis of findings from interviews, Stephen Ball (1984) argues that

> the processes and effects of market forces are related to social class and ethnic differences in access to and distribution between schools. I want to suggest that in an education market (a) the strategic processes of choice systematically disadvantage

> working class families and (b) the link between choices and resources (via per capita funding) disadvantages working-class schools and communities. In other words, the operation and effects of an education market benefit certain class groups and factions to the detriment and disadvantage of others. (pp.117–18)

He concludes: 'The market works as a class strategy by creating a mechanism which can be exploited by the middle classes as a strategy of reproduction in their search for relative advantage, social advancement and mobility' (p.126). Part of the problem, Ball argues, is that in order to work the school choice system, one needs to have 'certain types and amounts of social and economic capital', such as knowledge of local schools, access to information and the ability to decipher what is significant information, the skill to present oneself positively, the capacity to make direct approaches to schools, and the wherewithal to mount effective appeals against decisions. In short: 'The system of choice presupposes a set of values which gives primacy to comparison, mobility and long-term planning; it ignores those cultures which give primacy to the values of community and locality' (p.119). In effect, he says, 'we have to understand the market as a system of exclusion' (p.124). More recent evidence has confirmed that the policy of giving parents a wider choice benefits primarily the middle classes and more able children (Pennell and West, 1995; Smith and Noble, 1995).

The OECD report (1994, pp.50–52) makes a number of suggestions for addressing unequal opportunities. These are:

- *Intervention to create choices for educationally underserved groups* (e.g. better provision of information, including parent information centres; improving travelling facilities; performance indicators which refer to a wider range of factors; reserving some places for disadvantaged children regardless of residence)
- *A greater diversity of schools* to distribute choices more evenly and encourage innovation
- *Measures to improve the supply of chosen options* (e.g. helping less successful schools to improve as well as helping successful schools to expand)
- *Clear criteria for schools' choice of pupils* (including a more open debate about admission procedures to examine whether some school policies adversely affect others).

Lastly, it is important to recognise that parent empowerment is constrained by the role which children play in making school choices. According to research by Thomas and Dennison (1991), children have the 'biggest say' in selecting a secondary school, largely because parents want their children to be happy at school – though no doubt many parents subtly influence their children's 'preferences'.

Question for discussion

Do parents in your area have 'real' school choice? What changes would lead to greater parental empowerment in this respect?

---

3. Does school choice exacerbate racial and social segregation?

The answer to this questions is obviously linked to the issue just discussed. As some schools are able to fill their places with the children of street-wise middle-class parents who know how to procure the places they want for their children, so other less popular schools are left with the bulk of children who have special educational needs, who have been excluded from other schools, or whose first language is not English. The situation is then compounded as the popular schools attract funds and therefore better resources, which in turn attract favourable inspectors' reports and a high position in league tables, which in turn attract more pupils and more funds. In contrast, the less popular schools experience depleted revenue and poorer resources, which increases the likelihood of a low position in the league tables and adverse reports from Ofsted, which in turn leave the schools more and more with the children of parents whose exercise in school choice is a chimera. In the OECD (1994) report mentioned earlier, strong evidence emerged that gives substance to the concern that school choice reinforces social segregation. If this is the effect of the system, then 'whom one goes to school with is just as important as what happens when one gets there' (p.15), especially when the school you go to is linked with employment opportunities.

In a review of the relationship between parental choice and racism, Cumper (1994) points to two main problems. The first is a legal one. The law does not prohibit parent choice on grounds of religion – indeed, it facilitates it. But under Section 18 of the Race Relations Act 1976, an LEA must not do anything which constitutes racial discrimination. However, this is qualified in Section 41 which make clear that an act of discrimination would not be unlawful if pursued as a duty under another Act. The matter came to a head in 1991 when a High Court judge rejected the claim by the Commission for Racial Equality that Cleveland County Council acted wrongly in complying with the wishes of a parent who asked for her five-year-old daughter to be transferred from a school where 60 per cent of the children were Asian to one where almost all were white. The duty to comply with a parent's preference under the 1980 Education Act took precedence over the 1976 Race Relations Act – a ruling which was upheld in the Court of Appeal in 1992. In short, given the potential tension between parental choice and racial discrimination, the former has priority in law. Indeed, the Education Minister Michael Fallon rejoiced in the fact that the Cleveland Case was 'a victory for the right of parental choice over all others' (quoted in Cumper, 1994, pp.170–1).

The second issue which Cumper brings out is a practical one: the definition of 'discrimination'. How are transfers which are racially and culturally motivated to be distinguished? In the Cleveland Case, the parent had stated that she did not want her daughter coming home from school 'singing in Pakistani ... I just don't want her to learn this language ... I just want her to go to a school where there will be in the majority white children, not Pakistani' (quoted in Cumper, 1994, p. 165). The Commission for Racial Equality had taken the view that the parent's motives were racial, not cultural, but, as we have seen, the High Court ruled otherwise. As Cumper points out, articulate parents whose real motives are racial can easily formulate their case on cultural grounds, as happened in Dewsbury in 1987. Kirklees Education Authority had been forced, on a technicality, to allow some parents to send their children to schools which were predominantly 'white' instead of the one to which they had been allocated, where 85 per cent were Asian. Afterwards, the parents involved expressed deep hurt at the suggestions that their motives were racial, arguing that they simply wanted schools which provided a traditional Christian education.

Question for discussion

Should the law be changed so that parents cannot choose schools from racial motives? What about social class motives?

---

4. Does school choice improve standards?

One of the Government's main arguments for championing school choice is that competition in the education market will force schools to improve standards to attract more customers: 'The Government believes that school autonomy and parental choice – combined with the National Curriculum – are the keys to achieving higher standards in schools' (DfE, 1992, p.15). Much the same point was made by President Bush when he launched his 'America 2000' strategy in 1991. 'It's time parents were free to choose the schools their children attend. This approach will create the competitive climate that stimulates excellence in our private and parochial schools as well' (quoted in Sky, 1992, p.76). Another reason for the 'choice raises standards' argument is that the act of choosing will increase parental involvement in the child's education and school affairs.

The evidence to support or refute this hypothesis is not available, and indeed it could not easily be, given the difficulties of isolating the choice factor from others, such as the National Curriculum and the four-yearly inspection, both of which could have a bearing on educational standards. Moreover, schools' success can sometimes be attributed to their ability to attract the more able pupils rather than to improve their curriculum and teaching arrangements. Woods (1994), using data from the Parental and School Choice Interaction Study (PASCI) at the Open University, suggests that schools are certainly changing, and that these changes can in part be attributed to consumerism. Some changes are substantive and curricular, such as increasing the range of courses available (e.g. introducing vocational studies), more systematic policies on homework and closer links with feeder schools. There is also more evidence of structured 'environmental scanning' – finding out what influences parents' school preferences. However, Woods maintains that

> responses are limited and patchy. There is no evidence at present of major or sweeping changes in schools' central educational areas as a result of attention to parents' preferences. Indeed, it would appear that schools tend to be more willing to engage in promoting themselves than in establishing systematic means of being responsive to parents. (pp.133–134)

The argument that school choice improves educational standards presupposes that preferences are decided mainly on the basis of academic reputation. But is this so? In another paper, Woods (1993) found that while middle-class parents put a school's academic success at or very near the top of their priorities, working-class parents are more likely to consider social and personal factors. Overall, factors such as convenience for travel, the school's facilities, the school's general reputation and the child's wishes and happiness seem as or more important than standards of academic education. More recently, Hazel Pennell and Anne West (1995) found that among a sample of inner London parents, the majority maintained that exam results did not affect their choice of school. Coldron and Boulton (1991), who came to similar conclusions, argue that that 'more than anything else, parents wish their child to be happy and secure at the new school' and that this will mean concurring with the child's preferences:

> Being with friends; a safe and disciplined environment; caring teachers; proximity to home; these are criteria that are valued by parents. It is important that schools and LEAs in their increasing concern with marketing and concepts of school image, avoid a total preoccupation with academic standards. (p.178)

If, as the Government have proposed, popular schools are allowed to expand, less popular ones will have to close. Ironically, this would not only reduce choice but could endanger the popular schools maintaining their success rates with larger numbers of pupils and possibly larger classes too. On this argument, choice could endanger standards.

Question for discussion

In schools that you know, what changes have been made in response to parents' choice preferences? How much of this seems likely to improve standards?

THE FUTURE?

As a leader writer for the *Times Educational Supplement* (9 June 1995) has noted, parental choice may be controversial, but one fact is clear: the traffic tailbacks in the morning have lengthened. If the leader of the Labour Party shuns neighbourhood schools in favour of a GM school for his son, the policy of school choice is clearly here to stay no matter what party is in power. And if recent Government announcements are implemented, the school choice policy is going to be strengthened. However, the dual policies of wanting all schools to become GM and allowing GM schools to have greater freedom in their admissions could lead to 25,000 separate admission arrangements, a recipe for chaos (Dunford,1995). And for choice to be a reality, the weaker schools also need extra resources: if they are not given the means to improve, the scope for 'choice' in many areas will be reduced to the one or two 'good' schools and the others.

Some Tories would like a voucher scheme (which in 1995 became Government policy at pre-school level) to cover the 5 to 16 age-range in the state sector, even if this were to involve parents making some financial contribution. In outlining his ideas to set vouchers at rather below the average cost per pupil and allow schools to set fees above this level, Lord Skidelsky, chairman of the Social Market Foundation think-tank and professor of political economy at Warwick University, has provocatively opined: 'If John Major is serious about making the state sector so good that people will have no incentive to spend their money on private schools, the funding gap has to be narrowed' (*Guardian*, 16 March 1995).

Alongside such attempts which would confirm the trend towards Phillip Brown's 'parentocracy' (see pp.126–7), concerns remain about both the principle of school choice and its implementation; and with pupil rolls now rising nationally, competition for places in the more popular schools will be intensified. What needs to be done is to improve the chances of all sections of the community benefiting from the policy. The Labour Party (1995) wants policies 'to ensure that as many parents as possible obtain their first preference' (p.10): these would include a 'consultative partnership' whereby GM schools, the LEA and neighbouring authorities would consult to produce more homogeneous admissions criteria. Labour would also ensure that local appeal bodies are wholly independent of the LEA. However, measures such as these may need to be supplemented by ones which are designed more specifically to empower working-class parents and those from ethnic minorities, such as the possibilities outlined in Issue 2. We also need to know whether parents want choice between schools offering different wares, or whether 'there is a broad consensus of the "ideal school"' (Glatter, *et al.*, 1995, p.22).

FURTHER READING

Halstead, J. M. (ed.) *Parental Choice and Education: Principles, Policy and Practice*. London: Kogan Page.

Organisation for Economic Co-operation and Development (1994) *School: A Matter of Choice*. Paris: OECD.

REFERENCES

Almond, B. (1994) 'In defence of choice in education', in J.M. Halstead (ed.) *Parental Choice and Education: Principles, Policy and Practice*. London: Kogan Page.

Ball, S., Bowe, R. and Gewirtz, S. (1992) *Circuits of Schooling: A Sociological Exploration of Parental Choice of School in Social Class Contexts*. Swindon: Economic and Social Research Council.

Brain, J. and Klein, R. (1994) *Parental Choice: Myth or Reality?* Bath: Centre for the Analysis of Social Policy, University of Bath.

Brown, P. (1994) 'Education and the ideology of parentocracy', in J.M. Halstead (ed.) *Parental Choice and Education: Principles, Policy and Practice*. London: Kogan Page.

Coldron, J. and Boulton, P. (1991) '"Happiness" as a criterion of parents' choice of school', *Journal of Education Policy*, 6, 169–178.

Cumper, P. (1994) 'Racism, parental choice and the law', in J. M. Halstead (ed.) *Parental Choice and Education: Principles, Policy and Practice*. London: Kogan Page.

Department of Education and Science (1991) *The Parent's Charter: You and Your Child's Education*. London: DES.

Department for Education (1993) *Our Children's Education: The Up-dated Parent's Charter.* London: DfE.

Department for Education (1992) *Choice and Diversity: A New Framework for Schools.* London: HMSO.

Department for Education (1993) *Your Child's Next School: A Guide to Secondary School Admissions.* London: DfE.

Dunford, J. (1995) 'A recipe for chaos', *Times Educational Supplement*, 22 September.

Halstead, J. M. (1994) 'Accountability and values', in D. Scott (ed.) *Accountability and Control in Educational Settings.* London: Cassell.

Jowett, S. (1995) *Allocating Secondary School Places.* Slough: NFER.

Organisation for Economic Co-operation and Development (1994) *School: A Matter of Choice.* Paris: OECD.

Pennell, H. and West, A. (1995) *Changing Schools: Secondary Schools' Admission Policies in Inner London in 1995.* London: Centre for Educational Research, London School of Economics and Political Science.

Sky, T. (1992) 'Open enrolment legislation in the States and the United Kingdom: some comparative notes', *Education and the Law*, 4, 75–85.

Smith, T. and Noble, M. (1995) *Education Divides: Poverty and Schooling in the 1990s.* London: Child Action Poverty Group.

Walford, G. (1994) 'Weak choice, strong choice and the new Christian schools', in J.M. Halstead (ed.) *Parental Choice and Education: Principles, Policy and Practice.* London: Kogan Page.

White, P. (1994) 'Parental choice and education for citizenship', in J. M. Halstead (ed.) *Parental Choice and Education: Principles, Policy and Practice.* London: Kogan Page.

Woods, P. (1993) 'Parental perspectives on choice in the United Kingdom: preliminary thoughts on meanings and realities of choice in education'. Paper presented at the annual meeting of the American Educational Research Association, Atlanta.

Woods, P. (1994) 'School responses to the quasi-market', in J.M. Halstead (ed.) *Parental Choice and Education: Principles, Policy and Practice.* London: Kogan Page.

Part IV

MANAGEMENT POLICY

CHAPTER 11

School Management and Funding

Helen Johnson

INTRODUCTION

It is clear that what is expected of teachers in English and Welsh schools is now very different from what was regarded as their role as recently as ten or fifteen years ago. Their autonomy in terms of pedagogical practice has been structured and contained – some would argue curtailed – by Government policy in respect of what is to be taught, perhaps even how it is to be taught, and the success of this process is to be evaluated by governmentally prescribed pupil assessment and school inspection. But something else has happened to the role of the teacher. This pedagogical activity has been placed in a new context in terms of administrative structure, practice and funding. The teacher, whether a seasoned head or new entrant to the profession, is now to be seen not solely as a teacher but as a proactive manager of resources. The era of the teacher-manager has arrived.

The dramatic and very recent nature of this change can be seen by a quick visit to any university or good public library. The researcher will find a shortage of books about educational, especially financial, management that predate the watershed year of 1988. Any books before that date will tend to be directed at the administrator in the local education authority or in central Government, or for those occasional headteachers who sought clarification about some of the decisions that others had made about their schools. In contrast, from 1988 onwards, many books tackling educational management topics are to be found. Although some books have an academic interest, there are many that have a highly practical, everyday flavour. These books seek to help and support practitioners in what now has to be done in their new role as managers.

In tracing the background to the present funding policy, it should first be noted that state provision of education is comparatively recent. Prior to the nineteenth century, two-thirds of children in England and Wales received no formal education. Central Government was reluctant to interfere with the voluntary activity of private charitable bodies, but eventually felt compelled to make some gesture to indicate its concern. In 1833 this took the form of grants to assist the work of the two main voluntary bodies, the non-conformist British and Foreign Schools Society and the Anglican National Society. These societies received grants of a mere £10,000 each (Pile, 1979). As an indication of Governmental priorities and attitudes, in the same year British slave owners were awarded £20 million 'compensation' on the emancipation of their slaves.

It was not until Forster's Education Act of 1870 that education became regarded as a public service. This was in response to pressure for compulsory education from both trade unions and employers in the face of international, especially German, competition. From earlier Governmental reluctance to become involved, we reach unapologetic intervention. Forster himself urged the House of Commons to pass the 1870 Bill in the following terms: 'Upon this speedy provision of education depends also our national power'.

At a local level, school boards were established for each district, with the power to raise rates and build schools where voluntary provision was lacking. This emphasis on local control was reinforced by Balfour's Education Act of 1902 which put board schools under the control of borough or county councils. They were authorised to establish secondary and technical schools as well as develop the existing elementary schools. Fisher's Act in 1918 extended the range of ancillary (e.g. medical) services to be provided by local authorities. The same Act also formalised the relationship between central and local government, and introduced order into the confused system of central grant aid for local expenditure.

After World War II a Ministry of Education was established with far wider powers than its predecessor, the Board of Education. Under the terms of the landmark Education Act of 1944, local education authorities were set up 'to provide a varied and comprehensive education service' as appropriate to local circumstances. Charged with this task, it is not surprising that LEAs became one of the dominant institutions in educational policy-making and provision for the next forty years and they held tight control over the distribution of financial and other resources.

The debate on an open, national scale about the effectiveness of the English school system picked up considerable momentum with the intervention of a Labour Prime Minister, James Callaghan, who, in his famous speech at Ruskin College in October 1976, opened the debate on accountability in education. There were also the 'Black Papers' about education in which writers such as C.B. Cox and A.E. Dyson lead what Stephen Ball (1990) has called a 'discourse of derision' about the academic standards within the state system of schools, and attacked the professional competence and alleged political motivations of teachers. Both sides of the political divide contributed to a general public disquiet about the quality of the school system in the face of the ever-increasing amount of public funds spent on the nation's schools. (Contrary to some public perceptions, Government spending on education has increased. In 1987–88 education expenditure accounted for 4.7 per cent of GDP; five years later, it accounted for 5.4 per cent (Jackson and Lavender, 1994).

These concerns revolved around many factors. The most important were:

- the perceived underachievement of pupils
- the absence of standardised tests by which children's progress could be objectively monitored
- a curriculum perceived as unsatisfactory, irrelevant or varying in standards and opportunities offered, at least in part, depending on local education authority and even between schools in the same locality

Behind these criticisms, however, there was a deeper discontent. The schools system was seen as unresponsive and unaccountable to parents, having been captured by its 'producers' – that is teachers and other educational professionals. LEAs in particular were seen as too bureaucratic and perhaps with political agendas of their own that might be in conflict with central Government and, importantly, with the wishes and demands of parents for whom little or no choice was offered concerning the schools that their children attended. All in all, there was a public perception of a highly bureaucratised system that ran primarily for its own benefit. This view was certainly held among the New Right that was then gaining ground in the Conservative Party.

Given the accumulation of power and activities at LEA level by the late 1970s, the changes introduced by the Thatcher Government can seem – whether or not we agree with them – only the more remarkable. As part of her project, many of the institutions of the post-war political consensus about an interventionist role for Government both within the field of education and beyond have been dismantled or significantly redesigned. A country accustomed and conditioned to expect incremental, evolving adjustment in the public domain has experienced a radical and systematic New Right project to bring about fundamental changes in the relationships between the state institutions and its citizens.

Other national educational systems, especially in Australia, New Zealand, Canada, the Netherlands and the USA, have experienced similar changes in response to similar criticisms. According to Levacic (1992, p.17), the new organisational form had one or more of the following characteristics:

- decentralised decision-making and delegated budgeting at school level
- allocating the school's budget by formula and not by administrative discretion
- giving parents the opportunity to exercise choice of school, while making the school's budget determined mainly by the number of pupils enrolled
- the school is managed by a council or governing body with direct community representation.

THE POLICY

Local Management of Schools and formula funding

The Education Reform Act 1988 introduced the Local Management of Schools (LMS) scheme, the aim of which is to achieve the maximum delegation of financial resources to schools. Brent Davies (1990)uses a useful analogy:

KEY POINTS

- Local Management of Schools and formula funding
- The Education Reform Act 1988 as a watershed in educational administration and management
- The grant-maintained school as an 'independent business'
- A Common Funding Formula piloted
- Vouchers for pre-school education

> The LEA acts as the landlord responsible for capital expenditure, as represented by the school building and major structural work, while the school is responsible as the tenant for everything that goes on inside … The school therefore has in its budget funds for teachers' salaries and other staffing costs, equipment and books, heating and lighting, rates, examination fees and all internal maintenance associated with normal 'wear and tear'. (p.45)

The LEA no longer directs how much a school should allocate for items like those mentioned. It is for the school itself to decide how to set its priorities and to spend accordingly. In this way, the school positions itself in the market to attract pupils – and, as funding follows pupils, so determine its income. The introduction of needs-based formula-funding and the delegation of financial and managerial responsibilities to governing bodies are key elements in Government's overall policy to be accountable and responsive to parents and to improve the quality of teaching and learning in schools.

Funds are delegated on the basis of an LMS formula designed by the LEA. From the start, the Department of Education and Science (in Circular 7/88) insisted that each LEA formula, had to be:

- simple, clear and predictable
- based on an assessment of schools' objective needs, rather than historic patterns of expenditure
- determined mainly by the number of pupils, weighted for their difference in age, but also taking account of the additional costs of pupils with special needs and of maintaining the curriculum in small schools.

The DES also recognised that LEAs might wish to take into account other factors such as the socio-economic characteristics of school intake. Some items of expenditure – for instance premature retirement and dismissal costs and the administrative cost of statementing – were listed as 'mandatory exceptions' and could not be delegated to schools. For some other items ('discretionary exceptions') – for instance, pupil support and governors' insurances – the LEA could choose whether to delegate to schools.

The Education Reform Act 1988 can be seen as a watershed in the administration of schools in England and Wales. In educational, managerial and political terms it sits at the opposite end of the continuum to its highly influential predecessor of 1944. Effectively the all-powerful local education authority was dismantled as the management of the schools in its area was devolved to the schools themselves in the form of their governing bodies, who were now motivated to be more responsive to the school's customers.

However, with this delegation of managerial powers away from the LEA came an increasing centralisation of policy-making and pedagogical strategy, with central Government now very much in control. As is discussed in other chapters of this book, complementary initiatives have included the introduction of a National Curriculum, open enrolment, teacher appraisal, Records of Achievement, pupil testing and league tables of public examination results. With the overall depowering of local government and with the introduction of these initiatives, central Government has been able to implement its own political and educational agendas more effectively than in an earlier era when it might have been faced with a recalcitrant local education authority with a mind, purpose and a policy of its own.

So we arrive at a point where schools are now encouraged to compete against each other for pupils; and, since the funding follows the pupil, the good school will drive out the bad. Education is no longer to be producer-dominated; a quasi-market in education has been set up and customers have been empowered in various ways to make choices.

The major powers of the LEA, save for some important coordinating duties such as in special educational needs, were finally taken away by the Education Act 1993, specifically by Clause 1, which removed the reference in Section 1 of the 1944 Act to national policy being executed by LEAs under the 'control and direction' of the Education Secretary.

The grant-maintained school as an 'independent business'

This devolving/centralising tendency in education management is now well established and is seemingly going to continue. An important example of this is the grant-maintained school. There are few issues in the field of education or elsewhere where opinions fall neatly into either 'for' or 'against' categories. However, the Conservative Government's policy on grant-maintained schools would seem to be one of the few that allows no middle ground. As Davies and Anderson (1992) have noted, the grant-maintained school is effectively a small business. It is free to manage its day-to-day running and long-term future in a way decided by its governing body, and, most importantly of all, it has total control over the annual maintenance grant that it receives from the central funding body, the Funding Agency for Schools (FAS), since it is outside the control of the local education authority, which previously was the recipient, distributor and controller of those funds.

The calculation of the annual maintenance grant is based, for the moment at least, on the same LEA's LMS formula as it would have been had the school remained within the LEA umbrella. However, GM schools receive extra funding (now determined on an LEA-to-LEA basis) in respect of central LEA costs which are passed on to the school. These are meant to cover services such as personnel, payroll, educational psychology and in-service training, but in practice GM schools receive more for the loss of these services than their actual cost. So the figures of grant per pupil cannot be directly compared between LEA schools and grant-maintained schools within the same locality.

Despite this extra funding plus generous capital and special purposes grants (GM schools in England in 1994/95 received 14.1 per cent of total capital spending on schools although they account for only 5.6 per cent of schools), the policy has had a mixed success. By May 1995 only 1065 schools out of over 24,000 had opted out of LEA control. In November 1995, the Government proposed a 'fast track' for church schools seeking GM status; but according to a report in the *Times Educational Supplement* (17 November 1995), the churches were angry that their schools had been singled out to boost the number of GM schools. In the face of these protests, the proposal did not appear in the Queen's Speech which outlined the Government's legislative programme for the 1995-96 parliamentary session. Once again in the story of the grant-maintained scheme it is necessary to watch this space!

In its recent policy document *Diversity and Excellence*, the Labour Party (1995) seemingly moved its position by retaining grant-maintained schools, though the Funding Agency would be abolished and the schools would be given a new name, Foundation Schools, with funding routed through LEAs and made 'equitable' for all schools in the community. Meanwhile, the Government has a declared aim to develop a consistent basis for funding grant-maintained schools on a long-term basis. In a first move towards the development of a common funding formula for all grant-maintained schools, the Government initiated a pilot scheme with five LEAs (Bromley, Calderdale, Essex, Gloucestershire and Hillingdon) in 1994–95. This pilot has recently been expanded to include a further 16 LEAs in 1995–96 for areas which have more than 30 per cent of pupils in grant-maintained schools.

Vouchers

As progress is made to a common funding formula (and perhaps at some point a national funding formula), vouchers as a funding mechanism are perennially popular with New Right commentators. The idea behind them is apparently simple and takes devolvement of funding to its logical conclusion, with the Government issuing credit notes to parents for the education of their children. The New Right find this concept attractive because it gives parents the financial means to choose the school, whether in the private or state sector, that they really want for their children. Once again, market forces will decide which schools remain in the market and which ones fail and so exit from it. Vouchers now have their advocates in the ranks of the Labour Party too, where they are seen as an egalitarian device.

In July 1995, the Secretary of State for Education announced a £1 billion voucher scheme for nursery education, and the subsequent Queen's Speech announced an Education Bill that would give the parents of every four-year-old the right to a nursery place – envisaged to be worth £1,100 – to secure a pre-school place from April 1997. The scheme's reception has been mixed, and only four local authorities have agreed to participate in the pilot scheme. However, this policy move may be an indication that vouchers are being actively considered for other areas of education provision, for example, 16- to 19-year-olds in further education, and university students.

ISSUES FOR DEBATE

1. Is there fairness in a funding formula system?

The Audit Commission, which was set up as a non–departmental public body in 1983 to appoint and regulate the external audit of all local authorities in England and Wales, has an important role in ensuring that public funds are spent appropriately and well in education. In its 1993 publication *Adding up the Sums 2*, the Commission made the following point:

> Local authorities have some discretion over the composition of their funding formulae and over the size of the total budgets from which individual schools' budgets are drawn. Schools of the same size and with pupils of the same ages but located in different parts of the country may therefore receive different amounts of money. This can also apply to schools within the same local education authority. Local authorities also have some discretion over the proportion of the schools' budget which they delegate to schools. This also explains some of the differences in funding and the amount of delegated budget per pupil. (p.37)

So it is clear that within this 'discretion' there can be unfairness. How can neighbouring schools compete, for example, if one receives more funds than the other?

Yet the issue of 'unfairness' is more complicated than this. Rosalind Levacic (1995), a leading researcher in this area, argues that although formula funding makes the rules for distributing school budgets transparent, it seems that 'socially and educationally disadvantaged pupils have received proportionally less resourcing as a consequence of local management' (p.145). Using evidence from the LMS Initiative (1992), she notes that schools with a higher than average number of pupils with special educational needs have experienced more than a ten per cent budget loss. She goes on to note, however, that Sheffield spent between £170 and £350 more on inner-city schools, showing that, given the political will, schools can still be differentially funded because of social and educational disadvantage. The issue is, of course, whether the political commitment is there so to do. Some schools have also allegedly turned down non-statemented pupils with special educational needs since they are regarded as potentially more expensive. Moreover, because the formula for funding staff salaries is based not on actual cost but on an 'average salary' figure, what are the educational and managerial implications when older and more experienced teachers are 'too expensive' to employ?

Question for discussion

Can school funding be 'fair' if it is also to be 'simple, clear and predictable'?

2. Are schools managing their funds effectively?

Once again, the Audit Commission (1993) exposes the pertinent issues:

> If locally managed schools have balances of income over expenditure at the end of the financial year, they may carry these forward to the next financial year. Schools should not run into deficit at the end of the year, but occasionally this happens. Local authorities generally require schools to make good such deficits from the following year's budget. (p.18)

But does not this place a tremendous responsibility on school governors? Given the recent events in Warwickshire in 1995, where governors set deficit budgets, and resignations from governing bodies throughout the country that year, the situation is potentially serious.

Another issue in this area is the very contentious one of schools holding large balances 'just in case'. There has been much discussion in the educational press about this – but it does seem that the Department for Education and Employment has no powers to instruct schools to manage their funds more effectively. Levacic (1995) noted that in 1993 only 9 per cent of schools had run into the red and that financial reserves were 5 per cent of the budget in primary schools and 3.5 per cent in secondary schools. She goes on to comment:

> Apart from accumulating savings for a large capital project, the holding of excessively large balances means that resources have not been used for the educational benefit of the children for whom the funds were allocated by central and local Government. (p.157)

This is a telling point in educational terms. Could it be, as Levacic herself suggests, that schools are being financially prudent by 'saving' funds that might be needed in the future to pay teachers' salaries in case of future cut-backs by the Government? In this instance, we see an interesting clash between educational and financial values.

Question for discussion

With levels of funding being tightly held down, what set of values should take precedence – and what set is likely to?

3. Is devolved management improving the quality of education ?

The work of two Australians, Caldwell and Spinks, was very influential in the devising and implementing of the LMS policy. Their international best seller *The Self-Managing School* (1988) sets out a model of self-management for schools based on a cycle of six stages which are explicitly linked to educational improvements:

1. goal-setting and need identification

2. policy-making, with policies consisting of statements of purpose and broad guidelines for action in achieving those purposes
3. planning for programmes of learning and the support of learning, including the setting of priorities
4. preparation and approval of budgets for each programme in the school
5. implementing the learning and teaching programmes of the school
6. evaluation of the programmes.

Importantly, Caldwell and Spinks emphasise that LMS is not primarily about finance but about better education through improved management at the local level. They argue that the headteacher's role as an educational leader, far from being diminished and reduced to mere 'bean counting', is enhanced. All teachers in a school can be involved in decisions relating to their subjects, focus and expertise. Here we return to the point made at the beginning of the chapter about the emergence of the teacher-manager.

But what has been the actual experience in England? Rosalind Levacic (1992) found that the initial impact of LMS was determined, not surprisingly, on whether the school lost or gained resources under the funding formula. (Caldwell himself had said that this shift in the pattern of management requires five to ten years for successful implementation.). She goes on to say that there was a 'need for integrated financial, staff and curriculum planning and greater managerial responsibilities for headteachers in terms of developing management structures and processes for undertaking whole-school planning, implementation and review' (p. 26). But perhaps importantly she did note that some school staff had less time for class contact because of managerial functions. What are the educational implications of this? Could increasing numbers of teachers with managerial responsibilities become detached from 'where it's really at' in the classroom?

Question for discussion

Is the emergence of the teacher–manager likely to improve the quality of education?

---

4. Has the LEA coordinating and strategic role been missed ?

Much has been made of the bureaucratic nature of the 'old' LEA . It displayed, so it is argued in some quarters, the classic symptoms of dysfunctional behaviour in which officers showed a certain rigidity in their actions, following the rules for their own sake and being suspicious of the new and innovative. At an operational level most heads are now seemingly content with LMS, and there is considerable anecdotal evidence that few, if any, heads would wish to return to tight managerial controls from the LEA.

But what at the strategic level? Planning for school places does remain with the LEAs (save where the number of grant-maintained schools means that this responsibility is shared with the FAS or assumed by it entirely. There are other indications that schools are voluntarily looking to the LEA to buy from it certain specialist services (e.g. personnel management) or for support and assistance in the area of quality. The interventionist role of the LEAs has clearly gone forever in most if not all LEAs. However, if paternalism has gone out of fashion and is unmissed, it would seem that more collaborative, equal relationships are now being established between the 'reformed' LEA and the increasingly self-managing schools. Can the 'new' LEA develop a meaningful role, not as a 'controller' but a critical and supportive friend?

Question for discussion

If LEAs were abolished, would the quality of education be likely to suffer?

---

5. Is there a lack of democratic accountability by the FAS and other educational quangos?

As we have seen, grant-maintained schools are funded by the FAS. This is a quango (a quasi–autonomous, non-governmental organisation) and as such operates at 'arm's length' from central Government. A quango is an administrative body, whose board comprises unelected appointees approved by the appropriate Secretary of State. It has emerged as a feature of current British public administration. Education has its share of these quangos, which cover a wide range of activities from funding to inspection of schools.

It is clear that quangos carry many issues with them, including administrative and constitutional ones: On what basis are quango board members selected and paid? How do quangos make their decisions? How much do they shape policy? And most importantly of all, to whom are they accountable? As would be expected, the FAS is accountable to the Public Accounts Committee of the House of Commons. But what is its actual accountability to its customers at the local level, to grant-maintained schools themselves and to parents? This question is far-reaching and raises serious issues about policy-making and implementation in a democracy.

According to a recent report, Britain now has one quango for every 10,000 people. By May 1994, there were 5,521 of these, Government-appointed agencies and 65,000 unelected public appointees, whereas there are 25,000 elected councillors in the whole of the UK (*Guardian*, 2 September 1995). Public debate is becoming increasingly anxious about the proliferation of quangos, which, as Roy Pryke, the Director of Education in Kent, argued recently, make their decisions privately, untroubled by public observation of quite what does and does not go on. Quangos can be seen as an administrative device that not only implement policy but, in the manner of that implementation, shape and perhaps even create policy outside the usual system of democratic checks and controls.

Why does this matter? As we have seen, much of the criticism levelled at the public sector, including education, was seemingly made to justify the reforms of the Conservative Government. These criticisms were focused on the institutions of educational policy-making themselves, almost totally at local level: on the dysfunctional behaviour of bureaucrats in their supposed service of the public;

on the lack of genuine democratic control over elected members and bureaucrats; and finally and not least, on the prescriptions rather than choices offered to the public. There was a consistent and potent attack on the paternalistic, controlling, self-interested activities of local education authority bureaucracy which was alleged to deny parents the schools of their choice and responses to their other demands.

The strategy to address these criticisms has meant considerable structural reform to take away the powers the LEA enjoyed and to give them to schools and quangos. In so doing there would seem to be a return to the almost *ad hoc* nature of educational administration that preceded the unifying Education Act 1944 Act that put most administration under the control of the local education authorities. Has one unaccountable, dysfunctional bureaucracy, the LEA, merely been replaced by others, the FAS and other quangos, that make no attempt to be democratically accountable?

Question for discussion

Does the criticism that quangos lack democratic accountability mean that their responsibilities should be given back to the LEAs?

THE FUTURE?

As mentioned in the first section of the chapter, there are issues on the horizon in terms of funding mechanisms: the common funding formula is currently (1995) being piloted, a national funding formula may be on the cards, and the issue of vouchers has moved from debate to pilot schemes and national policy. What is perhaps significant is that the policies offered as alternatives by the Labour and Liberal Democrat Parties seemingly accept almost *in toto* the new structures brought about by local management of schools reforms.

It is clear that the area of schools management and funding, far from being the exclusive domain of 'bean counters' in grey suits, hosts a debate that is endless. This is unsurprising as the discussion raises all kinds of managerial, technical, political, constitutional and ethical questions, each of which have impact in the real world of schools and pupils.

FURTHER READING

Bush, T. C. M. and Glover, D. (1993) *Managing Autonomous Schools: The Grant-Maintained Experience*. London: Chapman.

Caldwell, B. and Spinks, J. (1988) *The Self-Managing School*. London: Falmer.

Davies, B. and Anderson, L. (1992) *Opting for Self-Management: Early Experiences of the Grant-Maintained School*. London: Routledge.

Johnson, H. and Riley, K. A. (1995) 'Education quangos', in F. Ridley (ed.) *Quangos*. Oxford: Oxford University Press.

Knight, B. (1993) *Financial Management for Schools: The Thinking Manager's Guide*. Oxford: Heinemann.

Levacic, R. (1995) *Local Management of Schools*. Buckingham: Open University Press.

REFERENCES

Audit Commission (1993) *Adding up the Sums 2: Comparative Information for Schools.* London: HMSO.

Ball, S. J. (1990) *Politics and Policy Making in Education.* London: Routledge.

Caldwell, B. and Spinks, J. (1988) *The Self-Managing School.* London: Falmer.

Davies, B. (1990) 'Resource management in schools', in B. Davies, L. Ellison, A. Osborne and J. West-Burham (eds) *Education Management for the 1990s.* Harlow: Longman.

Davies, B. and Anderson, L. (1992) *Opting for Self-Management: Early Experiences of the Grant-Maintained School.* London: Routledge.

Jackson, P. and Lavender, M. (1994) *The Public Services Yearbook 1994.* London: CIPFA, Public Finance Foundation, and Chapman and Hall.

Labour Party (1995) *Diversity and Excellence.* London: Labour Party.

Levacic, R. (1992) 'Local management of schools: aims, scope and impact', *Educational Management and Administration,* 20, 16–29.

Levacic, R. (1995) *Local Management of Schools: Analysis and Practice.* Buckingham: Open University Press.

LMS Initiative (1992) *Local Management of Schools: A Practical Guide.* London: LMS Initiative.

Pile, W. (1979) *The Department of Education and Science.* London: Allen and Unwin.

Pryke, R. (1994) 'Early experience of the FAS has been positive, but will it last?', *Education,* 1 July.

Sheffield City Council Education Department (1992) *Resourcing Sheffield Schools.* Sheffield: Sheffield City Council.

CHAPTER 12

School Governance

Michael Creese and Peter Earley

INTRODUCTION

Not the least significant of the changes which have taken place over the past ten years have been those in the composition and responsibilities of school governing bodies. These changes have largely been driven by a belief in the power of the market place and the voice of the consumer to raise standards. As part of this shift towards a consumer-led system of education there has been a reduction in the powers and influence of Local Education Authorities (LEAs). Teachers now find themselves accountable to, and dependent upon the decisions of, part-time unpaid volunteers (not professional Education Officers and elected Councillors). These changes have not been entirely without criticism. For example, speakers at the Annual Conference of the National Association of Head Teachers in 1995 drew attention to the increasing number of suspensions of headteachers by governing bodies and to anecdotal evidence of the interference by some governors in the day to day management of the school.

The 1944 Education Act made it a statutory requirement that all mainstream schools should have a Board of Managers (primary) or a Board of Governors (secondary). In the case of the secondary schools all of the governors were to be appointed by the LEA and in primary schools one third were appointed by the Minor Authority (that is the District or Parish Council where one existed) and the remainder by the LEA. Schools could be grouped together under one governing body and this – together with the largely party political nature of the appointment of governors in at least some parts of the country – led in time to governing bodies being seen as largely irrelevant to the life and work of the school.

The side-lining of governing bodies led to power being increasingly centred in the hands of headteachers and LEA officials. Growing demands during the 1960s for more parental accountability led to the setting up of the Taylor Committee in 1975. Their report recommended, amongst other things, that every school should have its own governing body, and the 1986 Education Act put many of the recommendations of that report into effect. The 1988 and subsequent Education Acts have given governing bodies considerably increased responsibilities, perhaps the most significant of these being the management of the school's budget.

THE POLICY

KEY POINTS

- The change in the composition of governing bodies
- The increased responsibilities given to governing bodies
- The increased accountability of governing bodies
- The increased accountability of teachers to the governing body

The change in the composition of governing bodies

The Taylor Report (1977) recommended that the membership of governing bodies should consist of equal numbers of local authority representatives, school staff, parents (with, where appropriate, pupils) and representatives of the local community, with never fewer than two members in any one category. The report's recommendations were largely implemented in the 1986 Education Act, although the proportion of teacher representation was significantly reduced due to a concern about the possible teacher domination of governing bodies. The composition of county, controlled and mainstream special schools is currently regulated by Section 3 of the Education (No 2) Act of 1986 and is dependent upon the size of the school (Table 12.1). Governors serve a four-year term of office.

Table 12.1 The composition of governing bodies in county schools under the 1986 Education Act

Pupil roll	Number of governors				
	Parents	LEA	Teacher	Co-opted*	Total
Fewer than 99	2	2	1	3	8
100–299	3	3	1	4	11
300–599	4	4	2	5	15
Over 600	5	5	2	6	18

*In county and controlled primary schools, where a Parish or District Council has the right to appoint a governor, the number of co-opted governors is reduced by one.

Co-opted governors are chosen by the other governors who are expected to ensure that the governing body reflects a balance of interests. In particular the local business community is to be represented by co-option or otherwise. The headteacher may choose whether or not to become a governor. Most currently opt to serve; a recent national survey found that eight out of ten headteachers are governors of their schools (Earley, 1994). In the case of controlled schools (most of which are religious foundations) Foundation governors replace the majority of co-opted governors. For aided and special agreement schools there are the Foundation governors, the head if serving, and at least one of each of the following: a governor appointed by the LEA, a parent, a teacher (two in schools with more than 300 pupils) and a governor appointed by the Minor Authority where one exists.

The governing body of a grant-maintained school is made up as follows:

- The headteacher (who must serve, as opposed to those in LEA schools who have a choice)
- One or two elected teacher-governors (this is a matter of choice and does not depend upon the size of the school)
- Five elected parent-governors
- A number of other appointed governors (First or Foundation governors) who must outnumber the other governors by at least one. This group must include representation of the business community and at least two members who have children in the school at the time of their appointment.

The term of office for First or Foundation governors is between five and seven years while the term of office for elected governors is four years. The governing body is responsible for filling vacancies amongst the First/Foundation governors as they occur.

The increased responsibilities given to governing bodies

According to the Department for Education and the Office for Standards in Education, governing bodies have three main roles (BIS/DFE/Ofsted, 1995). The first is to provide a strategic overview and to set, and keep under review, the broad framework within which the headteachers and staff should run the school. Secondly, the governing body should act as a critical friend, supporting the school while at the same time monitoring and evaluating the school's effectiveness. Finally, the governing body is responsible for ensuring good quality education. Accountability is ensured through reports by the headteacher and staff on the school's performance.

Specifically, the responsibilities of governing bodies are now as follows:

- helping to establish (with the head) the aims and policies of the school, and how the standards of education can be improved
- deciding the conduct of the school, that is, how in general terms, it should be run
- helping to draw up (with the head and staff) the school development plan which sets out the school's priorities for development in the coming year
- helping to decide how to spend the school's budget
- making sure that the National Curriculum and Religious Education are taught
- selecting the head
- appointing, promoting, supporting and disciplining other staff
- acting as a link between the local community and the school
- drawing up an action plan after an Ofsted inspection, and monitoring how the plan is put into practice
- in the case of LEA schools, considering once a year whether or not to ballot parents about applying for grant-maintained status. (DfE, 1994, p.15)

Although some of the responsibilities may be delegated (and nearly all governing bodies now operate with a system of committees and/or working parties to cope with the additional workload) many cannot, and must remain the responsibility of the governing body as a whole. It is important to note that the responsibilities are vested in the governing body as a whole. Individual governors have no power unless responsibility has been specifically delegated to them.

The increased accountability of governing bodies

At the same time as governors have been given wider powers, they have also, in theory at least, been made more accountable to the community and in particular to parents. The 1986 Education Act requires that the governing body publish an annual report to parents which will explain how the governing body has put into practice its plans for the school during the previous year. The governing body must also hold a meeting at least once a year at which parents may discuss the governors' annual report and any other relevant matters, such as the progress made on the points covered in the Action Plan produced following an Ofsted inspection. The report of an Ofsted inspection of the school will also refer specifically to the work of the governing body. Under the section 'Leadership and Management', inspectors should include an evaluation of the effectiveness of the governing body in fulfilling its legal responsibilities and the leadership provided by the governing body, headteacher and other staff in positions of responsibility (Ofsted, 1995).

The increased accountability of teachers to the governing body.

The idea that the school should be accountable to the governing body and through the governors to the local community and especially parents has regained ground in recent years. Staff have been made more accountable to governors in two ways. First of all, governors now have much more information available to them about the performance of their school and, for comparison, of other schools in the neighbourhood. Secondly, every governing body and its sub-groups receive regular reports from the head and other staff. The broadsheet *Governing Bodies and Effective Schools*, produced jointly by the Department for Education, the Office for Standards in Education and the Banking Information Service in 1995, points to ensuring accountability as one of the three main roles of the governing body: 'The governing body is responsible for ensuring good quality education in the school. ... It is not the role of governors simply to rubber-stamp every decision of the headteacher' (p.2).

'League tables' are now published which set out pupils' performance in terms of percentage GCSE and A–level pass rates of every secondary school together with attendance/truancy tables. As the programme of testing of National Curriculum subjects at the Key Stages when pupils are aged 7, 11, and 13 gets under way, these results too will be published. The report of an Ofsted inspection has to be made freely available to parents (as does the resulting Action Plan) and to any member of the general public who requests a copy, and schools are required to distribute copies to a number of local bodies.

The governing body now decides on the number of staff to be employed in the school, though the scope for decision-making is severely constrained by tight school budgets. In grant-maintained and aided schools, the governing body is the employer. Although the LEA remains the legal employer of the teachers in county and controlled schools, when a vacancy occurs the LEA must appoint the teacher selected by the governors unless the candidate fails to meet the legal requirements (qualifications and health) or is barred from teaching. In the case of the appointment of a headteacher, the Chief Education Officer or a representative can offer advice to the governing body which they must consider, but the final decision is the governors' alone. The governors must review the point on the salary scale at which the head and deputies are paid every year and they must also assess annually the points total available for above-scale posts. The governing body is also responsible for setting out disciplinary rules and procedures for staff and can decide (after proper process) to dismiss or make redundant a teacher.

ISSUES FOR DEBATE

1. How representative are governors of the community which they serve ?

Governing bodies form an important link in the system of democratic accountability in this country. They are seen as a means through which the producer, the school, is to be made responsive to the consumer, that is the parent, or perhaps more correctly, the child. Thus the governing body represents the community in calling the school to account for its actions (being representative *of*), but also provides a mechanism through which the community may be involved in deciding upon the school's policy on key issues (being representative *at*). However, Deem (1992) has pointed out that democracy, accountability and notions of active citizenship all imply that those involved in governing schools should include a cross-section of the population. In 1984 Kogan and his team found that the majority of governors came from the middle class, and similar findings have emerged from more recent national surveys (Keys and Fernandes, 1990; Earley, 1994). However, as Thody (1989) notes:

> The unequal spread of representation could be seen as a failure of democracy but it is a feature common to all attempts to extend stakeholder participation. Participation in public life is undertaken by classes with fairly high incomes and levels of education because their social background leads them to expect to undertake such service. (p.145)

There are issues of gender and race as well as class in the composition of governing bodies. Overall there are approximately equal numbers of male and female governors (Keys and Fernandes, 1990; Earley, 1994), but in secondary schools about 60 per cent of the governors are male. Streatfield and Jefferies (1989) found that among co-opted governors about two-thirds are male, suggesting that ensuring gender parity on the governing body is not a prime consideration when making co-options. The number of non-white governors across the country is very small – around two per cent. Deem and her co-workers (1992) found in their sample of ten schools that where governing bodies had set up Finance Committees (which often wield considerable influence), these committees were dominated by white men.

Question for discussion

How might governing bodies be made more representative of the communities which they serve?

---

2. How far are governors capable of fulfilling the role expected of them?

The new model for the relationship between governing body and school sees the governors as the board of directors, with the headteacher as the managing director and the parents as shareholders. This analogy is borrowed directly from the business world but, although there are some similarities, there are also considerable differences. Governors have to work within the limits set down by national and local government; they do not, for instance, have complete freedom over their total budget or over teachers' pay scales. Governors are unpaid volunteers, doing the job in their spare time with little in the way of administrative support. Working closely with the head and staff of the school, governors often find the support aspect of their role, as suggested in the BIS/DfE/Ofsted broadsheet (1995), much easier to perform than the monitoring.

During the 1960s and 1970s the role of school governor was perceived as something of a sinecure, albeit unpaid. As we have seen, legislation has since changed all that. Governing bodies typically now meet five times over the school year, with most meetings lasting about three hours (Earley, 1994). In addition almost all governing bodies have set up committees or working parties to handle matters such as finance, and governors can expect to serve on at least one of these. The conscientious governor will also wish to visit the school on a regular basis in order to meet the staff and to see the school in action, as well as undertaking governor training. It is no wonder that some governors complain about the time which they spend on governance or resign because they feel themselves unable to do the job properly. About two-thirds of governors take time off work to undertake their governing duties (some five hours per term) and 58 per cent of them received their normal pay for this time (Earley, 1994). However, although the law requires employers to give governors time off in order to undertake duties connected with governance, they are not entitled to time off with pay. This in itself makes it difficult for some people to be governors.

The extent to which governors are able to fulfil their role is still to a large extent dependent on the attitude of the staff and in particular of the headteacher. Governors may be constrained in their role by the way in which meetings of the governing body are conducted. It may also be very difficult for governors to obtain the necessary detailed information which they would need to offer alternative views to the teachers' interpretation of what is happening in the school and/or the proposed course of future action. The headteacher in particular plays a crucial role when choosing the issues which are put before the governing body for discussion. In theory the agenda for meetings of the governing body is under the control of the governors themselves, but in practice it is often left to the chair, clerk or headteacher or some combination of these three. In some cases the LEA still provides the agenda for governing body meetings. It can be difficult for the inexperienced or diffident governor to raise an issue of concern; often they simply don't know the questions to ask. For governors whose only experience of schools is as pupil or parent, no matter how often they visit the school and how much information is provided for them, they can only have a partial view of the work of the school and of current developments in education in general. Because these problems limit the independence of the governing body, they restrict the extent to which governors are able fully to evaluate the effectiveness of their school.

Whilst governors have been encouraged to become involved in financial and administrative matters, there has been a much greater reluctance to involve them in matters concerning the curriculum which still tends to be seen as the 'secret garden' – the exclusive province of the professionals (although governors are more often involved in the discussion of some cross-curricular issues such as sex education and behaviour). Even when the teachers would have welcomed a greater input from governors, the latter have been reluctant to become involved (Munn and Holroyd, 1989). In the nineteenth century governors had a clear role in curriculum decision-making, but that role lapsed and was obscured following the 1944 Act. The Taylor Committee, however, was quite definite in believing that governors ought to be fully involved in curricular matters and, indeed, in all aspects of school life:

> We take the view that the life and work of the school are indivisible: there is no area of the school's activities in respect of which the governing body should have no responsibility nor one on which the head and staff should be accountable only to themselves or the local education authority. (Taylor Report, 1977, para 3.15)

Governors who fail to involve themselves in curricular matters have opted out of consideration of the central function of the schools, that is the provision of learning experiences (the curriculum) for the pupils.

Burgess (1992) suggests that the chief function of the governing body is to be the body to whom the professionals, the head and staff, are accountable. In this the governors have a difficult balancing act to perform. As Elliott (1981) points out:

> When governors allow their investigation to become distorted by loyalty to the school they fail to carry out their 'representative at' functions, and when they allow it to be distorted by prejudices they share with their constituents they fail to carry out their 'representative of' functions. (p.165)

Question for discussion

How might the difficulties which prevent governing bodies fulfilling their role be overcome?

---

3. How far has a partnership between lay governors and professionals been established?

Crucial to the effective working of the governing body is the nature of the relationship between governors and staff and, in particular, the relationship between the chair and the headteacher. The Taylor Report (1977) envisaged the governing body as a partnership. However research into the work of governing bodies (e.g Deem *et al.*, 1992; Shearn *et al.*, 1993; Creese, 1994) has shown that the partnership has tended to be more of a myth than a reality. Shearn and his co-workers looked specifically at responsibility for financial matters within a small sample of schools and found that in the majority of cases the head was essentially in charge of the school, with the governors having little impact upon its direction. This situation either arose with the governors' approval or by default, with the governors either unwilling or unable to play their full part. Deem and Brehony (1992) take an even more pessimistic view:

> We feel that, partly as a consequence of the greater degree of autonomy between schools and governors, brought about by new responsibilities ... conflict rather than partnership is becoming a common feature of relationships between governors, headteachers and schools. (p.3)

The headteachers in the ten schools studied all claimed, in various ways, that they managed their governors as well as the school; indeed management of the governing body has long been seen as one of the criteria of successful headship. Part of the difficulty may well lie in the absence of a clear demarcation between the roles of the lay volunteer governors and the paid professional staff.

Few, if any, governing bodies appear ever to have discussed their role in a formal way, and the governing body may still be seen as largely peripheral to the real work of the school. In a study of 41 governing bodies in eight LEAs by Baginsky and her co-workers (1991), some of the governors from those schools expressed the view that they should not be presented with a *fait accompli*, and that they wanted more involvement in decision-making within their schools. However, while those governors might want to have a greater share in decision-making, there were very few ideas about how this would be achieved in practice.

Question for discussion

What are the difficulties which inhibit the establishment of a strong governor-teacher partnership and how might they be overcome?

---

4. How far and to whom are governing bodies accountable?

The key mechanism through which the governors' accountability to parents is exercised is the annual report to them and the subsequent meeting. However, research (Arden, 1988; Hinds *et al.*, 1992) shows that these meetings are, in general, very poorly attended. Why is this? Parents readily go to meetings which are perceived as directly involving the education of their own child. The problem may lie in the rather formal nature of the governor–parents meetings (a formality which has been deliberately fostered in some cases), or in the fact that the report is concerned with past events rather than future possibilities. More significantly, perhaps, many parents have failed to recognise the changed role and responsibilities of the governing body. However, even if the parents are dissatisfied with what they see as the unsatisfactory performance of the governing body, there is little they can do about it. There is no mechanism by which elected parent or teacher governors may be removed by their dissatisfied constituents before their term of office is over, any more than a Member of Parliament may be voted out before a general election. Governors may be asked to step down if they fail to attend meetings of the full governing body for six months, but there is no evidence of this sanction being widely applied. Governors can be prosecuted either individually or collectively (governing bodies were incorporated on 1 January 1994) for financial malpractice or criminal negligence. Beyond such extremes it would appear that there is little anyone can do short of appealing to the Secretary of State to remove the governors *en bloc.*

Question for discussion

How might the accountability of governing bodies be increased?

THE FUTURE?

Although governing bodies may be making some progress towards embracing their increased responsibilities (Earley, 1994), they have, so far at least, failed to live up to the expectations of the Conservative Government, which had hoped to see schools, led by their governors, opting out *en masse* from local authority control. Not only that, but governors have tended to side with the teachers over issues such as the work-load imposed by the new assessment arrangements, class-size and teacher redundancies. For example, in Warwickshire in 1995, the local authority was forced to take back responsibility for the budget in some schools because governors refused to set a legal budget which would have meant making teachers redundant. Elsewhere governors have resigned *en masse* rather than implement cuts. There are some 300,000 governors in this country and they could, if properly mobilised, become a significant political voice. So far, however, an organisation truly representative of all governors across the country has failed to emerge. It is possible that the National Governors Council, set up in 1994, will come to be that organisation, but there are very significant practical difficulties in consulting with, and presenting the view of, so many individuals spread over such a wide area.

Governing Bodies and Effective Schools (DfE,1995) seeks to draw governors into the debate about school effectiveness. There is now considerable evidence regarding the factors which lead to effective schools and a list of these is provided. It is perhaps unfortunate that, in a document aimed specifically at school governors, not one of the eleven factors listed makes reference to the governing body! The nearest one gets is a reference to the importance of the home–school partnership. Although much research has been done on effective schools, there has been much less on effective governing bodies, although there are some published criteria on what makes an effective governing body (AGIT/NAGM, 1993; Creese, 1995). The link between effective governance and effective schools is much more tenuous, and further research is urgently required in this field.

The 1986 Education Act requires LEAs to provide free of charge such training for governors as 'seems necessary'. A considerable amount of time and effort has been expended in providing such training. To date, however, the training has not reached all governors, and much of it has been aimed at providing governors with basic information about their role and responsibilities. Comparatively few courses have been offered which enable governors to engage with the fundamental issues of school effectiveness and school improvement. In recent years there has been a significant move towards providing training for the governors of one school together on a topic of their choice. Such training, although expensive in terms of the commitment of LEA trainers, does perhaps meet the needs of the whole governing body more effectively. The Action Plans produced by governing bodies following Ofsted inspections should give governors a meaningful monitoring role in reporting progress to parents. It remains to be seen, however, whether, schools will be able to improve significantly through the intervention of the governors. In the case of schools deemed to be 'at risk', additional governors may be appointed by the Secretary of State, but it is hard to see how part-time governors, however able and experienced, can have a major influence on what happens in the classroom day by day.

It may well be that it is impossible for volunteer governors to carry out effectively the work currently expected of them. In a recent national survey, about two-thirds of heads, half of the chairs and one-third of the governors felt that the extent of governing body responsibilities under recent legislation was too wide-ranging (Earley, 1994). There have been attempts in recent years by headteacher associations to limit the power of governing bodies and to enhance that of headteachers. If this were to be the case, given the much reduced powers of the LEA, headteachers would be in a very powerful position indeed, and the sort of accountability as envisaged by the Taylor Committee seriously affected.

How far will less effective governing bodies be able to improve their performance? Thody (1994) suggests two possible avenues of development. Either governors will effectively hide where power really resides in our educational system and, by providing an illusion of democracy, serve only to legitimise the power of headteachers and principals, as for instance in the schools examined by Shearn and his colleagues (1993). Alternatively, Thody suggests, governing bodies will gradually empower themselves, learning by experience and organising their own training and development. Governors nationally could then become an effective lobbying group, standing between the teachers and central government. They would also be able to establish genuine working partnerships with the staff in their schools and together would be able to affect decisively the standard of education provided in our schools.

FURTHER READING

Creese, M. (1995) *Effective Governors, Effective Schools: Developing the Partnership*. London: David Fulton. Chapters 1, 3 and 5.

Esp, D. and Saran, R. (eds) (1995) *Effective Governors for Effective Schools*. London: Pitman.

Sallis, J. (1994) *Heads and Governors: Building the Partnership*. Coventry: Action for Governor Information and Training (AGIT). Chapters 3, 4 and 6.

Holt, A. and Hinds, T. (1994) *The New School Governor: Realizing the Authority in the Head and Governing Body*. London: Kogan Page. Chapters 1, 4 and 5.

Thody, A (ed.) (1994) *School Governors: Leaders or Followers?* Harlow: Longman. Chapters 2, 4, 6 and 14.

REFERENCES

AGIT/NAGM (1993) *How Effective Is Our Governing Body?* Coventry: AGIT and NAGM.

Arden, J. (1988) 'A survey of annual parents' meetings by the London Diocesan Board for Schools', in P. Earley (ed.) *Governors' Reports and Annual Parents Meetings: The 1986 Education Act and Beyond*. Slough: NFER.

Baginsky, M., Baker, L. and Cleave, S. (1991) *Towards Effective Partnerships in School Governance*. Slough: NFER.

Banking Information Service/Department for Education/Office for Standards in Education (1995) *Governing Bodies and Effective Schools*. London: Department for Education.

Brehony, K. (1994) 'Interests, accountability and representation: a political analysis of governing bodies', in A. Thody (ed.) *School Governors: Leaders or Followers?* Harlow: Longman.

Burgess, T. (1992) *Accountability in Schools*. Harlow: Longman.

Creese, M. (1994) Governor-teacher relationships following the 1986 and 1988 Education Acts. Unpublished PhD thesis, University of East Anglia

Creese, M. (1995) *Effective Governors, Effective Schools*. London: David Fulton.

Deem, R. (1992) 'Governing by gender?: school governing bodies after the Education Reform Act', in P. Abbott and C. Wallace (eds) *Gender, Power and Sexuality*. Basingstoke: Macmillan.

Deem, R. and Brehony, K. (1992) Consumers and education professionals in the organisation and administration of schools: partnership or conflict? Paper presented at the American Educational Research Association annual meeting, San Francisco.

Department for Education (1993) *Good Management in Small Schools*. London: HMSO.

Department for Education (1994) *School Governors: A Guide to the Law*. London: HMSO.

Earley, P. (1994) *School Governing Bodies: Making Progress?* Slough: NFER.

Elliott, J. (1981) 'School accountability to governors', in J. Elliott, D. Bridges, E. Ebbutt, R. Gibson and J. Nias (eds) *School Accountability*. London: Grant McIntyre.

Keys, W. and Fernandes, C. (1990) *A Survey of School Governing Bodies*. Slough: NFER.

Hinds, T., Martin, J., Ranson, S. and Rutherford, D. (1992) *The Annual Parents' Meeting: Towards a Shared Understanding*. Birmingham: Centre for Education Management and Policy Studies, Birmingham University.

Kogan, M., Johnson, D., Whitaker, T. and Packwood, T. (1984) *School Governing Bodies*. London: Heinemann.

Munn, P. and Holroyd, R. (1989) *Pilot School Boards: Experiences and Achievements*. Edinburgh: Scottish Council for Research in Education.

Office for Standards in Education, (1995) *Framework for Inspection*. London: HMSO.

Shearn, D., Broadbent, J., Laughlin, R. and Willig-Atherton, H. (1993) Headteachers, governors and the local management of schools. Paper presented at the British Education Research Association Annual Conference, Liverpool.

Streatfield, D. and Jefferies, G. (1989) *Reconstitution of Governing Bodies: Survey 2*. Slough: NFER.

Taylor, T. (1977) *A New Partnership for Our Schools* (The Taylor Report). London: HMSO.
Thody, A. (1989) 'Who are the governors?', Educational Management and Administration, 17, 139–146.
Thody, A. (ed.) (1994) *School Governors: Leaders or Followers?* Harlow: Longman.

CHAPTER 13

Staff Appraisal

Di Bentley

INTRODUCTION

The appraisal of teachers is an issue which, in policy terms, has been developing for over a decade. The early debates concerned the fact of appraisal itself – should teachers be appraised at all? More recently, the arguments have become divided. Arguments in schools, local authorities and the academic papers have concerned themselves with the 'how' of appraisal, whereas arguments nationally have been more concerned with the links between appraisal and pay. This is not to say that the pay-linked debates do not also take place in schools, but the 'what' of appraisal is still in its infancy in the teaching profession. Since most schools are really only just ending their first cycle of appraisal for staff, the 'how and what' are of more immediate interest.

This chapter explores the early controversies surrounding appraisal; some of them, such as the links with 'getting rid of bad teachers' are still rumbling on. It examines the actuality of the policy and the different interpretations of that. It also looks at a variety of models for appraisal and raises some questions regarding such models. The controversies which are explored focus around the role of appraisal in schools: Is it to reward good teachers who reach their targets? Is it to help staff develop? Is it, as was once claimed, to weed out bad teachers?

'Joseph is poised to purge Britain's schools of bad teachers using Government legislation … Whitehall want to see the worst teachers penalised by not receiving pay increments or even forced out of their jobs.' These were the words that greeted the readers of the *Mail on Sunday* on 30 December 1984. The newspaper was taking a pre-emptive look at the probable statement on appraisal of teachers which Sir Keith Joseph, the then Secretary of State for Education, was to make in the New Year at the North of England Conference. The article encapsulated some of the difficulties faced by the Government, local education authorities and schools in dealing with the recent pay and salary structure disputes.

Between 1984 and 1986, an industrial dispute over pay and salary conditions had been disrupting Britain's schools. In a nutshell, the employers (LEAs and the Government) were seeking agreement on a new salary structure and a contract of employment which set out teachers' duties and responsibilities – the now famous 1265 hours. The Government for its part, whilst supporting the move to more precise conditions of employment, was, as ever, concerned at the cost. Differences in philosophy on the way in which schools should be structured, which had knock-on effects on the new salary structures, were also evident between LEAs and the Government in their joint role as employers. The Government wished to have a framework which would reward good teaching through a structure of posts of responsibility with an emphasis on management; in contrast, the employers wanted a greater emphasis on rewarding the main professional grade. The long-running industrial action culminated in the Teachers' Pay and Conditions Act 1987 and the suspension of arrangements for negotiating teachers' pay.

Sir Keith Joseph, in subsequent speeches to the North of England Conference, whilst not denying the possible links between appraisal and incompetence, made efforts to reinforce the positive staff-development views of appraisal which the White Paper *Teaching Quality* had laid out:

> Those responsible for managing the school teacher force have a clear responsibility to establish, in consultation with their teachers, a policy for staff development and training based on a systematic assessment of every teacher's performance and related to their policy for the school curriculum. (DES, 1983, para.92)

The industrial dispute continued to be the background to the moves made on appraisal. As a result of the intervention in the dispute by the Advisory, Conciliation and Arbitration Service (ACAS) in 1986, a report was produced which laid down a framework for appraisal and training. This framework formed the basis of the pilot project set up by the Department of Education and Science in 1987. It involved six LEAs, and aimed to develop programmes in which appraisal, as conceived by the ACAS framework, might be put into practice. A National Steering Group (NSG) was set up to monitor the progress of the pilot study, which culminated in two documents – Bradley *et al.*, (1989) and the report of the National Steering Group (DES, 1989).

When the NSG reported in 1989, it did so with a proposal for an agreed national framework which placed appraisal firmly within the staff development philosophy. John McGregor, who was Secretary of State for Education at the time, did not accept the scheme outright, but agreed to consultation. Morris (1991), a member of the NSG, reports on three reasons for the Government seemingly dragging its feet:

> a. a feeling that it [the scheme] presented an overly supportive model of appraisal, having insufficiently demonstrated links with quality, teacher promotion and so on;
> b. concern about the costings, which envisaged a scheme of over £40m. annually;
> c. the fact that appraisal was the scheme of the last Secretary of State but two and the world had moved rapidly since January 1987. (p. 168)

Rather abruptly following the consultation period, the subsequent Secretary of State, Kenneth Clarke, decided that appraisal would become mandatory in 1991. A statutory instrument and a DES Circular (1991) were issued, and phased introduction for all teachers, including headteachers (with some financial support) came into being in 1992. All teachers were to have had their first appraisal completed by 1995.

THE POLICY

KEY POINTS
• Appraisal involves 'the evaluation of the professional performance of an appraisee by an appraiser together and the establishment of targets for future action and development' (DES, 1991 p. 6) • Appraisal should be clearly separated from disciplinary procedures • All teachers are required, under the Pay and Conditions Act 1991, to take part in appraisal • Appraisal schemes are under the direction and responsibility of designated appraising bodies • It is expected that the appraiser should be the line manager of the teacher • The process of appraisal is a cyclic one over two years • There are four components to the process: classroom observation, an appraisal interview, the preparation of an appraisal statement and a review meeting • Complaints regarding the process take place at first within the school but ultimately are the responsibility of the appraising body

The main features outlined here are taken from DES Circular 12/91. The circular interprets the statutory framework laid out in the Pay and Conditions Act 1991, but is most likely to represent what teachers will find in operation in their schools. Because it is guidance only, it leaves schools some areas of flexibility in how they interpret the parts of the process of appraisal.

Requirement to take part in appraisal

The requirement to take part in appraisal arrangements applies to all qualified teachers employed on a contract of at least one year's duration full time or on a contract of 40 per cent or above. The regulations do not apply to unqualified teachers, teachers in their first year of teaching, articled or licensed teachers, supply teachers, advisory teachers, peripatetic teachers or teachers employed in the school for less than 40% of the time. However, within available funding, headteachers are advised to consider how they might arrange appraisal for those who are exempt, since the appraisal scheme aims to recognise the achievements of all teachers and help them identify ways of improving skills and performance.

The appraising body and the role of governors

The LEA is the appraising body responsible for LEA schools and the governing body that for grant-maintained schools. This means the LEA is responsible for producing a common appraisal scheme for all its schools which is cost-effective and manageable and which implements the Regulations enshrined in the Act and the Guidance in Circular 12/91. It also means that the LEA is the body ultimately responsible for any appeals against the process brought by individual teachers. In grant-maintained schools the governing body is also responsible for drawing up the scheme of appraisal within the Regulations and thus for organising any appeals procedures.

Teachers have to be consulted by appraising bodies when schemes are drawn up. Where the school is a voluntary-aided (church) school, the LEAs should also consult the relevant diocesan board about the appraisal arrangements. The Department expects local variation between LEA schemes and also between schools in how they apply both the statutory regulations and the LEA scheme. This permits a fair degree of flexibility to schools and to individuals, an issue which will be returned to in the next section.

The arrangements made within a school are expected to be approved by the governing body, which should receive regular reports on the progress of appraisal of teachers; but governors are not permitted to see actual staff appraisal reports. The role of governors is slightly different in respect of headteacher appraisal. For this, the governing body should be informed and the chair should have the opportunity to submit comments to the appraisers. If the appraisers intend to approach the governing body for information (as opposed to just the chair being given an opportunity), the Regulations require that the appraisers consult appraisees first.

Choice of appraiser

Circular 12/91 states that wherever possible the appraiser should already have management responsibility for the teacher. However, it also states that no appraiser should be responsible for more than four appraisees. Clearly in large secondary school departments this creates difficulties. In cases where the appraiser is not the line manager, the head is responsible for the appointment of an appraiser who is 'by virtue of his or her experience and professional standing to ensure that appraisal serves the need of the school teacher and the school' (para. 21). There is some leeway, however, for choice by the individual. The Circular reminds heads that they 'should not refuse requests from staff for an alternative appraiser if there are circumstances which suggest this might be appropriate' (para. 22).

As far as heads are concerned two appraisers are required, typically another head and an LEA officer or inspector. Headteachers are not allowed to choose their own appraiser, but again reasonable requests should not be refused. No headteacher should be involved in the appraisal of more than three other heads.

Deputy heads for the most part are covered by the regulations governing teachers, not headteachers. There is normally only one appraiser appointed, though Regulation 8(6) of the Act allows for headteachers to appoint two appraisers for deputies, assuming that the appraising body approves. One of these is expected to be the headteacher.

The appraisal process for teachers

Circular 12/91 describes four basic parts to the two-year appraisal cycle and suggests other aspects which could also be carried out. For example, there might also be self-appraisal and an initial meeting between appraiser and appraisee. The circular is careful to point out that self-appraisal is not compulsory.

The four essential parts are:

1. *Classroom observation.* This should normally be for at least one hour in total spread over two or more occasions. Observers are urged to ensure that they are fully briefed on the context by the appraisee before the observation, and that they present feedback within two working days of this. The observation may be supplemented by the collection of information from other sources relevant to the role of the appraisee – for example, the work and progress of pupils. If other information is to be collected, the Regulations require that the appraisee be consulted, particularly if it involves consulting others in the school. Appraisees should be given the opportunity to state their views on the principle of the collection of such information as well as the method of collection. The period of information collection/observation, should normally be completed within one term, and the appraisal interview should normally take place as soon as possible after the observation/collection.
2. *Appraisal interview.* Circular 12/91 suggests that the interview should involve:
   - consideration of the job description
   - review of work, including successes and areas for development
   - discussion of professional development needs including career development
   - discussion of the appraisee's role in relation to school policies and any constraints the school engenders
   - identification of targets for action
   - clarification of points to be included in the appraisal statement.

   There is also guidance on the conditions which might be most appropriate for the interview, such as prior preparation by both parties, discussion on information gathered and observations undertaken, and freedom from interruption with clear time limits.
3. *Appraisal statement.* This is in two separate parts: a record of the discussion at interview, and the appraisal targets. Copies are confidential and are provided for appraiser and appraisee, and the headteacher. The headteacher, on request, has to provide the chair of governors with the targets for action; for LEA schools, the CEO must receive the whole statement. The targets should also be given to the person in school responsible for staff development activities; for church schools this would be the diocesan board. Appraisees may record their own comments on the appraisal, particularly where there is disagreement, but this must be done within 20 days of the interview. The Circular recommends that the appraisal statement form should invite both parties to show that they are content with the statement. The Regulations state that the whole statement may not be shown to anyone other than those stated without the consent of the appraisee, except where it is relevant for a Court or tribunal or for a police

investigation. The Regulations allow the people in possession of the statement to use them to advise on decisions about pay, promotion or disciplinary matters. Apart from the statement, any documents produced during an appraisal, including records of observations, should be destroyed. The appraisal statement should be kept for a minimum of three months after the next statement is produced to allow time for complaints, but they may be kept longer, depending on the conditions set by the Appraising Body.

4. *Follow-up meeting*. The appraiser should assist the appraisee to achieve the targets set and schools are required to set up systems to help achieve this, such as release from teaching, in-service courses or further observations. In the second year of the appraisal cycle, a follow-up meeting should be scheduled. This is to review progress, reconsider targets since they may no longer be appropriate, consider training and its usefulness, discuss career development, and allow the appraisee to raise any issues. The date of the meeting is to be recorded on the appraisal statement as are any revised targets and the reasons for their revision.

Appraisal process for headteachers

The processes are almost the same for teachers and headteachers, but there are three aspects in which they differ significantly.

First, whereas a prior meeting is optional for teachers, headteacher appraisers have one as a scheduled part of the process. This is because the appraisers will not be members of the school and need to acquaint themselves with how it operates. Appraisers must also be given access to a variety of information for that meeting. This includes: the school development plan, statements on policy and the structure of the school, calendar of meetings, examination results, assessment and recording systems, staff development arrangements, financial and management systems, and the headteacher's job description. The initial meeting with the appraisee should be to consider the job description in the light of the policies and other information, agree the timetable and scope of the appraisal, and agree on classroom observation or other methods of information collection such as assigned tasks. Information for the interview may be collected from a variety of sources, including the chair of governors. It is likely that appraisers will also want to collect information from parents, other governors and LEA advisers/officers, but the appraisee must be consulted about its nature and collection.

Secondly, the appraisal of headteachers need not involve classroom observation but may involve a task, such as conducting a senior management team meeting, or preparing and presenting a report to the governing body. However, headteachers should be observed in the classroom if 'their current responsibilities involve teaching on a regular basis' (para.49).

Thirdly, appraisers of headteachers supply the chair of governors and the CEO with the whole statement, not just the targets.

Targets for action

These should relate to the professional performance, training and development of the teacher or headteacher. They should be designed to help, but must be realistic in terms of available resources and support. They should also be stated in precise language and be monitored. Ideally, targets should be mutually agreed, but the Regulations give the appraiser the right to set the targets in the case of non-agreement provided that they are shown to the appraisee, who can then formally record her or his comments on the appraisal statement within 20 days of the interview.

Procedures for complaint

Complaints are dealt with within the school in the first instance. The Regulations require that schools appoint a review officer in cases of complaint. The review officer should be an impartial person of sufficient seniority in the school, who should be given access to the appraisee's record. The review officer has the authority to take the final decisions with regard to the complaint raised by the teacher, and to interview the teacher and the appraiser to elicit further information. The Regulations require that the school draw up a procedure for dealing with complaints. However, the Appraising Body must agree these procedures.

Disciplinary procedures

The Circular notes that 'appraisal may be one, although not the only, opportunity where inadequacies in performance may be discussed with a senior colleague and remedies suggested' (para. 68). It also makes it plain that disciplinary procedures should be kept separate from appraisal. However, persons with access to the appraisal record may use information from this where it is relevant, provided that the appraisee is consulted.

ISSUES FOR DEBATE

1. The staff development model and others

The extract quoted from Morris (1991) on page 164 indicates that whilst, under guidance from professionals, the model of appraisal adopted was one predominantly of development for individuals, the Government might have been better satisfied with a model which clearly linked performance to progression or discipline. In fact, recent critics of the system question whether the model is a development one or an evaluative one which has within it the seeds of links to pay and dismissal. Fidler (1995) draws attention to this debate when he points out that 'In common with schemes in other organisations in the UK, it is performance enhancement which is the clear primary purpose of the appraisal scheme ... whatever the rhetoric, there is an evaluative aspect to the process' (p.98). So even what was thought of at the time as in principle a developmental process, with hindsight critics are regarding in actuality as evaluative. Fidler also points out that the process of appraisal omits such crucial aspects as self-appraisal, which he claims would be a 'vital preparatory process' if it is a developmental activity.

Other writers within this field take a less jaundiced view than Fidler, pointing out the possibilities of real developmental approaches to appraisal which are still possible within the current Regulations. For example, Metcalfe (1994) states that, 'It is my impression from recent contacts with schools that, within the legislative framework, appraisal is being introduced in a variety of ways, and that approaches to appraisal are generally consistent with the existing organisational cultures of the schools concerned' (p.96). Metcalfe goes on to describe a peer appraisal process in six LEAs which has been in operation alongside the Regulations. He claims that these LEAs demonstrated 'considerable scope for pragmatic, eclectic approaches to a school's approach to staff development and the place of appraisal within it. This is itself fully consistent with developments in more forward-looking commercial organisations' (p.107). This is the nub of the debate. From contemporary reporting, the original intent of the Government when appraisal was brought into being seemed designed to 'weed out bad teachers'. This is not what the final proposals from the NSG brought to light. Rather, teachers were to be given help to improve and develop. However, critics seem to be saying that, even within a so-called developmental policy, evaluation of performance was evident and the Government's intent to link the process to pay and dismissal was still visible.

However, the Regulations are loose enough to permit a great deal of developmental activity if that is what appraising bodies such as LEAs and individual schools want. The intention of the Government seemed to be a hierarchical approach in which appraisal was by a line manager (still evident), and non-achievement of targets could be linked to dismissal. Teacher professionals mitigated this to encourage an approach in which individuals and their development were important. The debate still centres around which of these two models is the more appropriate: the industrial one which claims to be harder and performance-related; or the developmental one, such as many schools have brought in alongside the Regulations, in which evaluation plays a part. The Regulations do allow for a more self-development approach, and several of the methods have been tried (see Hughes and Jones, 1994). Humphreys (1992) speaks persuasively of a system which allows for the empowerment of teachers, rather than one designed to punish the bad or reward the good. In fact the systems which are more evaluative and less developmental, may not, in the experience of industry, be the best way forward. As Handy (1989) remarks, in advocating for industry a change of approach to one which is more developmental, 'appraisal sounds like judgment, not help, looking backwards, not forwards, smacking of authority not partnership' (p.184).

Question for discussion

Would the public standing of the profession be enhanced by a more unashamedly evaluative and performance-linked approach to appraisal?

---

2. The linking of appraisal to pay

Some of the major protagonists in this debate, are, not surprisingly, the unions. The NUT (1994) have argued from the start that appraisal should be established only for the purpose of professional development. Their argument is that appraisal linked to pay and performance is divisive and 'would cause resentment, demotivation and a neglect of the particular education needs of children'. In spite of listening to evidence from teaching unions, individuals and other bodies, the most recent School Teachers Review Body (1995) recommended that for heads and deputies pay be linked in future to achievement on four essential performance indicators:

- year-on-year improvements in a school's examination or test results
- year-on-year improvements in pupil attendance
- evidence of sound financial management
- if there had been a recent Ofsted inspection, progress in meeting the requirements of the resulting action plan.

All the respondents to the Review Body, with the exception of the Government, pointed out that the performance indicators were simplistic and that funding would be problematic. Leaving aside the last point, it is clear that the Government continues to press on with the notion, for heads and deputies at least, that performance should be rewarded. The major problem, of course, lies in the suggested performance indicators. What, for example, if there has been no Ofsted inspection? The indicators are then reduced to three. What if, as for example in many primary schools, the attendance is always very good? How do the performance indicators apply to special schools? The choice of the particular indicators gives clear messages about what is expected of schools. They represent a clear output model of education. There are no opportunities to consider excellence of teaching or professional development. One could argue, very successfully, that if performance indicators for headteachers were to be chosen, those relating to staff development are equally as important as those relating to indicators of pupil success. But what of teachers? The Review Body explored the possibility that their four essential performance indicators be adapted to apply to teachers and that governing bodies be given discretion to award excellence points. However, the advice they received from unions, and the reluctance of the Government to increase funding, led to no firm conclusions.

There is no doubt that the continued push to relate appraisal schemes to performance, based upon criteria of some kind, is going ahead. The unions already regard the appraisal scheme as one which is evaluative. Further links through the Pay and Conditions Act, with criteria to be met, would ensure its status as an evaluative tool in schools. One might argue that is no bad thing. However, the effects that this will have on appraisal will be to remove much of the flexibility from schools in operating their own schemes and direct very firmly the type of evidence to be collected. It may well also direct the kind of development opportunities and 'training' to which teachers are entitled. Certainly the current possibilities (in which appraisal interviews can include discussion on pretty much any area of a teacher's work, as long as this is negotiated between appraiser and appraisee) would be curtailed. What is interesting is that the Review Body has adopted a model for rewarding performance in keeping with other such schemes in operation, i.e. based upon common indicators. What it did not suggest was that heads and deputies should be allowed to select their own performance indicators and agree these with their appraiser and the governors. This would have been much more in keeping with a developmental approach.

Questions for discussion

1. Are the unions correct in believing that performance-related pay, linked to appraisal, is divisive? How could performance-related pay for teachers be managed?
2. What performance indicators might there have been if the model of education being explored were a developmental child-centred approach rather than an output model?

---

3. Links between appraisal and discipline.

This is really the other side of the coin from the last issue and draws together the threads of the purposes of appraisal. Guidance from the Department is clear about the links between appraisal and discipline: the two are not linked. However, it is naïve to suggest that, whilst disciplinary procedures are separate from the appraisal process, the judgements made in one forum will not be taken into account into another. As Fidler (1995) says

> Where there are poor performers ... there will be a dilemma. Appraisal procedures are going to generate the evidence to show such cases are in need of more urgent and more demanding assistance than are associated with appraisal. Where there are no other evaluative processes diagnosing those in need of professional support procedures, the appraisal process has to carry out this function and it would be disingenuous to pretend otherwise. (p.103)

This is the nub of the issue. Whilst the Department may claim that appraisal is only one of the methods by which teachers in need of support are identified, it is the only one in which there is a requirement to seek evidence prior to full disciplinary stages being implemented. Schools do not generally collect evidence about their teachers, outside of appraisal, as a matter of course. Thus whilst appraisal may be only one source of evidence, it is likely to be the first and the most influential. To place appraisals in such a position could undermine their status as a staff developmental model as currently practised in many schools by reason of their careful and sensitive interpretation of the Regulations. It would be naïve to suggest that appraisal targets and progress would not be used to help inform the head and governors as to when the informal discipline stages should be commenced.

This is more dangerous ground than performance-related pay can ever be. It would be a disaster for any school to undermine the trust which teachers currently have in appraisal as a system that at the least does them no harm, provides a listening ear once in a while and at best may well do them some good.

Question for discussion

What are the problems in divorcing disciplinary procedures from appraisal? Do you agree with the comment above that to link the two would be disastrous for the profession?

THE FUTURE?

In a recent evaluation of the schoolteachers' appraisal scheme, Michael Barber and his colleagues (1995) concluded that appraisal had been implemented skilfully and resourcefully at both school and LEA levels. It had lead to improved classroom performance and school management, and more closely focused in-service training and professional development. Furthermore, the vast majority of the teachers were positive about the prospect of appraisal, the experience itself and the appraisal statement. However, the evaluators also highlighted a number of areas in which improvement is needed. In particular, they were concerned that both appraisers and appraisees found difficulty in pitching targets at an appropriate level, and that many schools failed to link appraisal results to their development plan for school improvement. The production of national and local guidelines on the management of appraisal is recommended.

The positive findings from this report certainly suggest that appraisal should continue, while the concerns identified should be given high priority by Government, schools and local authorities. Yet funding for the scheme ended in March 1995, and the responsibility for the continuance of appraisal has fallen on local authorities. It is important that lack of funds does not allow this important policy initiative to founder.

FURTHER READING

Barber, M., Evans, A. and Johnson, M. (1995) *An Evaluation of the National Scheme of School Teacher Appraisal*. London: HMSO.

Fidler, B. (1995) 'Staff appraisal and the statutory scheme in England', *School Organisation*, 2, 95–107.

Hughes, P. and Jones, J. (1994) 'Managing teacher appraisal: an exercise in collaboration', *British Journal of Inservice Education*, 20, 205–18.

National Union of Teachers (1994) *Performance Related Pay: Submission to the School Teachers' Review Body*. London. NUT.

Metcalfe, C.K. (1994) 'Re-appraising appraisal: a re-examination of some of the issues involved in staff appraisal in the light of experience of a scheme of peer appraisal', *British Journal of Inservice Education*, 20, 95–108.

REFERENCES

Barber, M., Evans, A. and Johnson, M. (1995) *An Evaluation of the National Scheme of School Teacher Appraisal*. London: HMSO.

Bradley, H., Bollington, R., Dudds, M., Hopkins, D., Howard, J., Southworth, G. and West, M. (1989) *Report on the Evaluation of the School Teacher Appraisal Pilot Study*. Cambridge: Cambridge Institute of Education.

Department of Education and Science (1983) *Teaching Quality*. London: HMSO.

Department of Education and Science (1989) *School Teacher Appraisal: A National Framework*. London: DES.

Department of Education and Science (1991) *School Teacher Appraisal* (Circular 12/91). London: DES.

Fidler, B. (1995) 'Staff appraisal and the statutory scheme in England', *School Organisation*, 2, 95–107.

Handy, C. (1989) *The Age of Unreason*. London: Business Books.

Hughes, P. and Jones, J. (1994) 'Managing teacher appraisal: an exercise in collaboration', *British Journal of Inservice Education*, 20, 205–18.

Humphreys, K. (1992) '"I must be crackers": teacher self-appraisal for professional development: reflections based on a case study of a group of teachers', *School Organisation*, 2, 115–25.

Metcalfe, C.K. (1994) 'Re-appraising appraisal: a re-examination of some of the issues involved in staff appraisal in the light of experience of a scheme of peer appraisal', *British Journal of Inservice Education*, 20, 95–108.

Morris, B. (1991) 'School teacher appraisal: reflections on recent history', *Educational Management and Organisation*, 19, 166–71.

National Union of Teachers (1994) *Performance Related Pay: Submission to the School Teachers' Review Body*. London: NUT.

School Teachers' Review Body (1995) *Fourth Report*. London: HMSO.

Suffolk Education Department (1985) *Those Having Torches*. Ipswich: Suffolk LEA.

CHAPTER 14

Inspection and Advice

David Rowles

INTRODUCTION

Prior to the Education (Schools) Act 1992, inspection practices, whether involving LEAs or HMI, had been generally irregular and included a wide range of patterns and procedures. LEAs tended to develop models very much in line with their own culture. Some, for example, operated a stringent model which involved the grading of individual teachers and lessons on a regular basis, whilst a number of other authorities preferred a softer approach, often replacing the word 'inspection' by friendlier terms such as 'survey' or 'school review', and conducting the exercise in a more low-key style. The process was carried out by local authority advisers and inspectors who were usually friendly and familiar figures and who were also responsible for offering support and advice to the school. HMI, on the other hand, with a complement of only 480 inspectors, had not found it possible to carry out regular inspections of the 24,000 or so schools in England and Wales. According to the Government, it would have taken around 200 years before each primary school received an HMI inspection.

Since part of the Government's philosopy, as an essential element of its market forces approach, was to obtain and publish as much information as possible about individual schools in order to inform and encourage parental choice, it was clear that a new and much more regular system of school inspections would be required, and much of the Education Act 1992 was concerned with this aspect.

THE POLICY

As a result of the 1992 Act, inspections of schools in England are the responsibility of a new non-ministerial department, the Office for Standards in Education, known as Ofsted, a word subsequently to become synonymous with terror and panic in the minds of many teachers, and one which has been transformed into a verb of sinister proportions – 'We're going to be Ofsteded!'. This organisation is led by a Chief Inspector, who is able to exert a great deal of independence in the role – though he must 'have regard to such aspects of Government policy as the Secretary of State may direct', a possible threat to a fully independent approach. Comparable arrangements exist for Wales (see Key Points).

Ofsted introduced its new inspection model based on a regular four-year cycle claiming that it gave priority to promoting inspection of the highest possible quality, for only in that way could schools be offered sound evaluation to use as a basis for improvement (Coopers and Lybrand, 1994). A Framework for

KEY POINTS

Education Act 1992

- Inspection of schools in England now the responsibility of the Office for Standards in Education (Ofsted), a non-ministerial department headed by HM Chief Inspector for Schools. For Wales there are separate but comparable arrangements under the Office of HM Chief Inspector of Schools in Wales.
- All maintained schools should have an inspection every four years.
- Inspectors are trained and contracted by Ofsted/Ohmci (Wales), and operate as independent teams, each under a Registered Inspector.
- Inspection teams must include at least one lay member
- Inspections must include a meeting with parents, an oral report to the Head, and a written report (with summary to parents)
- School authorities must prepare an Action Plan within 40 days of receiving the written report

Education Act 1993

- Special measures for schools failing or thought likely to do so

Inspection document and accompanying Handbook, containing some generally acceptable features of the new model, was widely welcomed by the profession:

- There were clear criteria and procedures
- Inspectors' judgements were to be firmly based on evidence gathered and cited
- The main thrust would be on classroom observation
- The inspection would be fully comprehensive and include all aspects of a school's organisation and performance
- Inspectors would work to a clearly established code of practice
- The local community would be involved both in the gathering of information and the dissemination of the report.

The original – and somewhat curious – intention that each school, through its governing body, would be able to make its own arrangements for inspection was defeated at the Committee Stage in the House of Lords, and responsibility for appointing Registered Inspectors to carry out inspections of individual schools was assigned to Ofsted. In a House of Lords Debate (11 February 1992), Lord Ritchie commented: 'I believe the prize must go to whoever thought up the idea that schools should choose their own inspectors. That seems to me to beat almost anything that I could think of if I were asked to think of the silliest provision possible'.

In order to ensure that the very extensive programme of inspections could be sustained, the Act provided for the creation of a large number of independent teams, all of whom would be required to submit tenders to undertake inspections as soon as schools were named. Ofsted insists that the allocation of inspections to Registered Inspectors is firmly based on the overall quality of the submissions made and whether they offer 'value for money' rather than the least expensive bid, although some of those whose early bids were unsuccessful did achieve a significant increase in allocations when they subsequently reduced their prices. The Government's initial expectation was that the vast majority of inspections would be undertaken by independent teams many of whom would be new to school inspection and would bring a fresh perspective to replace the traditional practice of HMI and LEA inspectors, whose views and judgements had in some instances come to be questioned and mistrusted by Government officials. However, consultancy firms such as Coopers and Lybrand, Deloitte, and Price Waterhouse, whose involvement had been anticipated, considered that the work would be uneconomic and did not become involved.

The practical issue of who would carry out the inspections was therefore largely resolved by pragmatism. LEA inspection teams, who saw this as an opportunity to extend their earning capacity and also retain a professional involvement in the process, have provided the bulk of the personnel, and they have been supplemented by former HMI and ex-LEA inspectors operating either as a consortium or on an individual basis. (HMI were reduced from 480 to 175, with 40 inspectors being given responsibility for the monitoring of inspections.) All those who wished to become inspectors, whatever their previous experience, were obliged to undertake a rigorous and exacting one-week training and assessment programme; those wishing to lead inspections as Registered Inspectors received additional training and were monitored in action by HMI prior to their registration. These procedures have since been modified. For inspections of denominational education in voluntary-aided schools, a specifically trained inspector (usually a member of a diocesan team) is selected by the governing body to carry out a full inspection of the school's RE provision under Section 13 of the 1992 Act.

At secondary school level, the Registered Inspector is supported by a core team of two or three colleagues who concentrate on whole school and management issues, whilst subject specialists (known as team inspectors) inspect individual departments. An innovatory requirement is that each inspection team (primary and secondary) must include at least one person 'without personal experience in the management of any school or the provision of education in any school (other than as a governor or in any voluntary capacity)' (Education Act 1992, Schedule 2). In this way it was anticipated that each team would benefit from the 'outside view' of a lay inspector, but there was considerable concern initially from both schools and inspectors that such a presence could interfere with the professionalism of the exercise.

Inspections typically last for the best part of a week and most teachers are observed on two or three occasions. Opportunities must be created for structured interviews with senior and middle managers, and a sample of pupils' work must be examined in depth prior to the pupils themselves being interviewed. Shortly before the inspection takes place, schools are asked to submit for scrutiny all existing policy documents, handbooks and schemes of work, and these, in addition to other evidence such as examination and test results, are evaluated in the light of observed practice. Prior to the inspection week, parents are invited to complete a questionnaire about the school and asked to attend a parents' meeting where a set agenda of key issues is discussed – without the presence of the headteacher.

When setting up its Ofsted structure, the Government made a clear distinction between the functions and processes of the carrying out of inspections and the giving of advice, a division which has proved to be a major feature and bone of contention (see Issue 2). The responsibility for follow-up lies with the governing body, which is obliged to draw up an action plan to address the issues raised within 40 days of the inspection report.

Special provision is made for schools considered to be 'at risk'. If the Registered Inspector's view is subsequently confirmed by HMI, the governing body is required to draw up its action plan to a more urgent timetable, and this plan is very carefully monitored by Ofsted. As an ultimate sanction, the 1993 Act empowers the Education Secretary to set up bodies known as Education Associations to conduct the affairs of a 'failing' school.

As the secondary inspection programme was being implemented in the autumn of 1993, a number of striking features were immediately apparent. It became clear that the very short timescale for preparation allowed to schools was inadequate, and Ofsted agreed to provide at least two term's notice in future. (Subsequently, schools have rued the apparently interminable length of time that the Ofsted 'sword of Damocles' hangs over their heads.) It also became apparent that some modifications were required to the Ofsted Framework and Handbook, and updated versions were produced in 1994 and 1995. At the same time, many primary schools were finding the inspection model inappropriate with its secondary approach and terminology and its insistence on reviewing practice in terms of specialist subject provision. Because early inspections revealed undue pressure experienced by individual primary school teachers, who were likely to be seen by four or five different inspectors, Ofsted was eventually obliged to guarantee that in each class for at least one session during the day there would be no inspector present. But apart from a few concessions such as this, the approaches established in secondary school inspections were retained for primary schools (although there is now a separate handbook for primary school inspectors), with the main thrust centred upon the same four principal areas of concern:

- the quality of education provided by the school
- the educational standards achieved in the school
- whether the financial resources made available to the school are managed efficiently
- the spiritual, moral, social and cultural development of pupils at the school.

Ofsted was aware of the scrutiny to which its procedures would be exposed and ensured that during the first term all inspection teams were closely monitored by HMI, and that detailed feedback was obtained from a representative sample of headteachers whose schools had been inspected. The report by Coopers and Lybrand (1994) testified to the efficiency and effectiveness of the vast majority of inspections carried out in the autumn term of 1993. In particular the Framework and Handbook had not only enabled inspectors to deliver focused judgements but had also proved to be extremely useful documents to help schools to undertake their own review and to plan school improvements. As the inspection process became more widely experienced, views began to crystallise. These can be summarised as follows:

- The vast majority of headteachers felt that, although the inspectors' report and findings had not usually informed them on matters of which they were unaware, it had often given helpful precision and sharpness and added a confirmatory element.
- The rare chance to have such a full and detailed external audit (or, as one head described it, 'an enforced consultancy') had been extremely informative and beneficial.
- An impending inspection provided schools with the impetus to 'spring clean' their policies and schemes of work and to explore the link between stated policy and current practice.
- The fact that the inspections involved such a thorough and structured review of classroom practice was widely welcomed. Inspectors spent at least 60 per cent of their time in school observing lessons – a major change of emphasis for a profession where classroom observation after the induction year had not been a major feature, apart from the relatively limited element involved in teacher appraisal schemes.
- The governors' action plan, required by Ofsted as a follow up to the main findings and key issues of the inspectors' report, was based on a clear list of priorities and provided a basis for the school development plan for the next three years or so. It was a particularly useful lever in schools or departments reluctant to change.

Many heads, however, expressed concerns about the new model:

- Judgements had often been too broad and were too tightly tied to rigid criteria, with insufficient heed being paid to the individual school context or the progress that the school had made in the past few years, starting perhaps from a low baseline.
- The emphasis on evaluation without advice was questioned, as was the lack of feedback to individual teachers. In many instances, there had been no real professional dialogue and little chance to question interpretations. Heads claimed that change was inevitably less likely if conclusions were not explained or tested for accuracy.
- The Ofsted model meant over-reliance on two or three days of observation, and this snapshot took relatively little note of previous work.
- The value of grading lessons was challenged, involving, as it must, a strong subjective element. Moreover, how significant was an overall judgement such as '67 per cent of all lessons seen were found to be satisfactory'? Other heads felt that by attempting to focus on the measurable, inspectors often ignored process.

- The language of inspection reports was often thought to be bland or to contain too many repetitions of the word 'satisfactory' without any clear indication of its import. Ofsted, via its regular newsletter to inspectors, advised that 'satisfactory' should be avoided as far as possible, and where appropriate replaced by 'sound'.
- Universally schools felt that there had been an over-emphasis on the amount of documentation to be produced by schools and that this might have rendered the inspection something of a cosmetic exercise.

Following a major consultation process in the early part of 1995, three 'streamlined' versions of the Handbook, with quite specific approaches and documentation for primary, secondary and special schools, were published in October 1995 with a view to the changes being put into operation from April 1996. Ofsted claimed to have heeded the criticisms made of the original model and insisted it was attempting to make what was accepted as being a very burdensome exercise more manageable for inspection teams and more worthwhile for schools by contributing more effectively to their strategies for improvement and development.

Apart from the introduction of a phase-related approach, the main differences in the new guidance are:

- An increased focus on the four main strands (see p.178)
- In order to ensure that the essence of individual schools is captured, only 'significant' features, strengths and weaknesses will be reported, and particular attention will be given to the school's self-evaluation of its own performance, its development plan and identified priorities.
- Judgements about attainment will be more systematically based on national standards and expectations of what children know, understand and can do in relation to National Curriculum requirements. An important addition will be a reference to pupil progress in relation to prior attainment.
- There will be increased importance attached to attainment in the core subjects of mathematics, science and English. Variation in the progress of different groups of pupils will be highlighted.
- Increased attention will be paid to equal opportunities and special educational needs although, controversially, these will no longer be treated as discrete areas.
- There will no longer be a separate section on the Quality of Learning but there will be a new emphasis on the quality and effectiveness of the teaching, children's response to it, and their attainment and progress. A number of commentators regret this departure since the previous specific concentration on outcomes as well as teacher input had been widely welcomed.

ISSUES FOR DEBATE

1. Is the new inspection system improving standards?

In their review (1995) of the first hundred primary school inspections, Professor Michael Barber, from the University of London Institute of Education, and Paul

Fuller from the consultancy firm Touche Ross, concluded that most of the schools involved benefited. However, they queried whether the present process maximises the improvement that might result from inspection: although there was considerable evidence of improvement before the inspection, as schools strove to prepare for this trial, the evidence of improvement as a result of inspection was less convincing, partly because it was too early to gather definitive data. There was an indication that some, at least, of the adjudged 'failing schools', estimated to be about 2 per cent of the total number of schools inspected, and a further 10 to 15 per cent which revealed serious weaknesses, had made sufficient progress to be taken off the 'at risk' list. But some other schools which received a satisfactory report had said that after such a 'shattering experience' there was a long-lasting feeling of flatness and apathy among staff and an inability to pick up and move forward with any degree of enthusiasm. As Cathy Byrne from a school in Hull put it (*TES*, 2 June 1995)

> After months of preparation you still can't get it right. The inspection week was you at your best. The school had been tarted up, all the documentation was in hand, lessons had been prepared for three hours every night, all the resources were on tap, everything was under control – and still it wasn't good enough!

In the Barber and Fuller report, some of those involved – including inspectors – claimed that the model was too authoritarian and static and did not encourage the self-motivation, flexibility and responsiveness needed to ensure professional growth. Others were much more positive about the outcomes. Two-thirds of headteachers and three-quarters of school governors had been happy with the overall inspection judgements, believing that drafting and revising documentation had helped to focus both thinking and practice and that there was a real value in having access to an informed outside view.

Questions for discussion

1. From your own knowledge or direct experience of an Ofsted inspection, to what extent did it prompt the school to improve its standards?
2. To what extent is an independent inspection report essential information for school governors if they are to carry out their statutory responsibility to guarantee high standards of education in their school?

---

2. Is the policy of separating inspection from advice a sound one?

When the Ofsted formula was being devised, the Government had a clear view that the process of inspection should be quite separate from that of advice. It was felt that in this way a further set of data and results could be provided for school governors who, working alongside the school senior management team, would then undertake their legal responsibilities and decide what action should be taken and by whom. Moreover, it was hoped that in this way there would be no clash of vested interests among inspection teams who might previously have been involved in offering professional development to the school staff, or who might be tempted to offer their services to the school in terms of follow-up activities after the inspection. At the outset, Ofsted stessed very strongly that no inspector who had previously had significant contacts with a school should be included in its inspection team since they were likely to be 'contaminated'. This indeed persuaded some larger LEAs to divide their inspectorate into two groups, each of which carried out different functions in different parts of the county. A survey by the Royal Society has found steep drops in the number of specialist subject advisers, with no adviser posts at all in some authorities (*TES*, 5 January 1996).

There has been widespread criticism of this particular aspect of the inspection process, and Tony Blair, leader of the Labour Party, has insisted that his party's model would emphasise the need to associate inspection with advice, and that schools required a combination of support and pressure (*TES*, 8 September 1995). This view has been supported by a report based on research commissioned by the Organisation for Economic Cooperation and Development. According to the report's author, Caroline St John-Brooks (1995), schools have to be not only provided with a rigorous assessment of strengths and weaknesses but also advice from understanding professionals ('critical friends') who can devise workable strategies for improvement. She points out that in other countries, particularly Spain, where the team includes the local inspector, it would appear that schools have a more positive approach and that it is easier to capitalise on the insights provided by the inspection.

Question for discussion

How can inspection judgements and advice most effectively be delivered to schools in a manner which pinpoints ways forward whilst preserving objectivity? Would it be more appropriate for post-inspection advice to be offered as a matter of course by a specific support agency such as an LEA team?

---

3. How accountable, manageable and effective is the Ofsted inspection model?

The original criteria drawn up by Ofsted for making inspection judgements were generally acceptable to the teaching profession. The training and selection procedures for prospective registered and team inspectors were extremely demanding and rigorous, with a surprisingly high failure rate during the initial stages. All of the early inspections were closely monitored by an HMI, who reported back to Ofsted, which also summoned regular feedback from headteachers and teacher associations. Both the Coopers and Lybrand (1994) and Touche Ross (Barber and Fuller, 1995) reports indicated general satisfaction with the way in which inspectors carried out their tasks.

In his introduction to the Touche Ross report, Professor Barber stated that there was a high degree of professionalism amongst all those involved, but also warned that questionnaires about customer satisfaction were inherently limited since there was a strong correlation between those who were satisfied with the process and those who received a satisfactory inspection report. In the longer term he wondered whether the system of private inspection teams would always be subject to some form of market pressure, and highlighted the need to have ways of monitoring the quality of the inspections and the consistency of judgements amongst the teams. Ofsted admit that they do not have the resources to monitor every Registered Inspector (which would be their ideal) but insist that they do scrutinise every written report.

Schools were originally (and to some extent still are) apprehensive about inspection reports, which have very clearly and intentionally been placed in the public domain. However, most reports are prone to err on the side of blandness, a criticism which flies in the face of early fears that inspectors would be too harsh. The pressure not to find a school failing is quite high, according to Professor Barber, since it means more work for the inspection team without additional payment.

A much more unsympathetic view of the whole Ofsted initiative has been taken by Ted Wragg and Tim Brighouse (1995), who have berated inspectors for producing reports which are mechanical, written to a formula, full of empty phrases like 'generally satisfactory' and 'sound', and which are too vague to be influential. They maintain that an Ofsted inspection is regarded as a one-off ordeal, with little long-term use: a 'hoop to jump through' rather than the central part of a programme of improvement. In addition, it assumes that all schools are the same, and attempts to measure them against a suspect interpretation of national norms whilst ignoring the successes of those schools who operate in difficult circumstances. The authors propose a new five-point model which would involve a re-established HM Inspectorate working in partnership with LEA inspectors and possibly primary and secondary school headteachers who, within a context of core factors, would treat each school as a unique establishment and concentrate much more on the quality of teaching.

In a reply, the current Chief Inspector, Chris Woodhead (1995), rejected these criticisms, saying that many improvements had been made in the updated Framework and Handbooks, which now give greater emphasis to the school's own circumstances and to the quality of classroom teaching. He admitted, however, that in 1994/95 Ofsted had had to reduce the target number of schools to be inspected because of a shortage of inspection teams at primary level and hundreds of inspections were rescheduled. In 1995/96 it was anticipated that 2400 schools would be inspected out of an original target of 3600. Bearing this in mind, perhaps, and also aware of the undoubted strain suffered by schools during the inspection (and especially pre-inspection) period, Woodhead suggested that in future perhaps only schools which received a poor report during the initial cycle would be subjected to a further inspection within the following four years.

Question for discussion

Is it feasible to devise a collection of performance indicators which can be applied to all schools throughout the system, regardless of individual circumstances?

---

4. Should individual teachers be identified as part of the inspection process?

Although many inspectors would admit that it is a nonsense to pretend that when inspecting schools they are not inspecting teachers, there is no requirement in Ofsted's legislative specification to vet individual teachers, and the English tradition of inspection (unlike the French) eschews individualistic public judgements. This principle is, however, somewhat stretched when it is difficult to disguise individual identities. Such written comments as 'This school is poorly led' or, in a school where a single specialist undertakes all the teaching, 'The teaching of music is of an unacceptable standard' require little guesswork to establish *who* is being evaluated.

The Ofsted findings during the first two years of the inspection programme, that teaching was unsatisfactory in one quarter of the lessons observed in primary schools and one-fifth at secondary level (HMCI Annual report, 1995), has given rise to a lively debate on this issue. Criticisms levelled at teachers include the claim that some have only a hazy grasp of the subject they are teaching, and that in certain instances the lessons are poorly structured. Chris Woodhead (1995) has no doubts at all that individual 'failing' teachers should be identified:

> We have tolerated incompetent teachers for years and years in a way we simply wouldn't anywhere else like, say, the airline industry. If you had an air traffic controller saying 'Well, nine out of ten seem to land safely' we would be appalled and rightly so.

He believes that the real casualties of education are found in the 2 per cent of schools which have failed the inspection and the further 10 to 15 per cent which have serious weaknesses; but he also draws attention to the fact that, in the course of a series of regional conferences during the summer of 1995, he was very surprised by the vehemence with which many primary headteachers spoke about the problems of competence in their schools: 'I think it is definitely a minority of teachers,' he says, 'but your child or my child has only one chance at school and if they get a lousy teacher for a year, it matters'.

As a result of such concerns, from April 1996 inspectors were told to report to headteachers on the very worst and best standards of teaching, although whether inspectors' reports might be used as part of disciplinary or even dismissal procedures is still a very controversial area. Some concern has been expressed about this proposed change of emphasis since it is claimed that the Ofsted model imposes 'a tyranny of orthodoxy' in schools, and that rather than establishing a core of judgemental values it can smother schools with a culture of uniformity. Bob Moon and Tim Brighouse (1995) argue that the era of development plans, Ofsted-focused policies and teaching to criteria has tended to obscure the way in which teachers individually (and, perhaps even more successfully, in teams) can strike out in new directions, generate new ideas and set new benchmarks for everyone to follow.

Articles in the *Times Educational Supplement* sometimes give glimpses of the excitement that surrounds an outstanding teacher, but there should be greater recognition of such achievements which are all too often marked by promotion into managerial roles, distancing the teacher from the classroom. Within the school, the inter-personal balance of the staffroom makes such recognition difficult, and school governors have almost unanimously rejected the idea of offering salary enhancement points for 'excellence', seeing this Government proposal as being potentially divisive. Moon and Brighouse suggest that under the blanket Ofsted inspection programme it is impossible not to be aware of brilliant performance by teachers, and that these should be celebrated in the Ofsted inspection report. Such vignettes could not only enliven the anodyne clichés and mechanistic format that currently characterise many reports but would also highlight the achievements of thousands of outstanding teachers. This could have a significant impact on public perceptions of and confidence in schools, and redress an imbalance markedly prevalent in recent years whereby alleged failure and underachievement have dominated media interests.

Questions for discussion

1. Would it be appropriate to name teachers formally in a report or during the verbal feedback to headteachers and governors, with evaluations given of individual performance?
2. What stategies and procedures should be applied in order to make the process of identifying and dealing with incompetent teachers more effective?

THE FUTURE?

Although the advent of Ofsted has created a number of inherent tensions, a whole school audit is generally accepted as a useful starting point for school improvement, and the extremely thorough Ofsted procedures can potentially provide the best review the school has ever had. However, it is only one of several evaluation mechanisms; to be fully effective evaluation needs to be regular and ongoing, not just (at best) every four years. Any beneficial outcomes of inspection are likely to be the result of steady determined effort rather than instant transformation.

Schools are for the most part wholly responsible for the implementation of their post-inspection action plans since Ofsted currently merely carries out a sampling follow-up exercise except in those schools which are deemed to be seriously at risk. This means that they will need to establish their own procedures for monitoring, review and evaluation and may well lead to an agreed and structured form of school self-review as a future alternative to the Ofsted model, which is seen by some as being in danger of crumbling under its own weight. Some observers speculate that Ofsted may in future need to restrict its inspection activities to the core subjects of the National Curriculum, that inspection teams may visit groups of schools rather than concentrating so intensely on individual institutions, and that a second four-year cycle (if ever implemented) might apply only to those schools which were deemed to be unsatisfactory during the first cycle.

The future of Ofsted is unclear both for professional and practical reasons. Already, however, in just over two years of operation, there is clear evidence that it has had a marked effect on the thinking, aspirations, anxieties and planning of schools – including the 70 per cent who have not yet had first-hand experience of an Ofsted inspection. The current involvement of many LEA inspectorates and advisory teams in helping schools to prepare for Ofsted could well be extended in the future to carrying out supportive monitoring and evaluation activities to ensure the effective implementation of the post-inspection action plan.

Any future Labour Government would certainly wish to reform the present system. The Labour Party, because it favours external scrutiny of schools, does not believe that Ofsted should be abolished but it would wish to explore different models and also undoubtedly to increase the role of local authority advisory services in both carrying out inspections and in supporting follow-up activities.

FURTHER READING

Earley, P., Fidler, B. and Ouston, J. (eds) (1996) *Improvement Through Inspection?: Complementary Approaches to School Development*. London: David Fulton.

Ouston, J. and Earley, P. (eds) (1996) *Ofsted Inspections: The Early Experience*. London: David Fulton.

See also References.

REFERENCES

Barber, M. and Fuller, P. (1995) *Inspection Quality: 1994/5*. London: Ofsted.

Coopers and Lybrand (1994) *A Focus on Quality*. London: Ofsted.

Moon, B. and Brighouse, T. (1995) *School Inspection*. London: Pitman.

Office for Standards in Education (1995) *Guidance on the Inspection of Nursery and Primary Schools/Secondary Schools/Special Schools*. (three versions) London: HMSO.

St John-Brooks, C. (1995) *Schools Under Scrutiny: Strategies for the Evaluation of School Performance*. London: HMSO.

Wragg, E. and Brighouse, T. (1995). *A New Model of School Inspection*. Exeter: Exeter University School of Education.

Woodhead, C. (1995) Interview in the *Observer*, 15 October.

CHAPTER 15

Performance Measurement and Targets

Helen Johnson

INTRODUCTION

It is a widely accepted view that it was Margaret Thatcher's New Right government that first seriously challenged the quality of public services, including education, and set about introducing performance indicators and achievement targets. But concerns about effective public management were around before the 1970s. In 1968, the Fulton Report on the British Civil Service defined accountable management (and argued for its introduction) as 'holding individuals and units responsible for performance measured as objectively as possible'. In terms of central government itself, however, Fulton's recommendations about performance assessment were mostly ignored by the Wilson Government. Yet, as we saw in Chapter 11, it was a Labour Prime Minister, James Callaghan, who began openly questioning the performance of the public sector in general and of the education service in particular. In his famous speech at Ruskin College in October 1976, he expressed concerns about the relevance and the effectiveness of the education offered to Britain's children, remarking 'Where there is legitimate public concern it will be to the advantage of all involved in the educational field if these concerns are aired and shortcomings or fears put to rest' (quoted in Lello, 1993, pp.2–3).

From this it can be seen that there were cross-party currents of dissatisfaction in Britain about education and other public services that had been established in the early 1940s mould of Beveridge and Butler. It is also necessary to acknowledge that there were real public dissatisfactions about the standard of public services and about the degree to which they were accountable to the service recipients at the point of delivery. The British public thus had a marked reluctance to go on paying large amounts of personal income tax for such public services. Overall, there was a sense that there was a need to modernise and better manage Britain's governmental and public service institutions, be they government departments, local authorities or individual units such as schools.

The Conservative Government came to power in 1979 with a clear mandate for change: public services were to be made economical, efficient, effective and, most of all, accountable. Resources were to be managed instead of simply being used. 'Producer' power, in which the public service bureaucracies and professionals allocated resources as they saw fit, gave way to 'consumer' rights where customer sovereignty was to hold sway. This 'sovereignty' in the market place demanded that customers should be more informed about the services on offer so that they could make rational choices. The era of performance management and information was upon us. Both here in the UK and in Reagan's America, New Right governments had nailed their ideological colours to the mast. Money supply was to be tightly controlled, tax cuts were to be made, and, in a much-repeated remark, the 'frontiers of the state were to be rolled back'.

LeGrand and Bartlett (1993, p.1) remark that 'when a new Conservative Government came into power in Britain in 1979, the welfare state was the biggest area of non-market activity in the British economy'. In all, the public services of the welfare state accounted for 23 per cent of the Gross National Product in 1979. Yet the desire for a more efficient (and less expensive) public services sector was seen by some as more than a commitment to a better public management. As Jackson (1988) has pointed out by quoting the 1976 US Committee for Economic Development, there was also a serious political purpose behind such moves:

> The importance of improving productivity goes beyond the issue of costs and even beyond the desirability of achieving higher quality and effectiveness in the important services that government provides. It goes directly to the need for restoring confidence in government. (p.11)

In short, unless the public see government spending taxes well and to some purpose, governments and possibility even democracy itself are tarnished, perhaps even threatened.

Performance measures and performance indicators

According to Jackson (1988), performance measures in the public sector are substitutes for profitability measures in the private sector since they seek to measure productivity and efficiency. An immediate objection to performance measures in the public services (discussed at greater length in the 'Issues for Debate' section) is that it is sometimes very difficult to quantify the outcomes of a public service; and, when suggestions are made, they are never satisfactory to everyone involved because of the relativity of the viewpoints that we will all express. Since it is often not possible to measure performance accurately and so arrive at a precise interpretation of the data in question, a performance indicator is commonly used. This, as Jackson puts it, acts as 'an alarm bell', a managerial device that alerts management that there might be an issue that requires closer attention. He illustrates the point with this example:

> The per pupil costs in one school might be three times those in another. That piece of data (per pupil cost) is not a measure that one school is three times more efficient than the other. Instead it is an indicator that further investigation is required to find out why this so. (p.11)

However, although it is possible to make a conceptual distinction between 'the measure' and 'the indicator', in practice the two terms tend to merge as we see from Jackson's example.

Given the subjective nature of the exercise, can a set of criteria be developed to help in the creation of satisfactory and reliable performance indicators? Nuttall (1989) suggested the following guidelines:

- Indicators should be regarded as diagnostic and suggestive of alternative actions, rather than judgemental.
- The implicit model underlying the indicators must be made explicit and acknowledged.
- The criteria for the selection of indicators must be made clear and be related to the underlying model.
- Individual indicators should be valid, reliable and useful.
- Comparisons must be done fairly, in a variety of different ways (for example, with like groups, with self), over time and using dispersions and differences between sub-groups as well as averages.
- The various consumers of information must be educated about their use.

Gray, Jesson and Sime (1991) have devised a set of criteria that concentrates on measuring performance at school level. They have argued for a set of only three or four to be developed initially, and to be based on empirical evidence drawn from school effectiveness research. They identify these as academic progress, pupil satisfaction and pupil–teacher relationship.

It is clear that performance indicators are not a neutral managerial tool. As with most models, techniques or tools in the management area, we have to ensure that the value that they carry with them is recognised and acknowledged. If this can be achieved, they become the foundation of good management practice, supplying managers with the information necessary for sound decision-making. Supposition can turn into hard evidence once the data has been collected and used in planning and policy-making. Then, with performance indicators as a benchmark and once decisions have been made about what should be done and policy designed and implemented, it is possible to monitor actual performance. When the dust has settled it also possible to use performance indicators to evaluate the overall effectiveness of a programme or policy. Subjective judgement gives way to objective assessment.

Additionally, it must be underscored that information of this kind is not simply for managers. Riley (1990) has emphasised that the process of developing school indicators should ensure that all the partners in education have a sense of ownership of the indicators. Even the quasi-market in education demands that information should be available for customers (be they students, pupils or parents), as well as governors, senior management teams, local authorities and the DfEE.

Much evaluation has gone on in education about what schools do it, why and how they do, and to what end. At the local level there have been many initiatives by local authorities (for example the Sussex Accountability Project in the 1970s); at a central level there has been the DES Better Schools Project in 1985, and an important development in the mid-1980s, the Guidelines for Review and Internal Development in Schools (GRIDS) project, described by McMahon *et al.* (1987). However, it is clear that much of what has happened recently, if not the direct result of government policy and pressure, has been initiated in response to a changing environment about evaluation and accountability in the public services generally, including education. The Audit Commission's report, *Towards Better*

Management of Secondary Education (1986) was followed by the Chartered Institute of Public Finance and Accountancy's *Performance Indicators in Schools* (1988). Interestingly the latter argued that qualitative as well as quantitative performance indicators could be explored, for example the management of the quality of teaching and learning, pastoral management, and liaison with other agencies and the community.

In the same year the Audit Commission reinforced the quantitative emphasis of performance indicators by proposing a range of indicators to be used by local authorities. Those for education included:

- *resources*, e.g. total cost per pupil
- *customers*, e.g. numbers of pupils; parental choice/appeals satisfied
- *service delivery organisation*, e.g. average school size; average school occupancy; average class size
- *services delivered*, e.g. pupil/teacher ratio; teacher/contact ratio; books/equipment per pupil; subjects in the curriculum
- *end results/outcomes*, e.g. examination results; places gained at university/FE/employment; truancy rates; complaints; HMI and local inspectorate reports

As Stewart and Walsh (1994) remark, 'such measures will allow judgments within services, say, between schools, but not with other services' (p.46).

KEY POINTS

- Performance indicators and output measures for all Government departments to assess achievement of objectives
- Monitoring of educational services, for example by Ofsted
- School league tables
- The Parent's Charter
- National education targets
- Similar trends in other countries

THE POLICY

It is with the Financial Management Initiative introduced in 1982 that the bandwagon for performance management in the public sector was truly set to roll. Each government department, including the then Department for Education and Science, were told in the White Paper,

> Where practicable, performance indicators and output measures [will] be developed which can be used to assess success in achievement of objectives. This is no less important than the accurate attribution and monitoring of costs; the questions the

departments will address are 'where is the money going and what are we getting for it?'. (Treasury and Civil Service Committee, 1982)

Previous chapters have illustrated how the Education Reform Act 1988 radically changed the organisation of education services at local level. Schools were to offer open enrolment, parents were to be offered a real choice in terms of the schools available for their children, a National Curriculum was to be taught, and most schools were to be managed through a system of delegated budgeting called Local Management of Schools. What was significant in administrative terms was that (save for LMS) most of these initiatives were to be monitored by a series of non-departmental quangos. One of the better known of these is the Office for Standards in Education (Ofsted), which was set up in 1992 to manage the national programme of school inspections. A lengthy and bulky handbook was published setting out for a number of areas the performance indicators that would be used by Ofsted inspectors. The indicators in the latest (1995) edition, which comes in three versions (primary, secondary and special schools) is discussed in Chapter 14.

In November 1992, the Government published its first league tables for all maintained and independent secondary schools. This it has done annually ever since, and the 1995 league tables, which included all independent as well as publicly maintained schools, listed each school's examination results for GCSE, A–levels, and vocational courses. Also included were each school's figures for pupil absence. To help the public interpret the tables in the light of schools' circumstances, the tables also included the numbers of pupils in each school and the numbers of children with special educational needs, both those with statements and those without. Chapter 3 has described the testing in place to assess the National Curriculum and these results are also published, although league tables have not yet been produced for primary schools. (Separate figures for sixth form colleges and FE colleges are also published.) Schools must distribute the league tables for their locality to parents.

In 1994, twenty million copies of the booklet *Our Children's Education: The Updated Parent's Charter* were distributed to all homes (including those without children) throughout England and Wales. The Government had expressed the wish to open up the 'secret garden' of education to the world beyond the education professions. National targets are laid down in this Charter. The first is the qualitative aspiration that education and training provision is to develop self-reliance, flexibility and breadth. Then the targets become more quantitative, and have since been revised upwards:

- By 2000, 85 per cent of young people are to obtain five A–C passes at GCSE or their vocational equivalent by age 19
- By 2000, 60 per cent of young people are to obtain two or more GCE A–levels, or advanced vocational qualifications by age 21.
- By 2000, one-third of all 18-year-olds will enter some form of higher education.

As can be seen, a culture that accepts goals and performance indicators has quickly become established in England and Wales. What about elsewhere ?

The use of performance indicators in education has not been unique to England and Wales. Most advanced economies (certainly those belonging to the OECD) have gone down this route in some way. Two examples will suffice.

Scotland possesses an education system that has developed from its own history and social and cultural values. In the early 1990s, the Scottish Office Education Department produced a wide range of performance indicators at national level. MacBeath (1994) tells us that in order to develop a balanced set of indicators, small teams were commissioned to work on different aspects. One team worked on the development of indicators related to exam performance, another on qualitative indicators, and a third took on indicators of attitudes to school. MacBeath's own special interest is in the latter; a set of indicators has been developed that a school could use to analyse its ethos and relationships with others. MacBeath lists them as follows:

- pupil morale
- teacher morale
- teachers' job satisfaction
- the physical environment
- the learning context
- teacher–pupil relationships
- discipline
- equality and justice
- extra-curricular activities
- school leadership
- information to parents
- parent–teacher consultation.

Further afield, the USA, which has a long history of pupil testing, started to develop a new set of educational indicators in the early 1970s. The federal Department of Education and the Centre for Education Statistics within it, issued a report called *The Condition of Education* which contained educational indicators. This report has become an annual event by which the performance of the American education service can be monitored. In 1983, the American National Commission on Excellence in Education published *A Nation at Risk*. This report was the impetus for a renewed interest in educational indicators that has not subsided. In 1984, the Secretary of Education published the first in a series of league tables which allowed direct comparison between the states for the first time. The following year, the American government set national goals for education in the year 2000. Selden (1994) lists them as follows:

- All young children will come to school ready to learn.
- Ninety per cent will complete secondary school.
- Students will master challenging subject matter in the academic subjects of English, mathematics, science, history and geography.
- US students will become the first in the world in mathematics and science performance.
- Adults will be literate and possess the knowledge needed to compete in a global economy and to exercise responsible citizenship.

- All schools will be free of drugs and violence and offer a safe, disciplined environment for learning.

In 1990, measures and indicators were identified for each of these goals, and the monitoring of progress is underway.

The difficulties with these types of qualitative indicators are obvious. We are aware that they cannot be effectively measured. What quantitative indicators (from MacBeath's list) could be used for staff morale? Would it be assessed on one particular day, or over a period of time ? Likewise with the ambitious American list, although some are clearly measurable (e.g. 90 per cent will complete secondary school) , what does 'Adults will be literate and possess the knowledge to compete in a global economy and to exercise responsible citizenship' really mean? Some of these indicators are clearly aspirational and highly relative in nature.

ISSUES FOR DEBATE

1. Is performance measurement as straightforward as some would like to appear?

One of the fundamental difficulties that confronts all rational managerial systems such as performance measurement is the political nature, in the widest sense of the word, of the public services themselves. To have a public service at all is a political decision, and therefore any public service has both a political role as well as the more obvious social and economic ones. So if the overall purpose of a public service is debatable, both what is meant by 'performance' and the evaluation of that performance is also open to public comment, and this can reflect any number of differing perspectives and value systems.

Since it is a political decision that 90 per cent of British children are educated in a system funded by public funds, and that system is under some form of democratic control (increasingly by central government in some form), the education service is 'political'. Also, since the service is paid for through general taxation, it is a service that can be held accountable not only to its customers and consumers (i.e. parents and pupils) but to the wider local community and to society as a whole. Indeed, because of its truly 'public' nature, the education service of today can and most certainly will be held accountable by future generations.

In short, services in the public domain are not the same as those services in the private sector. The stakeholders are limitless as is the time scale of their interest. So quickly we arrive at the pertinent questions: how are the aims of a public service ever satisfactorily agreed upon? And even if some sort of working definition can be agreed by a pragmatic consensus, how satisfactory will be the objectives that are set to obtain these goals? And to take this further, how can we be sure that the measures and indicators set to monitor and evaluate performance tell us anything that is both accurate and reliable?

The problem is particularly acute in the education service. The question 'What is education?' is itself a political one; and, if education resources are finite, definitions about education are endless. Shipman (1979) has warned against too much navel-gazing. Nevertheless there are important questions to be asked. What measures and indicators can conclusively claim to measure those targets? Issues of relativity must be uppermost in our minds. If we accept that precise measures are sometimes not possible, can proxies – performance indicators – used in their stead ever be satisfactory even in their admittedly limited purpose as, in Jackson's phrase, 'managerial alarm bells'?

Question for discussion

Within your discussion group, is there total agreement on any performance indicator for schools? What are the problems in arriving at a general consensus? Could any of these be overcome?

---

2. The 'value-added' debate

Difficulties can arise if the limited purpose of performance indicators is unobserved or ignored. What do league tables of examination results tell us and about whom? Is a set of results the reflection on the performance of the pupils as a whole or a set of pupils? Of all the teachers in a school or just some? On what timescale are these results to be evaluated? Do brilliant GCSE results reflect good teaching in just the fifth form, throughout the two-year GCSE course, throughout the school, or the child's whole total educational experience?

The problem is complicated because schools do not receive a uniform intake of pupils. They arrive at the school gate with different life histories, with differing levels of educational and social skills, from different socio-economic backgrounds – and most importantly with different expectations and aspirations. (Significantly, when Tony Blair, as Leader of the Opposition, spoke at the Institute of Education, University of London on 23 June 1995, he called for 'an educational crusade to tackle the poverty of aspiration'.) Is an average pass for 16-year-olds of five A-C GCSE grades a reflection of the same kind of performance by a school if its pupils are drawn from a poor, multi-lingual, inner-city London borough or from a leafy, well-ordered suburb, or from an affluent county where at least two cars are parked in every driveway?

It is with this kind of issue in mind that many LEAs have responded to central government's league tables, which at present show the crude examination results, by publishing tables that show the 'value-added' by their schools. This 'value-added' component takes into account the pupil intake of each school (essentially where things were at the start) and then assesses the progress that pupils have made during their time there (where things where at certain points or at the end). The difference between the beginning and the measuring point is the 'value-added'.

The concept of 'value-added' is not without difficulty, and much work is now being done in this area. Writing in the *Guardian* on 2 June 1992, Desmond Nuttall and Harvey Goldstein warned that valued-added data should be treated with care. This is what they said.

> The reason for this caution is twofold. First, the assessment of value-added is only as good as the information upon which it is based, in particular the measures of student

achievement when they start at the institution in question. In practice, it is often difficult to obtain such information in a reliable and consistent fashion. The second caveat is more fundamental. It is that, whatever methods are used, there will always remain some uncertainty attached to the estimates of each institution's 'value-added'. This is because there is year-to-year variation which may be large and unexplained and because the number of students in any one institution may be relatively small, so that unexplained random variation will force us to place a relatively wide interval of uncertainty about the estimate obtained.

Another study (currently underway) has been commissioned by the Schools Curriculum and Assessment Authority (SCAA). A group of academics at the University of Newcastle upon Tyne is examining ways to assess 'valued-added' from National Curriculum assessment results at the end of each Key Stage (i.e. at seven, 11 and 14 years of age) and from GCSE and A-Level results at 16 and 18 years of age. The three ways currently under examination are:

1 *Charting input against outcome.* Using data collected between Key Stages 1 and 4, an average performance is being calculated to allow pupils' performance to be assessed as below average, average, or above average. Some data is available to give a base line at age five, but the difficulties are obvious.
2 *Estimating the proportion of pupils who are doing better than expected.* Here the difficulties revolve around what progress can be expected. It can perhaps be assumed that the DfEE's own expectation is that pupils might progress through one National Curriculum level every year.
3 *Looking at overall school performance* to see in which schools pupils are achieving what might be expected of them, or less or more.

It is easy to see the difficulties that arise from attempting such measurement. For example, there are four years of schooling between Key Stages 1 and 2 and the National Curriculum levels are very broad. The research team is currently piloting a national study using 1995 National Curriculum assessment data (with a special emphasis on Key Stages 1 to 2, and Key Stages 3 to 4) and public examinations data.

Whatever method or combination of methods of assessing 'value-added' are considered to be 'the best', are they all likely to be too complicated for the average observer to understand? Can any system of performance indicators, even sophisticated 'value-added' ones, attempt to recognise the uniqueness of the individual child, the complexity of family circumstances and those of the community?

Question for discussion

Are indicators, including 'value-added' indicators, only a 'snapshot' that tell us nothing really meaningful? Or are they better than nothing at all?

---

3. Who chooses the indicators and decides what is information?

Pollitt (1993) has traced the development of 'managerialism' in the public services both in the UK and the USA. Managerialism essentially accepts the manager's right to manage. This becomes significant when we remind ourselves of the political importance of performance measures and indicators. Who should choose them, given their growing role in informing and shaping the debate about economic, efficient and effective performance in education and the other public services?

Some commentators such as Stewart and Walsh (1994) have argued that the choice of these measures and indicators cannot be left (as managerialism would expect) as the unquestioned activity of managers within the services themselves and elsewhere. They have expressed the view that, though it is unrealistic in the public domain to expect fully satisfactory measures of performance, performance measures do have a role. They go on to say, however, that the limitations of performance measures should be widely recognised. In addition to the supposedly 'hard' information supplied, 'all the information that surrounds a service' should be included in the discussion and evaluation of a service's effectiveness. They give the following examples:

- the softer views of opinion
- the pattern of complaints
- the experience of inspectors
- the understanding of public officials
- the views of politicians
- the processes of pressures and protest.

In this way, the political nature of the public services is acknowledged. The information surrounding a service can include the supposedly objective and the unrepentantly subjective and anecdotal (the power of which was discussed in terms of the public service strikes in the winter of 1978–79). With this variety of views in play the dominance of managers can be held in check, and the debate about the performance of a public service can become more representative of the community and of society as a whole.

Question for discussion

That the debate about what performance indicators should or not be used should be opened up would seem highly desirable. But is this just a fond wish? Who should be the interested parties? Given their number, how could this be done in practical terms?

THE FUTURE?

To have lived in post-war Britain is to have lived, as the Chinese curse would have it, 'in interesting times'. There has been much structural building in terms of social institutions and much demolition too. To make confident predictions about the future as far as performance measures are concerned would be a risky and foolhardy business, though on one point we can be sure: in contrast to its previous attitude, the Government as well as the opposition parties now seems to accept the need for value-added measures. What is also clear is that all major political parties are seemingly committed to the use of performance targets and indicators in education. Indeed, a Labour Party policy statement (1995) has proposed that, on top of national education targets, each LEA should draw up a three-year plan for raising standards in its schools, and these targets should be monitored by Ofsted.

All this can be seen to support the remarkable cultural change in British society which encourages and supports the citizen as an empowered customer. Whatever the limitations of a transactional, *quid pro quo* culture, customers need information with which to make decisions and choices. The future of performance measurement in some form or another would seem assured.

FURTHER READING

Glatter, R. (1986) 'The management of school improvement', in E. Hoyle and A. McMahon (eds) *World Yearbook of Education: The Management of Schools*. London: Kogan Page.

Jackson, P. (1990) *Measuring Performance in the Public Service*. Leicester: University of Leicester Press.

Murphy, R. and Broadfoot, P. (1995) *A Tribute to Desmond Nuttall*. London: Falmer.

Riley, K. A. and Nuttall, D. (1994) *Measuring Quality*. London: Falmer.

REFERENCES

Audit Commission (1986) *Towards Better Management of Secondary Schools*. London: HMSO.

Audit Commission (1988) *Performance Review in Local Government*. London: HMSO.

Chartered Institute of Public Finance and Accountancy (1988) *Performance Indicators in Schools*. London: CIPFA.

Fulton Report (1966) *The Civil Service* (vols 1–3). London: HMSO.

Gray, J. Jesson, D. and Sime, N. (1991) 'Developing LEA frameworks for monitoring and evaluation from research on school effectiveness: problems, progress and possibilities', in S. Riddell and S. Brown (eds) *School Effectiveness Research: The Messages for School Improvement*. London: Jessica Kingsley.

Jackson, P (1988) 'The management of performance in the public sector', *Public Money and Management*, 8, 11–16.

Labour Party (1995) *Excellence for Everyone*. London: Labour Party.

Lello, J (1993) *Accountability in Practice*. London: Cassell.

LeGrand J. and Bartlett, W. (eds) (1993) *Quasi Markets and Social Policy*. Basingstoke: Macmillan.

Macbeath, J. 'A role for parents, students and teachers in school self-evaluation and development planning', in K.A. Riley and D.L. Nuttall (eds) (1994) *Measuring Quality*. London: Falmer.

Nuttall, D. L. (1989) 'The functions and limitations of international indicators'. Paper prepared for the OECD/CERI INES project, Paris.

Pollitt, C. (1993) *Managerialism and the Public Services*. Oxford: Blackwell.

Riley, K.A. (1990) 'Making indicators consumer friendly', *Education*, 11 May, 470–2.

Shipman, M. (1979) *In-school Evaluation*. London: Heinemann.

Spiers, M. (1975) *Techniques and Public Administration*. Glasgow: Fontana.

Stewart, J. and Walsh, K. (1994) 'Performance measurement: when performance can never be finally defined', *Public Money and Management*, April–June, 45–9.
Treasury and Civil Service Committee (1982) *Efficiency and Effectiveness in the Civil Service*, Cmnd. 8616. London: HMSO.

INDEX

14/16–19 provision vii, xi, 56–70
  A-level viii, xi, xv, 56, 57–9, 61, 67, 68, 108–9, 191, 195
  AS-level 58–9, 61, 68
  Baccalaureate xv, 66, 67–8, 118
  Certificate of Extended Education 57
  Certificate of Pre-Vocational Education vii, 57, 59
  Certificate of Secondary Education 31, 57
  core skills 58, 61–2
  Diploma of Vocational Education viii, 58, 59
  'dual track' system 60–1, 66–7
  F-level 56, 57
  GCSE viii, 31, 51, 59, 105, 108, 191, 194, 195
  GNVQs viii, 63, 65–6, 67, 68
  NVQs viii, 58, 61–2, 63, 64, 65, 68
  O-level 31, 57
  proposals 66–9
  Q-level 56
  see also under names of awarding bodies

accountability 1–2, 7, 40, 130–31, 141, 148–9, 151, 154–5, 158–9, 182–3, 189
Acts of Parliament
  1902 Education Act 118
  1944 Education Act xiv, 1, 72, 73, 127, 149, 151, 152, 153
  1975 Sex Discrimination Act vii, 101–2
  1976 Race Relations Act vii, 86, 87, 134
  1979 Education Act vii
  1980 Education Act vii, 128
  1981 Education Act vi, 72–4
  1986 Education (No. 2) Act vii, 16, 18, 151, 152, 160
  1987 School Teachers Pay and Conditions Act 164
  1988 Education Reform Act viii, xiv, 2ff, 6, 7, 15, 72, 74, 80–4, 86, 103, 115, 128, 129, 141–2, 151, 191
  1988 Local Government Act viii, 16, 18
  1989 Children Act 87, 91
  1991 School Teachers Pay and Conditions Act viii, 165, 171
  1992 Education (Schools) Act viii, 129, 186, 176–7
  1992 Further and Higher Education Act 64, 103–4
  1993 Education Act viii, xiv, xv, 6, 16, 18, 72, 74, 75–6, 83, 103, 128
  1996 Nursery Education and Grant-Maintained Schools Bill ix, 46, 48, 145
Adam Smith Institute 1
appeals
  admissions vii, 128, 132
  special educational needs 74, 75, 78
appraisal of teachers xiv, 163–74
  development 163–2
  discipline xiv, 172–3
  headteachers 166, 168, 172
  models of xiv, 169–70
  performance-related pay xiv, 171–2
  purpose 163–5
assessment and testing viii, ix, 30–43
  10-level scale 31, 34, 35
  Assessment of Performance Unit 30, 106
  attainment targets 4, 5, 31, 33, 35
  by teachers 33–4, 35, 38–9, 41
  for selection 120
  level descriptors 31, 35
  National Curriculum viii, ix, xi, xii, xv, 4–5, 7, 11, 30–43, 81, 117
  purposes 32–3, 35, 115
  special needs vii, 73–4, 81
  standard assessment tasks xi, 31, 33, 36–9
  see also 14/16–19 provision, SCAA, SEAC
Assisted Places scheme vii, 127, 128
Audit Commission xv, 77–8, 145, 146, 189–90
Australia, education in xiii, 127, 141

Baker, Kenneth 6, 8, 9, 31, 59, 61
Bentham, Sir Jeremy xvi

Black, Paul xi, 32, 38–9, 40
Black Papers 6, 56
Blair, Tony 194
Business and Technician Education Council 57, 60, 64

Callaghan, James 1, 57, 187
Centre for Policy Studies xi, 1, 45–6, 47–8, 53, 117
church schools *see* voluntary schools
City and Guilds of London Institute 57, 59, 60, 64
City Technology Colleges viii, 116, 129
Clarke, Kenneth 9, 164
Commission for Racial Equality 86, 95, 134
Common Funding Formula ix, 142, 144, 145
compensatory education 47
comprehensive schools vii, xii, 57, 113, 120, 121
Confederation of British Industry 62, 65, 67
Conservative Party x, xv, 1, 2, 6, 31, 32, 53–4, 123, 128, 136, 141, 159
corporal punishment viii
Council for Environmental Education 19
curriculum
  balance 2, 12, 15, 21, 64, 68, 103
  'hidden curriculum' xii, 107–8
  politics vii, 16, 20
  purpose 2
  religious education and worship 1, 4, 6, 112, 153
  sex education vii, viii, x, 6, 15, 16, 17–18, 24
  specialism 115, 116–7
  see also National Curriculum

Daugherty, Richard xi, 30, 38, 40
Dearing, Sir Ron 2, 5, 10, 34, 56 *see also* Reports
diversity xii, 112–125, 126
  arguments 112–13
  of ability 119–20
  of curriculum 117–19, 123
  school choice 126, 127, 130, 133
  society 121–23
  standards 113–14

equal opportunities *see* gender, race, special educational needs
exclusion from school ix

'failing' schools and teachers viii, xv, 176, 178, 181, 183, 184
France xii, 113, 118
funding xiii, xv, 82–3, 119–20, 139–50
  Common Funding Formula ix, 142, 144, 145
Funding Agency for Schools viii, xiii, 103, 143, 144, 147, 148–9
Funding Council for Wales viii
Further Education Unit 57, 61

gender vii, xii, 100–11
  attainment 100, 103
  education policies 103, 104–5
  'hidden curriculum' xii, 107–8
  historical influences 100–1
  legislation 101–2
  National Curriculum and 103, 105–6, 107, 110
  Ofsted 104
  TVEI 101, 102
Germany xii, 113, 118–9
governing bodies xiii, 151–62
  accountability xiii, 154–5, 158–9
  annual report and meeting vii, 154, 158
  composition vii, 152–3, 155–6
  National Governors Council 159
  relations with professionals 154–5, 157–8, 160
  responsibilities vii, xiii, 18, 76, 143, 152, 153–4, 156–7, 159–60
  teacher appraisal 165–6
  training xiii, 160
Graham, Duncan x, 9, 26, 37, 40
grant–maintained schools viii, ix, xv, 1, 103, 115, 116–17, 127, 129, 136, 137, 142, 143–4, 148–9, 153

Halsey, Philip 10
Hillgate Group 1, 2, 94

independent schools and nurseries vii, xi, 47, 50–1, 113, 116, 127, 128
information, duty to provide vii, 128, 129, 133, 154

Inner London Education Authority viii, 87–8, 92, 103
inspection of schools viii, xiv, 175–86
advice xiv, 181–2
Her Majesty's Inspectorate for Schools xi, 9, 47, 50, 77, 175, 178, 183
individual teachers xiv, 183–5
LEA 175, 177
Ofsted viii, xv, 64, 86, 90–1, 104, 115, 129, 153, 154, 160, 175–86, 190, 191
Institute for Public Policy Research 67
Institute of Economic Affairs 1

Joseph, Sir Keith 30, 51, 163, 164

Labour Party xv, xvi, 119–20, 123, 136, 137, 144, 149, 182, 186, 187, 194, 197
Lawlor, Sheila 47–8, 51, 53–4
league tables viii, 7, 30, 39–41, 81, 82, 115, 121, 129, 154, 191
Liberal Democrat Party xv, 149
local education authorities
duties vii, 4, 44, 74, 75, 82, 86, 128, 134–5, 141–3
role viii, xi, xii, xv, 2, 44, 45, 115, 119–20, 143, 147–8, 151, 165–6, 175, 177, 182
see also Inner London Education Authority
Local Management of Schools viii, 2, 103, 115, 146–7
Lochrie, Margaret 47, 51

McGregor, John 9, 61
Major, John 86, 104
management, school 139–50
Manpower Services Commission 60, 102
market forces 2, 7, 47–8, 126–7, 129–30, 142, 144, 151

National Centre for Educational Standards 1
National Commission for Education 62, 67, 68
National Council for Vocational Qualifications viii, 62–3, 64, 66
National Curriculum viii, ix, x, xv, 1–43, 112, 115
assessment *see* assessment and testing
attainment targets 4, 5, 31, 33, 35
careers education 18–19, 22, 65
citizenship x, xiii, 20, 22, 25–7, 130–1
criticisms of 6–12, 21–2
cross-curricular themes x, 3, 4, 10, 15–29, 157
differentiation x, 3, 5
economic understanding x, 16–17, 22, 23–4
entitlement x, 2, 3
environmental education 19–20, 22, 25
foundation subjects 1–14, 23–6, 9, 11, 16, 21
gender issues 103, 105–6, 107, 110
governing bodies 153
health education 15, 17–18, 22, 24
ideology 6–8
key stages 4, 5, 33, 45, 53, 59, 64, 103, 154, 195
personal and social education x, 2, 15, 16, 21
pre-school, effects on 44–5, 46, 47, 47–8, 49–50, 51
programmes of study 4
race issues 86, 87, 90, 94–5, 97
revised 2, 3, 4, 5–6, 10–12, 106, 118 *see also* Reports, Dearing
sex education vii, viii, ix, x, 6, 15, 16, 17–18, 24
special needs 75, 80–2
National Curriculum Council viii, ix, 9–10, 15, 21, 34, 37, 61, 90, 94–5
Netherlands xiii, 106, 127, 141
nursery education *see* pre-school provision

Office for Standards in Education *see* inspection of schools
open enrolment viii, 82, 127, 128–9
opting out *see* grant-maintained schools
Osborn, Albert 46, 49–50, 51

parent choice *see* school choice
parental rights vii, ix, 16, 39, 72, 73, 74, 78, 120, 126
Parent's Charter viii, 78, 129, 190, 191
Patten, John 2, 5
performance measurement xiv, 39–41, 187–9

indicators 188–90, 191–6
league tables viii, 7, 30, 39–41, 81, 82, 115, 121, 129, 154, 191
value-added xiv, 121, 123, 194–5
performance-related pay xiv, 171–2
personal and social education 15, 21
political education vii, 16, 20
postmodernism xiii, 121–3
pre-school provision vii, xi, 44–55
character of 44–5
independent nurseries 47, 50–1
learning outcomes 48–9
National Curriculum and 44–5, 47, 47–8, 51
Pre-School Learning Alliance 47
Ofsted 46, 47, 51
purposes 46–50
types 45
voucher scheme ix, xi, 46, 48–9, 51–3, 142, 144–5

quangos xiii, 148–9, 191 *see also* Funding Agency for Schools

race and racism vii, xii, 86–99
concept of 91–2
education policies xii, 86, 87–9, 94–5
legislation 86, 87
National Curriculum and 86, 87, 90, 94–5, 97
Ofsted framework 90–1
school choice 134–5
statistics 93
underachievement 96–7
see also Reports: Rampton, Swann
records of achievement viii, 58, 59, 63
religious education and worship 1, 4, 6, 112, 153
Reports
Crowther (1959) 66
Dearing (1994) x, 2, 4, 5, 10–12, 34–5, 41, 64
Dearing (interim, 1995) 56, 62, 66, 67, 68
Dearing (1996) ix, 69
Fulton (1968) 187
Hadow (1933) xi, 44
Higginson (1988) viii, 59
Keohane (1979) vii, 57
Newsom (1963) 8
Plowden (1967) 44
Rampton (1981) vii, 89
Swann (1985) vii, 86, 89–90
TGAT (1987) viii, xi, 31, 32–4, 37, 38–40, 81
Taylor (1979) vii, 151, 152, 157, 158, 160
Warnock (1978) vii, xii, 71, 75, 76, 83
Royal Society of Arts 20, 60, 64

School Curriculum and Assessment Authority ix, 2, 48–9, 64, 117, 195
School Examinations and Assessment Council viii, ix, xi, 10, 11, 30, 34, 61
school choice vii, xii, xiii, 1, 113, 115, 121, 126–38, 141
admission policies 127, 129, 136
appeals vii, 128, 132
arguments for and against 130–1
assisted places vii, 127, 128
curriculum opportunities 131–2
diversity 126, 127, 130, 133
legislation 127–30
open enrolment viii, 82, 127, 128–9
other countries 127
parent empowerment 131–3
'parentocracy' xiii, 126–7, 137
segregation 134–5
selection 121, 132
social class 132–3
special schools 127, 129
standards 135–6
Scotland 9, 113, 192
selection 8, 120, 121, 132
sex education vii, viii, x, 6, 15, 16, 17–18, 24
Shephard, Gillian 51
special educational needs vii, viii, xi, xii, 71–85
assessment vii, 73–4, 81
Code of Practice ix, 72, 75–6, 78, 83
concept xi, 71, 72–4, 75, 76–7
funding 77, 82–3, 84, 142
integration 72, 74, 75, 79–80
National Curriculum 75, 80–2
school choice 127, 129
special schools 79–80, 81–2, 117
statements vii, ix, xii, 72, 73–4, 75, 76, 77–9

standard assessment tasks xi, 31, 33, 36–9
standards in schools 1, 2, 7, 11, 30, 48, 56, 57, 108–9, 113, 135, 180–1, 191

Tate, Nick 11, 94
Technical and Vocational Education Initiative 58, 60, 101, 102
technical schools xii, 113
technology schools and colleges ix, 116–17, 119
Thatcher, Margaret 44, 60, 93, 187

underachievement xii, 40, 96–7, 108–9, 141
USA xiii, 44, 46, 49–50, 51, 94, 123, 127, 135, 141, 192

value-added information 188–90, 191–6
vocational education xi, xv, 4, 56ff, 115–16, 118–19
voluntary schools xv, 115, 127–8, 152–3, 155, 166
vouchers
  for 5–16s 136, 145
  pre-school ix, xi, 46, 48–9, 51–3, 142, 144–5

Warnock, Mary vii, xii, 71, 75, 76, 77, 78, 79, 83
White Papers
  A Framework for Expansion (1972) 44
  Better Schools (1985) vii, 58
  Choice and Diversity (1992) xv, 2, 75, 113–15, 116–17, 118, 119, 120, 121, 122
  Competitiveness Forging Ahead (1995) 65
  Education and Training for the 21st Century (1991) viii, 58, 62, 63, 65, 117
  Education and Training for Young People (1985) vii, 65
  Teaching Quality (1983) 164
Williams, Shirley 87
Woodhead, Chris 47, 50, 51
World Commission on Environmental Development 19